Praise for HappiNest

"I don't say this lightly: this book could save your life. With middle-aged adults, particularly women, dying younger than previous generations from 'diseases of despair,' finding a renewed sense of purpose and zest during the empty nest period is a recipe for happiness and meaning. Judy Holland has brilliantly woven together stories, research, and checklists that will appeal to anyone who wants to find out how to fill the empty nest in important ways." —**Caroline Adams Miller**, author of *Creating Your Best Life and Getting Grit*

"Beautifully written, interesting, and compelling. Holland teaches us about the challenges that empty nesters face, and, ultimately, about life itself. Highly recommended!" —**Annette Lareau**, Professor of Sociology, University of Pennsylvania; author of *Unequal childhoods: Class, Race and Family Life*

"In her book *HappiNest*, Holland presents a vivid road map to help you navigate uncharted territory when your last child leaves home. This thought-provoking and evidence-based book presents valuable insights and practical advice such as how to set ground rules if your child 'boomerangs' back into the household, how to prune and cultivate friendships for more soul per square inch, and how to add spark, novelty, and joy to your empty nest marriage. *HappiNest* entertains, enlightens, and eases the passage into the second half of life." —**David J. Pollay**, MAPP, best-selling author of *The Law of the Garbage Truck*

"With the variety of stories included in *HappiNest*, Holland provides a wealth of support and suggestions to help readers effectively manage this transition. Just like the title promises, the book absolutely delivers engaging and inspiring ideas that will set the reader on a path to a new type of personal fulfillment." —**Suzanne Degges-White**, professor and chair, Department of

Counseling and Higher Education, Northern Illinois University; author of *Sisters and Brothers for Life: Making Sense of Sibling Relationships in Adulthood*

"When the children finally leave the nest, women and men can find themselves challenged by a new stage in their lives. Holland's book tells these parents not to despair! There are many roads to happiness, and Holland provides them with insightful tools and tips for self-fulfillment as they take this exciting new journey." — **Jocelyn Elise Crowley**, PhD, author of *Gray Divorce: What We Lose and Gain from Mid-life Splits*

"We have been in the empty nest for thirty years and work with couples dealing with empty nest issues. Holland's book, *HappiNest*, is by far the best resource available today for all those who want to prepare for and enjoy this stage of life. She has done her homework and gathered the best research, advice from experts, and good commonsense tips to guide you through the challenges of the empty nest years. A must-read if you are near or in the empty nest—or even if your nest has refilled!" —**Claudia and David Arp**, MSW, authors of *The Second Half of Marriage*

"Holland has written an exceptional book balancing personal narratives with sound empirical evidence focusing on the complex and dynamic process of the empty nest. She offers a thick description of the struggles, rewards, and multiple challenges that parents face as their children leave home (and sometimes return), while simultaneously maintaining and managing their own intimate relationships with each other, friends, and their children. Holland gives sound advice that can help us successfully make our way through this inevitable and significant life transition. I highly recommend this book to all parents, and departing children as well, who will soon, or who are in the lifelong process of transitioning to the empty nest." —**Jon F. NussBaum**, liberal arts professor of Communication Arts and Sciences and Human Development and Family Studies, Penn State University

"*HappiNest* is a great resource for those parents who find they have been successful at what they have been working toward for almost two decades (getting their children out of the house) and yet, when the time actually comes, find it may not be as easy to deal with as they thought." —**Elizabeth Lombardo**, PhD, best-selling author of *Better Than Perfect: 7 Strategies to Crush Your Inner Critic and Create a Life You Love*

"Very few people in the past felt either the luxury or the loneliness of having an empty nest. Holland perceptively analyzes why this stage of life has become a problem for many people and offers practical suggestions for how to deal with it." —**Stephanie Coontz**, author of *Marriage, A History: How Love Conquered Marriage*

"We live now in an era where most people have only one or two children and live to be at least 80 years old. That means there is a lot of life left once the kids leave home, as most do by their early twenties. This wise book provides a road map for how to make the most of the opportunities ahead once the nest has emptied out. and how to handle the challenges, too." —**Jeffrey Jensen Arnett**, author of *Emerging Adulthood: The Winding Road from the Late Teens Through the Twenties*

"A wealth of information based on research and interviews done by an expert journalist; *HappiNest* will help navigate you out of the lonely post-kids woods into a joyful next chapter." —**John "JW" and Pamela Gaye Walker**, EmptyNestersPlay.com

"A thoughtful meditation on living as an empty-nester, this book is chock full ideas inspired by philosophy, social science, and hundreds of real-life experiences. Holland has written a rich and compassionate work that will surely help the many who will read it not only avoid despair and isolation but, more importantly, lead increasingly meaningful and fulfilled lives. An inspiring and sorely needed work." —**Mario Luis Small**, PhD, Grafstein Family Professor of Sociology, Harvard University

HAPPINEST

HAPPINEST

Finding Fulfillment When Your Kids Leave Home

Judy Holland

ROWMAN & LITTLEFIELD
Lanham • Boulder • New York • London

Published by Rowman & Littlefield
An imprint of The Rowman & Littlefield Publishing Group, Inc.
4501 Forbes Boulevard, Suite 200, Lanham, Maryland 20706
www.rowman.com

6 Tinworth Street, London SE11 5AL

British Library Cataloguing in Publication Information Available

Library of Congress Cataloging-in-Publication Data

Names: Holland, Judy, 1959– author.
Title: HappiNest : finding fulfillment when your kids leave home / Judy Holland.
Description: Lanham : Rowman & Littlefield Publishers, 2020. | Includes bibliographical
    references and index. | Summary: "HappiNest provides a road map to help parents
    navigate new paths, evolving relationships and existential challenges when their kids
    leave home. This book distills the latest research and presents vignettes from inter-
    views with more than 300 experts, including psychologists, sociologists, seasoned empty
    nesters, and fledglings"—Provided by publisher.
Identifiers: LCCN 2019048449 (print) | LCCN 2019048450 (ebook) | ISBN
    9781538130582 (cloth) | ISBN 9781538130599 (epub)
Subjects: LCSH: Empty nesters—Psychology. | Parent and child. | Separation (Psychology)
Classification: LCC HQ1059.4 .H645 2020 (print) | LCC HQ1059.4 (ebook) | DDC
    306.874—dc23
LC record available at https://lccn.loc.gov/2019048449
LC ebook record available at https://lccn.loc.gov/2019048450

For my husband John
And the three lights of my life:
Lindsay, Maddie, and Jack

CONTENTS

Foreword   xiii

Introduction   1

SECTION I: FINDING YOURSELF IN THE EMPTY NEST
  1 Empty Nest Awakening   9

SECTION II: EMPTY NEST RELATIONSHIPS
  2 Reinvigorate Your Marriage   27
  3 The Dreaded D-Word: Divorce   43
  4 Don't Suffocate Your Spouse   59
  5 Empty Nest Birds of a Feather   79

SECTION III: GUIDING YOUR FLEDGLINGS
  6 Now That Your Kids Have Moved Out   95
  7 What Young Adults Really Want and Need   111
  8 Obstacles in the Way   129
  9 The Nest That Never Empties   147

SECTION IV: WORDS OF WISDOM
  10 Words from the Wise   169
  11 Lessons Learned   193

Notes	211
Bibliography	223
Index	229
About the Author	241

FOREWORD

I generally don't agree to write blurbs or forewords for friends' books because part of my job for years was to do author interviews for National Public Radio. I felt that it was best to stay out of the book promotion business because I might be creating a conflict among my many bosses and my many friends. However, exceptions must be made for friends who are also neighbors, and I am happy to be making an exception now. Some years ago, Judy Holland and her family moved in across the street from us and although we didn't know it, the move was a step toward the empty nest, an effort by Judy and her husband, John Starr, to make their lives a little easier by living near schools. We watched from over the road as the family staggered out of the house with sports equipment and loaded it into the car for road trips. We watched as the children had big noisy parties and we wondered whether their parents knew. But then the kids grew up and one by one went away to college. We watched the nest grow empty. And because while she was dragging gear bags and driving kids somewhere, Judy had always studied what was happening around her and written about it, we should have predicted that a book about this experience would be a logical next step—and here it is.

Judy's ideas about empty nesters and how they fare, moving as she says "through one of life's most daunting transitions," immedi-

ately made me think of the baby boom. Before we had the boomers and all they have disrupted in our lives, I doubt we thought
much about empty nesters. I imagine that American families with
girls hoped they would marry and helped as best they could to
make that happen. The parents of boys, even in the period between the world wars, hoped for their sons to be prosperous and
to support their families. Now, the more than 65 million
Americans born between 1943 and 1960 have changed all that and
taught us to look differently at what young men and women will do
with their lives. They have also forced us to always keep them in
mind, those boomers, and what they're up to, what they need
(housing, health care), how they are doing, and what else they may
change about this country before they are done. And now that we
have a term for the "daunting transition" to the time after the
children leave home, we have looked even more closely at what is
going on with the aging generations following the baby boom
decade. Judy's book, *HappiNest*, lays it out for us with the good
parts and the bad and with some guidance for making the best of
what is ahead when children leave home and parents find themselves living in an empty nest.

Let me get one thing out of the way early on: My husband and
I have no children. We have always lived in an empty nest and we
will never experience the change that the departure of children for
the wide world brings. Therefore, I do not come to this book as a
helpful read on how to redecorate my nest or reorganize my much
less busy life. But although this book will surely be helpful for
people looking for that kind of guidance, it goes in a quite different direction. Judy is interested in making a spiritual investment in
the lives of people she will touch with this book. Big Hint: the
literary/philosophical quote that heads each chapter gets rolling in
chapter 1 with Khalil Gibran. Judy suggests that the wrenching
experience of seeing your last child depart the family home could,
with some effort on your part, "trigger spiritual awakening." She
returns often to the life of the spirit, without being at all preachy
about it, and slips her ideas into the book along with anecdotes
about people who have been stressed by the difficulty of seeing

their children off to a new life but have found a way to manage
their unhappiness by looking around for their own new beginning.
Not everything works for the empty nesters Judy writes about.
Many of them look around their empty nest and notice this old
man or old woman grumbling somewhere over there and wonder
why the bright and beautiful child left and not this nasty old crea-
ture. Some of them look around and find their mate of many years
is preparing his/her own exit, unnoticed until this minute by the
other parent deeply engaged with children. Sometimes that works,
freeing both parents, and sometimes it doesn't, leaving one person
without sufficient emotional or financial support. Judy suggests, by
anecdote and example, that if effort is required to repair the relationship overshadowed by children, it is often well worth the probably painful effort to try. And she has some amusing and sometimes surprising ways to do that. One of them appears at first
glance to come out of *Good Housekeeping* or perhaps some version of *Cosmo for the Older Gal*: take dance lessons. But again,
Judy surprised me by offering research that suggests a sweet and
sexy graduation from a course in ballroom dancing.

Perhaps the best-covered new phenomenon caused by the
empty nest is that it doesn't always stay empty. We're not talking
about the spinster daughter returning home to live on the fringes
of the parents' lives and help around the house. That's what happens in nineteenth-century novels. These days the kiddies cruise
back into the home and settle in, expecting and generally getting
the same kind of care and attention they had in their younger days.
Laundry figures prominently in the conversations I have had with
friends in formerly empty nests. Judy says that one of the most
dangerous aspects of this reentry is that the young people are
hoping to re-up their relationship with The Bank of Mom and
Dad, and unless parents take a firm line they may find that their
own retirement will not be happening. Judy's thorough research
on this and the other topics she covers is enlightening if sometimes a bit chilling. She notes that children often truly need their
parents' help and there is no choice but to give it, but of course it's

also possible a child raised by responsible parents will be responsible about money, especially Mom and Dad's money.

This is, it seems to me, one of the most interesting generational changes; much as I loved my parents it never occurred to me to move back in with them after college. I went a great distance in the opposite direction and moved to London to take my first job in broadcasting. My mother retaliated by telling me that if I could afford to go overseas to live I could certainly afford to do without the allowance of my college years. I found out much later that she was even more furious when I agreed with her. But, again, Judy's research puts up a blinking yellow light aimed at parents who may be offering help that may not help either the parents or the child.

This book is generally optimistic about refilling the empty nest perhaps with visiting grandchildren, with new jobs, with returning to a previous passion, but makes clear that it is a lot of work. And of course the fledglings that fly out of the empty nest grow up and grow stronger and my observation is they often become more interesting. They reengage with their families as adults to adults. And parents grow older and will likely find it necessary to reinvent their own lives more than once. It's not exactly another empty nest moment, but with age comes loss of friends and family members and a need to find a way to survive that experience. Transcendence is what Judy suggests; pursue a course of action that will inspire and be good for other people, something that will add meaning to your life. It would be a good idea, she says, to get started early on this mission, maybe right after the kids leave home. After all, you will have leisure time for the first time in forever. And Judy, who never stops moving, would not want us to waste that precious time.

Linda Wertheimer
Former host of All Things Considered
National Public Radio

INTRODUCTION

There is no friendship, no love, like that of the parent for the child.

Henry Ward Beecher

Parenthood isn't like other close relationships. The whole point is that the other person is going to leave you—and that can be heart-breaking. After years of building a nest for your kids, you realize that you don't *own* them, you are just renting them for a while. And although it can feel natural to swoop down and protect them after they leave, you must step back and allow them to handle life's challenges so they can learn to live on their own.

Not only must you trust that they will find their way, but you also need to reinvent yourself—a complex and multifaceted task. Re-feathering the nest involves reassessing your values and prior-ities, resurrecting interests, setting new goals, cultivating relation-ships, adjusting parenting, and contributing to something larger than yourself.

The transition to the empty nest is unsettling and can throw you into existential crisis, sending you searching for purpose and meaning. After you finish the daily grind of child-rearing, you may be relieved, but also feel a visceral void. Your zeal for climbing the career ladder, striving for social status, and collecting material things is likely to subside, as is common in middle age. Friends and relatives may suffer from illness or pass away, igniting an urgent need to make sense of it all.

But the empty nest is different for everybody. While some parents celebrate as their fledglings soar, others fret as their off-spring struggle or join the one in three young adults who "boome-rangs" back home. Most young adults hover in between, taking a winding road to adulthood: going to school longer, settling on careers later, and finding mates further down the road than their parents did, if at all. Some parents remain on call from afar when their kids face extra challenges, such as serious illness, depression, or a learning issue. Some couples who have led lives wedded to their kids instead of each other are headed toward the empty nest rocks. Many empty nesters are stretched to the breaking point as they assist their kids as well as their parents, who are living longer and requiring lots of help. As life expectancy continues to climb, many of today's empty nesters are siphoning off retirement funds and staying in the workforce longer than ever to make ends meet.

You will face a different kind of empty nest depending on how old you are. If you are among the 65 million Americans born between 1943 and 1960, you're considered a baby boomer and should be well poised to reinvent yourself sans enfants. Boomers are known as rugged individualists, living lives full of interests and passionate causes. After their kids leave, many are returning to earlier pursuits such as painting, dabbling in politics, or playing the piano, according to Robert W. Levenson, a psychology profes-sor at Berkeley.[1] But boomers tend to be less financially secure than their parents in the so-called Silent Generation, who came of age in a thriving economy, when conditions were ripe for amassing great wealth.[2] Boomers weathered the financial storm of the mid-1980s, and are retiring later, with less money and fewer benefits, according to Neil Howe, a historian, economist, demographer, and coauthor of *Generations*.[3]

Born in 1959, my husband John Starr and I straddle two gener-ations, feeling like we have one foot with baby boomers and the other with Gen-Xers. If you are a Gen-Xer, born between 1961 and 1981, you are more likely than a boomer to be financially shaky, but also more inclined to be self-reliant. With more women in the workforce, many Gen-Xers were "latchkey kids," coming home after school to an empty house, chores, and responsibility. Hard hit by the Great Recession, they have struggled to buy homes.[4] Unlike those in the Silent Generation, who held mortgage parties at age 45 to 50 to celebrate paying off their homes, Gen-Xers "have pumped cash out of their mortgage, are leveraged to the hilt, and have no idea how they will retire," Howe says, "and that's going to hugely influence what the empty nest experience is."[5]

Despite these challenges, today's empty nesters have far more opportunities than those in previous generations. We can find information in a flash on the Internet, connect to others around the world instantaneously, work remotely, and travel faster and more efficiently. Better nutrition, more exercise, and advances in health and medicine have led to increased longevity, prompting many empty nesters to prepare for a second or third act. We have a longer time horizon to rediscover ourselves than our parents did, which can lead to greater fulfillment.

Regardless of how old you are, transitioning to an empty nest is tricky and requires moving mindfully. You are far from alone: 22.5 million couples were empty nesters in 2014, with their youngest kid older than 18 and no longer living under their roof, according to the U.S. Census Bureau.[6] To get a grip on the reality of empty nesters today, I have interviewed more than 300 people, including therapists, social workers, psychoanalysts, neuroscientists, psychologists, sociologists, and empty nesters who have shared with me their wisdom, struggles, and strategies. In *HappiNest,* I have distilled research that has been buried in broader studies on aging, romantic love, emerging adulthood, and long-term relationships. I am deeply grateful for these sources who have enlightened me and helped create a pool of wisdom on empty nesting.

As my husband and I adjust to life without kids under our roof, we are experiencing the themes of every chapter in a personal way. We are learning to listen more and lecture less to our oldest child Lindsay, a singer/songwriter who writes "Americana" and is aiming for the charts in Nashville. I have persuaded my music-loving husband to stop trying to "improve" her lyrics to satisfy his middle-aged sensibilities. We frequently drive our 155-pound Great Dane, Hudson, and yellow lab puppy, Babboo, to visit our middle child Maddie, who is on the mend from a head injury and finishing college. We tell ourselves she is just as happy to see us as she is the dogs, although it doesn't look that way. When she joined her college equestrian team as a beginning walk/trot rider, I was terrified she could fall. But I also applaud as she pursues a new passion, while preparing to enter the nonprofit world. John and I are both getting better at calming our jitters as our son Jack plays top-level college lacrosse, attempting to stop 100 mph balls from slamming into the goal—or him. I have learned to stop nagging him about homework, eating right, and getting enough sleep, now that he has become an NCAA championship goaltender and his lifestyle is more disciplined than my own.

To better understand our young adult kids and live with grace in the empty nest, I have tapped my journalist's skills, honed from decades in newsrooms, including as Capitol Hill correspondent for Hearst Newspapers. I have discovered a treasure trove of wisdom that has helped me reinvigorate my relationship with my husband and remember why I fell in love with him in the first place. I have placed a higher priority on my most important relationships, tak-ing time to both prune and broaden my social network to include new friends who soothe my soul. My relentless research to find wisdom in the empty nest has helped me transform childhood passions into new pursuits and muster the courage to march to-ward my dreams. I find joy aiming for the Aristotelian idea of *eudaimonia*—working to become the best version of myself, seek-ing purpose, and serving others. In so doing, I have found deeper meaning and fulfillment than ever before. Researching and writ-ing *HappiNest* has changed the way I approach each and every day. By reading this book, you too can gain a deeper understand-ing of how to move gracefully through one of life's most daunting transitions. As you travel through this new territory, you can use the tools in this book to better navigate the journey ahead.

A few days before my last child left for college, it was those pint-sized boxes of chocolate milk that got me, the ones I bought by the case for my kids. Who would drink them now? A week later, I found a solution: My husband and I would add those chocolate milks to our coffee and make mocha. Now we stock those cartons for us. That's what you do: reinvent with a twist.

Section I

Finding Yourself in the Empty Nest

I

EMPTY NEST AWAKENING

Ever has it been that love knows not its own depth until the hour of separation.

Khalil Gibran

When your last kid leaves home, you can be caught in a swirl of emotions: emptiness, excitement, and existential angst. You grasp in a profound way that your time on Earth is finite and that life really *is* impermanent. You notice more gray hair gracing your temples. Your peers look better in softer evening light—and you guess you do, too. You get this uneasy feeling that what remains of your youth is slowly slipping away. It suddenly makes more sense to weed out your possessions rather than add new stuff. That's because you realize that you can't take it with you. You feel a growing sense of urgency: How do I use my time in a way that really matters?

But here's the great news: While the departure of your last child is jarring, it also can deepen your sense of self and trigger spiritual awakening. Although you might hover in limbo at first, this is an opportunity to come to really know yourself. By being mindful, cherishing the time ahead, and heeding the wisdom of those who have gone before you, you can chart your course toward much more meaning and fulfillment. This can become the best time in your life. In the empty nest, "we have more of an opportunity to experience contentedness, deep appreciation, and love that's within our own heart and mind," says Matteo Pistono, a Buddhist scholar and author of *Meditation: Coming to Know Your Mind*. "We can do that in a deeper way because we have more relative freedom and no longer the same pressure we had before."[1]

EMPTY NEST EUDAIMONIA

> The ultimate end of human acts is eudaimonia, happiness in the sense of living well, which all men desire; all acts are but different means chosen to arrive at it.
>
> Hannah Arendt

As an empty nester, you are well positioned to find purpose, challenge, and growth—the elements of *eudaimonia*, a term Aristotle used to describe human flourishing, or the happiness you attain when working for something beyond yourself. *Eudaimonic well-being* requires doing something you believe in and pushing your limits to achieve it. For many of us, helping our offspring thrive and become independent brings an incomparable sense of satisfaction and well-being.

But raising kids is also a time when stress levels skyrocket. "Being responsible for someone's health and welfare brings forth challenges, time demands, and stressors," says David Almeida, a professor of human development and family studies at Penn State University.[2] Getting kids out of bed, making sure they have lunch and do homework, and preparing them in myriad ways brings potential for lots of tension, says Almeida, whose research shows intrapersonal relationships are a leading source of stress. Tending to the constant demands of kids also reduces *hedonic happiness*, or fun and pleasure, because there just isn't much time for that, he says.

When your kids go, it can be traumatic, because you are vacating a daily role that can be intense and all-consuming. But once you adjust to this mother-of-all transitions, you can see bright new vistas. "The empty nest is a very positive time of life," Almeida says. Once the kids leave, "you can maintain *eudaimonia* without the small irritations of day-to-day child-rearing that make you feel grumpy, angry, and irritated," he says. Empty nest distress is a signal that it's time to shift your nurturing elsewhere, to cultivate other relationships, check in more often on siblings or aging parents, and ease existential angst by identifying and acting on your values and priorities.

Collecting Spiritual Tools

Since she became an empty nester, Michelle has come to truly understand that "everything is impermanent," which has enabled her to value and savor what is right in front of her. She says accepting the idea that things—including life—are impermanent has helped her find joy in "meaningful moments of connection every day." She's come a long way since she went to Europe pregnant and alone at age 26, terrified and considering suicide. Back then, she was panicked and "wanted everything to end." Now that her only child Joe is in college, she is redoing that European trip, but this time she is "utterly thrilled to be alive and for the gift of who mothering made me."

Before Joe left, she decided to upgrade her faith in herself, others, and God to help her face the unknown in the second half of her life. So she embarked on a solo eighteen-day pilgrimage along the Camino de Santiago in Spain, hiking 15 to 17 miles a day in the mountains, staying in hostels, and carrying her possessions in a 12-pound bag. Along the route, she found she was "moved a million times a day by beauty, nature and human kindness."

As she walked in nature and considered the path to her empty nest, Michelle pondered the gifts she has gained from parenthood. She is now able to focus on what she has, rather than what she is missing. She says her struggles have taken her from "living in fear to living in faith." And while fear still sometimes creeps toward her, Michelle no longer lets it consume and control her as it once did. "Before I was white-knuckling everything, trying to control, direct, orchestrate, and manage," she says. She has learned to "relinquish control, let go, trust, appreciate little things, and find what brings joy."

Michelle had lots to rattle her. Her journey to motherhood started with an unplanned pregnancy followed by a stroke when she was nine months pregnant. When her son Joe was ten weeks old, she and his father split up. "If I didn't have faith, fear would have consumed and paralyzed me," she says. "In fact, many times, it was the very thing that got me through, particularly during times of stress and financial duress." She did her best to support her son, surviving the first three years of their life together on $12,000 a year.

As a single mother, she struggled for years with scant time for herself. Determined to create a stable home, she moved both of them to a Los Angeles apartment before the first day of kindergarten and found or created jobs including writer, filmmaker, executive coach, and advertising executive. When middle school classmates called Joe a "faggot" because he was acting and singing on stage, she encouraged his passion for performance and attended every show. She coordinated his transportation with trains and carpools to the Los Angeles County High School for the Arts 30 miles away. When he gained too much weight and the kids called him fat, she altered their diet, cooking proteins and vegetables, serving fruit, nuts, and eggs, and hiring a trainer/mentor to do boot camp with him in the backyard. Joe lost 65 pounds and developed a trim, muscular physique, qualifying him for leading-man roles in musical theater.

When he graduated from high school, she packed up their home of thirteen years, left her job, and drove across the country to Pace University in New York, where he was awarded a scholarship. Dropping him off at school felt easier than she had anticipated. "It was time for his life to take a new direction," she says. "And mine, too. I embraced this new beginning."

Michelle says she watches parents worry about "every little thing with their children," even when they leave the nest. But through her own journey, she has realized that kids are going to struggle and that they must grapple with difficulties in life to fully develop. It's a natural impulse as a parent to want to shield them, but it's also those irritations, the sand in the oyster shell, that help create the beautiful pearl. On the second day of her trek along the Camino, Michelle badly bruised her foot and was forced to learn to receive help from others. She initially was dejected because she had set out to be of service to others, not to seek help for herself. "I am a giver," she says. "There is great vulnerability in receiving." But on that bumpy trail she learned that spirituality is about "that which connects all people."

Michelle's current goal is to refocus on herself and find "clarity and connection." She likens this phase to the final performance of a stage play. "After the last performance, the whole set is struck, and the theater is returned to a black box and that world goes away," she says. "It almost feels like it is appropriate to strike the set and create a new play."

ANOTHER CHANCE AT LIFE

Just when the kids leave, middle age has a way of throwing crises your way that prompt you to reassess your priorities. That's not all bad, because reconsidering your goals and how you spend your time is a critical part of making the best of the empty nest. Just ask Jenny. Shortly after her only child went to college, she had two near-death experiences. First, after being doubled over for two days with searing stomach pain, she landed in the hospital, where doctors found her gallbladder was gangrenous and about to rupture. They removed the organ in the nick of time.

Shortly afterward, she was flying home to Washington, DC, after visiting her son in college, when the pilot's voice burst over the loudspeaker. "Prepare for impact," he warned. "Brace yourself as hard as you can." The plane had been damaged after hitting a flock of birds and they were headed for an emergency landing. Just as life shifts into slow motion when the protagonist in great literature faces a critical moment, Jenny's world seemed to slow way down and she felt "extraordinarily calm" as she sat in the exit row reviewing emergency instructions. A divorced 53-year-old World Bank economist accustomed to leading teams, Jenny clicked into gear and helped compose her seatmates, telling the flight attendant she was fully prepared.

She texted her son about the emergency landing and reminded him: "I love you." She told him where the important papers were and assured him, "You will be fine." He texted back in shock and said he loved her too. "Basically, that is all you can say in the end," she says. She sent her sisters a final goodbye, determined not to leave them with a distressing vision of the end of her life. "I didn't want them to think my last moments would be fear."

And then, the plane touched down safely.

Later, Jenny lost the calm she had found when she thought she was meeting her maker. "It completely freaked me out," she says. She came to realize in a profound way that life and its many trials and joys can end at any moment. "It's good to imagine what life would be like without you," she says. "I am so happy my son still has his mother."

These near-death experiences changed Jenny's approach to living in the empty nest. She is now determined to enjoy life to the fullest and focuses on the bright side. After eighteen years of lugging groceries home after work, she is delighted to skip formal meals. "I have a dish of butter, condiments, and a bottle of rosé" in the refrigerator, she says.

She has switched off the part of her that wished for other things in life, like being happily married instead of divorced. She has learned to savor what she has, not mourn what she lacks. More than ever, she is looking forward to what's next. She is open to connecting with others and appreciates humanity more. As we sit and talk at a tapas restaurant with a glass of wine, she jokes with the young waitress who has forgotten details of our order. Rather than reprimanding the young woman, Jenny teaches her a memory game. She laughs and chats with the waitress as she passes by, savoring the interaction. The waitress is twenty-something, like Jenny's new classmates in the improvisation group she recently joined. Jenny struggled with acting classes in college, then set aside her love of performance and focused on studying economics. But as an empty nester, she realized she had left part of her soul behind. Now she spends time with young adults who meet after work to invent jokes off the cuff, training in improv and preparing to perform. She's enthralled with this form of comedic acting, and delighted she has found another compelling purpose. "Whatever pity party I might have had has evaporated," she says. "I am on a new mission. I am going to use whatever time I have left."

THE GIFT OF GRATITUDE

Lisa is also on a mission: to be grateful for every day since her kids were born. After miscarrying twins at nineteen weeks, she swore off hormones and infertility drugs and figured she wasn't meant to be a mother. As a devout Catholic, she would light a candle at church and pray for a child. When Josh was born, the maternity ward nurse said words that echoed in her ears: *The ultimate job in parenting is unemployment.*

Realizing that parenthood is fleeting, she resolved to savor it right from the start. She quit her job in advertising in New York and devoted herself to raising Josh, and later Emma. Without a babysitter or relatives nearby, she spent thousands of hours with them in the backyard, enjoying simple things like finding four-leaf clovers, which brought serenity and taught her to live more in the moment. She pressed the clovers with her kids and fit them into books. "Whatever was going on, I embraced it," she says.

Sending her children to college was an adjustment, but now she views their young adult faces with gratitude instead of a sense of loss. "Yes, I miss them," she says. "But I am so grateful for who they have become." She can't relate when friends fret over their kids growing into young adults, despondent that the childhood years are past. Lisa says she knows exactly where the time went. "I've been here," she says. "I've been living it, breathing it. I've been fully in. I've been in the trenches with my children and now I get to see them be independent."

She's able to enjoy the moment more than ever, now employed as an instructional aide at a New Jersey preschool. After work these days, she skips the many hours in the kitchen she logged for her young family, instead slapping a sandwich together or grabbing a quick bite with other empty nesters. When she's walking the dog, she doesn't worry about tomorrow and revels in details like the color of a leaf or the fragrance of a flower. She practices yoga unhurriedly and feels a new level of connection between body and mind, continually seeking signs on her spiritual journey. Says Lisa: "If you search for it, there's always a place of joy. You just have to look for it."

SPIRITUAL GIFTS

Gratitude like Lisa's goes a long way to making us tranquil and centered. "When we appreciate things we have or are yet to have, it helps them become part of our lives," says Martha Simkins Davis, a life coach in Laguna Beach, California, who teaches meditation and other ways to dig into the subconscious mind.[3] "Gratitude is like a prayer," she says. "It helps draw out all the amazing things, the miracles in our lives."

Picturing what we want and being thankful in advance helps us focus on the positive, rather than worrying about the negative. If we experience ten positive things and one negative, the brain tends to remember the negative one and that produces even more negativity, triggering stress hormones like cortisol, which increases blood sugar and suppresses the immune system. Negativity also triggers the fight-or-flight response, a physiological reaction to a perceived threat.

Gratitude, on the other hand, produces endorphins, a morphine-like substance from the central nervous system and pituitary gland that triggers a feeling of euphoria. Gratitude also releases oxytocin, which induces healthy, positive feelings and plays a role in social bonding. If you focus on gratitude, or something positive, you bring more of that into your life. "Gratitude is a very simple way of creating positive thinking," Simkins Davis says.

A TIME OF AWAKENING

If every day is an awakening, you will never grow old. You will just keep growing.

Gail Sheehy

Gratitude is great, but mark my words: The empty nest transition is tricky. For the better part of two decades, many parents, myself included, have been focusing on their kids in extraordinary ways. Guiding a young family can make a parent feel like Hans Brinker, the legendary Dutch boy who stuck his finger in the dike to stop a leak and was afraid to change what he was doing for fear that the whole balancing act might come crashing down.

When you are a parent with kids at home you can feel like your work is without end. Always needing to take care of things creates "deep mental grooves, deep habitual grooves," says Pistono, the Buddhist scholar and meditation teacher.

So when the kids go, it's hard to get out of those well-worn grooves and just "rest there for the moment and not be focused outwardly," he says. It's very difficult to stop, pause, and examine the moment during this transition because chances are you've been so busy with kids that you chose not to focus inward.

The space that's left when the kids leave home can make empty nesters feel uneasy or dissatisfied. They may feel they can't ever be completely fulfilled. Many begin filling that space with lots of things to do like volunteering at an animal shelter, feeding the homeless, playing golf or tennis, joining the church choir, writing a memoir, or learning to play the piano or paint.

But those positive activities may not bring the contentedness they seek, Pistono says. That's because, even with their new freedom and no more wet socks on the floor, empty nesters often avoid focusing on themselves. Pistono says people avoid looking inward because searching inside yourself "is not ever a super peaceful and comfortable place to look into because we encounter ourselves nakedly."

For empty nesters who are ready to explore new forms of spirituality, Pistono says meditation is the simplest way to start. Meditation is about retreating to a quieter and calmer place in your mind. It can involve techniques such as watching your breath, scanning your body, or doing yoga, which can help you slow down so you can respond more mindfully. Instead of feeling unhappy or stressed because of something outside us, we can learn to create a gap between stimulation from the outside world and our reaction to it. We learn to let things come and go in and out of our mind without having an opinion about every thought. We learn to control how we react. "Through meditation, we're able to arrive at a place that is calm and collected," Pistono says.

But meditation is far from a panacea. And it isn't the only way to find peace and spirituality. Many people find that sense of calm by running, dancing, swimming, stretching, singing, or listening to music.

Ministry to Others and Self

Some empty nesters find order and spirituality by providing service to others. After Gigi's two sons left for college at Ole Miss, she says she felt a "huge responsibility" to find a new purpose. She had "honored God and served him" by raising children, and was determined to do more when they left home.

When she heard about a Christian ministry at a prison in Lock-hart, Texas, a half hour from her Austin home, the 52-year-old real estate agent was ready to volunteer, even though she had never been in a prison and had some reservations. It was outside her comfort zone because the people she would visit had broken the law. But, she says, she "felt the Lord wanted me to do it." She went through background checks and six months of training, and signed an agreement acknowledging that she could be taken as a hostage. "It was quite daunting."

A sixth-generation Texan, Gigi was nervous about walking into a "serious prison," but determined to answer God's call to serve there. She was scanned in, patted down, and turned in her cell phone. The prison was home to 150 women who took showers in a large, common area and were locked in their rooms at night. She followed the prison's strict guidelines: nothing sleeveless, close-toed shoes, no sandals. Nonetheless, when she walked in, she felt every eye on her in street clothes. "I was acutely aware the second I stepped on the property that everywhere I went, they were watching me and wanted to see what I was wearing and every action I took. Every kindness was under huge scrutiny." The in-mates would touch her clothes and comment on them. Once, when she was racing to get there by the 7 a.m. start time, she threw on a pair of warm-up pants and left the house without makeup. When she arrived, she saw dropped faces. "They were disappointed that I was not dressed up."

She felt particularly needed in the women's prison. Male pris-oners often have women who come to see them on visiting day, she said, but "no one comes to see the women ever." The women in the Lockhart prison were "desperate for someone to say they matter," Gigi says, and she tried to fill that role.

It was a humbling experience. Many of the women were deter-mined to make a life change and devoted themselves to studying the Bible. Most had struggled with addiction to drugs and alcohol. They had been incarcerated for crimes including check fraud and prostitution. She mentored them, helping them prepare to be re-leased and coming up with plans so they would not fall back into the activities that got them in trouble. Gigi would ask them, "How are you going to break the chains and keep away from the people who got you in here?" She recalls one woman who had become a prostitute to earn money for drugs. She was in a bike gang and had nine children, all with different fathers; one son was in prison for murder. Like many of the other female inmates, she would join Gigi to pray for her children and learn God's word. Gigi says her prison ministry has brought her tremendous wisdom and fulfillment. "You've got to keep growing and having a purpose and making a difference," she says. Gigi's leap out of her comfortable and usual space into a world vastly different from her own helped her see her own life with greater clarity.

SPIRITUALITY IN NATURE

> I went to the woods because I wished to live deliberately,
> to front only the essential facts of life,
> and see if I could not learn what it had to teach.
>
> Henry David Thoreau

While meditation, chasing a passion, and connecting with like-minded people can help you find spirituality, so too can nature. Nature was a soothing presence for Simkins Davis, the Laguna Beach life coach, when her last child was in her final year of high school and she found herself at odds with her husband. After more than a decade of counseling, they were "dancing to different music and different rhythms." She knew she had to dissolve the marriage, but it was terrifying. She was sure her husband agreed, but both couldn't make the change. They felt stuck in "negative patterns" and something had to give. Separation seemed to be the only alternative. "Drastic change is scary because it's unfamiliar," she says. "It's like falling off a cliff. But you've got to get your feet off the cliff and do it sometimes."

When Simkins Davis found her marriage faltering and she knew the kids were leaving soon, she says she needed to find herself and her soul to survive, so she dove into things she loves to do, such as teaching yoga after two decades of practice—leading classes in postures, breathing techniques, and meditation methods aimed at finding physical and emotional well-being. She also trained to teach tai chi and qigong, the predecessor to the martial arts that is aimed at aligning ourselves with "universal life source energy." Simkins Davis says the goal of much of her practice is to train the mind "to return to the being you really are," beyond social labels and personal identity.

She now leads retreats in a North Carolina rain forest where the Appalachian, Blue Ridge, and Smoky Mountains come together, taking people past pines, oaks, hickories, dogwood, and maples, in a ritual known as "forest bathing."

"I go back there often and that's where I really ground myself," she says. Hiking in the forest, she guides others "to find out what their soul is calling for." Hiking is "a meditation in and of itself, because you are moving your body and your breath to the rhythm," she says. She grew up in a Southern agricultural family with parents who could identify every wildflower and tree they encountered. On her walks, she says, she notices "each little thing, each little plant, and to know the names is really magical." She also finds spirituality in that beauty. "It's a reflection of that beautiful God force in the world. When we put ourselves into nature, it helps us stop worrying about what we have and don't have." Nature, she says, provides a change in perspective. "You are kind of stepping out of time and space. That's what spirituality is all about."

She coaches empty nesters to find something they love, which will bring new people and learning into their lives. "You get involved in something that makes your heart sing and everything else falls into place," she says. "It's like you are getting nods from the universe." For those who are hesitant to try new activities, she suggests going into it with "little turtle steps."

The empty nest, she says, is a perfect moment to cultivate our souls because we can take the time to go back into ourselves. "By stepping out of our day-to-day existence and slowing life down, we find a grounded, peaceful place of ease and greater knowing, inspiration, and creativity," she says. "That's where you stay in the eye of the storm." Whatever chaos rages around you in the world, spirituality, combined with a sense of purpose and service to something larger than yourself, can bring a deep sense of meaning and fulfillment. It can keep you at the calm center.

The Ticket to Happiness

Laurie Cameron learned at age 16 that life is finite when her father, a rocket scientist, had a heart attack while she was standing next to him. When he died that day, she "perceived the impermanence of all things."[4] Many people experience this concept of impermanence much later, after their kids leave home. The visceral sense of loss prompts them to reflect deeply on what really matters to them—often for the first time. Facing a void, many empty nesters read stacks of articles and talk to others about how to navigate this phase of life. But Cameron, author of *The Mindful Day: Practical Ways to Find Focus, Calm, and Joy from Morning to Evening*,[5] suggests you start by focusing internally, to gain a better understanding of your interests, strengths, and values and where your passions and strengths intersect with what the world needs.

Each morning, instead of jotting down a to-do list, Cameron follows a deliberate and purposeful routine, which includes journaling, a great way to bring forth insight and clarity on what matters most. You can ask yourself, "Where should I serve?" "What might be my next project?" "What's my vision for the life I want to lead now?" During the day, Cameron also takes a "mindful pause," asking herself if an action is bringing her closer or further away from her vision.

After the kids go, you need to clarify your vision. While many parents think that taking a trip, buying a new car, or getting a facelift will help fill the void, these are fleeting pleasures. "The way we create sustainable, optimal states of well-being and happiness is living a life of meaning, purpose and connection," she suggests. The key is to shift our thinking from an "I or me" mind-set to thinking more about "we," and how our lives and actions are benefiting the greater good. A grateful, compassionate life and serving others is "the guaranteed ticket to happiness," Cameron says.

Instead of viewing the empty nest as a hole to be filled, reframe and re-envision what life looks like, she says. Take a conscious step back and determine how you envision your ideal life. Look deliberately at habits and behaviors that you want to stop, such as ruminating, obsessing, or thinking in negative ways. "What we want to do is put the brakes on habits and mindsets that don't serve us anymore and put the gas pedal on habits and practices that do fulfill us," Cameron says. If you move purposefully into the empty nest, you have an opportunity to find eudaimonia.

Section II

Empty Nest Relationships

2

REINVIGORATE YOUR MARRIAGE

There is no more lovely, friendly and charming relationship,
communion or company than a good marriage.

Martin Luther

After the marathon of child-rearing, it's time to turn toward your
spouse and nurture the bond you share. If the marriage is solid
after all these years, you can focus on the *two* of you. You can look
forward to navigating this transition with novelty, fun, and a sense
of adventure.

There's never been a better time to be an empty nester: Most
parents today are experiencing a renaissance in their relationship
when their kids leave, says Berkeley psychology professor Robert
W. Levenson, who has been conducting an ongoing study of baby
boomers and their parents since 1989. His research shows that
baby boomers who are together with their spouses after the kids
leave are finding their connection gets stronger and "they are reminded of the reason they got married in the first place. . . . This is
a chance to go back and rediscover that person who got pushed
aside."[1]

The quality of your connection to your mate is a huge predictor
of how happy you will be in life. More so than smoking or being
overweight, it also affects how long you will live. An unhappy

marriage can do more damage to your sense of self than other relationships can. We might not choose our parents, siblings, or kids, but we *do* choose our mates—and if we're not happy in those relationships, it can be devastating.

Having fun together is vital to the health of a marriage. Just ask Elizabeth Rubin, a relationship therapist who has counseled couples for forty years and is on the clinical faculty of the Department of Psychiatry at the Yale School of Medicine. When couples appear in her office, she immediately asks them about the "f-word," and they assume she is referring to their sex life. After an awkward silence she tells them she is talking about *fun*. "When is the last time you had *fun* together?" she asks. Fun can lead to intimacy, a reflection of strong emotional connection. "Emotional and sexual intimacy are both an essential part of any marriage," Rubin says. "When sex is good, it's 10 percent of the relationship. When sex is bad, or not happening, it's 90 percent of the relationship." When you find yourself in the empty nest, you should try to resurrect the intimacy you once had or make a mutual decision to recreate the warmth that has been missing. Rubin also recommends that you "approach the world with curiosity and don't let your fears determine your decisions."[2]

You might take a trip to a new place or go on double dates with another couple. It need not be expensive or time-consuming: You can wander together through a new part of the city, learn to cook an ethnic cuisine, go bowling, or practice the tango. If you strive to broaden your own horizons, the energy it creates will make you more attractive to your partner. There's nothing sexier or more magnetic than having "a strong sense of self, a lack of dependence, and a willingness to be engaged in the world," Rubin says.

SENDING SIGNALS

> To keep your marriage brimming,
> With love in the loving cup,
> Whenever you're wrong, admit it;

Whenever you're right, shut up.

Ogden Nash

You can reignite the spark in your empty-nest marriage by sending better signals to your spouse. This is particularly important after the kids leave because as many as two-thirds of parents experience a marriage downturn during child-rearing years, according to the Gottman Institute, a Seattle-based couples counseling and research center known as the Love Lab.[3] Relationships often strain when couples develop kid-centric marriages that revolve around jam-packed schedules and kids' interests, leaving little time for the romantic partner. Many couples turn away from each other because they are weary and stretched in too many directions. They no longer make or respond effectively to what Donald Cole, clinical director and master trainer with the Gottman Institute, calls "bids" for attention.[4]

Strong couples turn toward each other, making frequent bids, such as asking how the other is feeling, Cole says. For instance, a husband who hears a song on the radio might say something about it to his wife, inviting her to interact. According to Cole, she might "turn toward the bid," engaging in conversation about the song. However, she also might turn against his bid, saying, "You play *stupid* music," or keeping her eyes on the road and ignoring him, Cole says. Successful couples turn toward each other and make bids for connection in 86 percent of their interactions, while failing couples turn toward each other just 33 percent of the time,[5] according to John Gottman, cofounder of the institute that bears his name. If the husband reaches out and his wife rebuffs him, he will fear rejection and be less likely to try to connect the next time. But if she responds nicely, he is more likely to engage her on other topics. Says Cole: "Bids lead to more bids, while turning away leads to more turning away." When couples start blowing off each other's bids, they enter a negative cycle that spirals downward.

While empty nesters may have had fun and positive interactions with each other during activities like high school dance recitals and football games, the connection revolved around the kids. In overly child-centered marriages, "You pull the kid out and now there's nothing," Cole says. "You can't wish away the downward spiral by force of will. That would be like saying you are going to be in shape physically without doing what the in-shape people do," such as exercising and changing diet. "If you want to have a positive marriage or relationship, you have to do the things that successful people do in this regard," Cole says. "You can't wait until you feel close, that's an illusion." Many empty nesters need to actively repair their relationships, especially if they haven't taken time to maintain them, he says.

Cole recommends finding "hundreds of little ways to connect," such as talking about your day in positive ways or scheduling a weekly date. Cole and his wife Carrie, also a therapist, created a Friday ritual they call *lupper*. They meet at 2 p.m. for the lunch/supper combo, starting the weekend together before the children get home. And each morning, Cole gets up first to feed the kids. Then he takes scrambled eggs or yogurt and fruit to Carrie in the bedroom, cracking the same joke each day. She answers daily with the same response and they watch the news and eat breakfast together. One morning when he entered the room, she skipped her usual line and said "thanks" instead, disrupting the ritual. Cole asked if she was upset and learned that he had inadvertently blown her off earlier, coming across as dismissive. Cole realized there was a problem and apologized. The willingness to use such corrective behavior is the biggest predictor of relationship success, he says.

GIVE AND TAKE

Marriage is not just spiritual communion and passionate embraces: marriage is also three meals a day, sharing the workload and remembering to take out the trash.

Joyce Brothers

A happy empty nest requires give and take on both sides. Cole's wife Carrie, who loves to sing, pines to go to the Houston Grand Opera, which is definitely not on the top of his fun list. While Cole would prefer to see the Houston Astros, he opts instead for season tickets to the opera, which thrills his wife. When the couple goes to Grenada to help out at the medical school there, she swallows a Dramamine and goes deep-sea fishing with him despite her sea-sickness. "I know if I give to my wife, I will get," he says. "She will look for opportunities to give to me."

If each spouse is interested in the performance of this team of two, rather than just their own success, the marriage can thrive. But when couples fail to show interest in each other's lives outside the relationship, the union can end in divorce. "Instead of seeing our partner as someone interested in our well-being, we start seeing our partner as selfish," Cole says. Happy partners say, "I care about you and you care about me," he says. "We are committed to each other's needs, not just our own."

Flickering Flame

Long-term romantic relationships continue to evolve over time. In her book *Gift from the Sea*, author Anne Morrow Lindbergh likens a couple that is struggling to create a home, raise children, and find a place in society to an oyster that clings "tenaciously" to a rock. The couple, like the oyster, forms ties, roots, and a firm base, which is hard work and not always pretty. During these busy years, the oyster is "humble, awkward and ugly," she writes, "slate-colored and unsymmetrical" with a form that is "not primarily beautiful but functional."[6] Once the kids leave for lives of their own, Lindbergh suggests it is time to move to "another form," and new experiences. We must carefully select only a few goals in the empty nest, just as it is not possible to collect all the shells on the beach. We must select the ones that are the most meaningful to us.

Denise finally found beauty in the empty nest after a tough transition. When her only child got a scholarship to Texas A & M University, becoming the first in the family to go to college, she cried tears of joy. "I fell on my knees and bawled when the acceptance letter arrived," she recalls. But her tears kept falling for more than a year after her daughter Liz moved from her home in Corpus Christi to College Station, three and a half hours away. "I wasn't afraid for her," Denise says. "I was more afraid for me. I cried for the entire school year. And maybe even six months after. When I'd pass the high school, I'd cry again. . . . I'd think, 'Who am I going to be now?'"

Her husband Tommy, who built scaffolding and suffered from chronic headaches, was often groggy from migraine medication. He gained weight and preferred to spend his non-working hours on the couch. But out of her frustration came impetus for change. Denise researched her husband's headache meds and found a way to wean him off them and ditch the couch for the beach at North Padre Island, where the couple gathers often with friends to throw horseshoes. "I see him at his happiest," she says. "I never knew how competitive he was." They wear pedometers, a gift from their daughter, and measure the steps they take each day. Denise is delighted when her husband points out that he is winning the walking contest. "Now he is the one I knew before," she says. "Now we really like to be with each other."

NOVELTY KINDLES THE FIRE

> Of all the passions of mankind, the love of novelty most rules
> the mind. In search of this, from realm to realm we roam.
>
> Shelby Foote

We all yearn to grow and experience new things, which bolsters the human spirit. "A basic human motivation is the desire to expand your ability to accomplish goals, and when that happens it's really rewarding,"[7] says Arthur Aron, a professor at Stony Brook

University on Long Island who studies the psychology and neurobiology of romantic love. Aron's research shows that when you do things with your partner that are novel and challenging, you become elated and associate the good feelings with your mate.[8] Aron divided 53 couples who were married an average of fifteen years into three groups. He assigned the first third to spend 90 minutes a week doing something new and exciting, the second third to an activity they deemed pleasant, and the last group to nothing new. Those participating in novel and exciting activities reported "a big boost in their relationship quality," Aron says.

In another study, couples in Aron's research lab were tied together with Velcro straps at their wrists and ankles and crawled across a long set of gym mats, pushing a cylindrical pillow without using their hands, arms, or teeth.[9] The goal was to make it across the room and back quickly. Couples who took part in this edgy activity reported feeling much more love and satisfaction afterward than those who participated in a more mundane exercise.

Novel activities needn't be pricey. For example, going to the movies fits the bill because the visual material is new. Aron and his wife Elaine, also a psychologist, collaborate on new research projects, which adds spark to their relationship. They also kayak together, avoiding rivers with heavy rapids because they are novices. "One thing you do have to be careful about is not overdoing it," he says. "You don't want to take on a challenge you can't handle." For example, if you're afraid of heights, hiking the Matterhorn could stress, rather than bolster, the bond.

There's no question that novelty triggers a chemical boost. Those are the findings of Xiaomeng Xu, an assistant professor of psychology at Idaho State University who used MRI neuroimaging techniques to scan brains of people playing computer games or looking at something new. The scans show that participating in novel activities increases blood flow to areas of the brain rich in dopamine, the feel-good neurotransmitter associated with reward, motivation, and learning.[10]

Xu, who grew up in New York City, recalls the excitement of moving to Pocatello, Idaho. When she went bowling with her boyfriend for the first time, she felt her mood lifted by a release of dopamine, which would have been larger than that experienced by her boyfriend, who had gone many times. She was similarly thrilled to go with him to her first state fair and witness mutton busting, which is like bull riding, but with young children trying to ride sheep. She recalls acting "like a little kid squealing and grabbing him because it was such a fun thing to watch."[11]

Still Dancing

Relying on each other can reinforce your empty-nest relationship, as the Deals discovered once they began taking dancing lessons together. As they moved belongings from their old house into a new one in Falls Church, Virginia, the couple kept passing a dance studio. They had loved dancing in their dating days but had started and stopped lessons when their careers and kids were going full tilt. With the kids out on their own, they had more time and a new house with room to practice. While the prospect of learning intricate patterns and positions seemed daunting at age 60, it also was exciting, says Kathleen Holtz Deal, a retired assistant professor at the University of Maryland School of Social Work. Mastering the fox-trot and tango required clear communication and "wasn't always pretty," she says. But it was "a real rush" when it worked, she says. "It felt good to do this together. It was encouraging to have each other to remember things and to rely on."[12]

Her husband Dave, an attorney and mediator, says learning dance patterns was fine, but mastering the framing—how you hold yourself relative to your partner—was the hard part. "For several months or so our dancing was kind of clomping along," he says, but over time the movements became fluid through focus and repetition. Proficiency on the dance floor requires many of the skills involved in maintaining a strong marriage. When you "misstep" and end up "out of whack," you learn not to stop, but to keep moving through it, communicate, collect yourselves, and step out of the problem, he says.[13]

Kathy says dancing "made me pay attention to our bodies in relation to each other," since each dance requires a different frame and nonverbal communication to create a stylish flow. She learned to follow her husband's lead and body movement by closing her eyes and paying close attention to how things felt. For two people whose jobs were largely cerebral, learning to dance better was great, she says. There was no room for tentative moves. Dave says good dancing requires "firming up your frame, staying in close contact, maintaining the tempo, and never rushing through the steps." It has provided a sense of novelty and excitement, Kathy says. "Now we have this ability to do something together that we were not able to do before," she says. "When we get out there and we move across the floor, it's so much fun." Twelve years after they hit the dance floor as empty nesters, the Deals are still going strong.

Connecting Dots

Stepping into your spouse's space can make the heart grow fonder. After their only child Dawson left for college, Kim convinced her husband Todd to enroll in a drawing class together at Florida State University. Kim says the experience "shook up our regular routine" and allowed him to "come into her world," which tends to be more creative and freewheeling. She was amused to see differences in the way they approached the class. Todd, who is precise and scientific, with a PhD in biology and ornithology, insisted on buying a how-to book on drawing before the class started, so he could practice his skills. Kim took a more hands-on approach, preferring to enter the class without any prep and looking forward to sketching whatever the teacher put on the table. Their shared experience helped them appreciate the contrast in their styles and enhanced the relationship. "I love that he was open to this," she says.

Next, it was Todd's turn to take the lead and expose his wife to his hobby. He bought Kim a kayak for her birthday, so she can join him on the river enjoying the wildlife around them. Kim says she admires that he knows every bird and can identify every natural sound he hears. "Being with him in his world makes me really, really appreciate him."

A RENEWED GAZE

Diversions like ballroom dancing, taking a drawing class, or learning to kayak foster "mystery, intrigue, and unpredictability,"[14] allowing partners to view each other with a renewed gaze, says Amy Muise, an assistant professor of psychology at York University in Toronto. While sexual desire can be high in the early stages of a relationship because partners are getting to know each other and having many "self-expanding" experiences, these opportunities tend to decline over time.

But you can reignite the spark. In a study Muise led in Canada, researchers asked couples to find joint pursuits that provide "a sense of newness and self-expansion." The couples completed questionnaires for 21 days about activities they agreed on, such as teaching the other to make a cherry pie, playing beer pong, shucking oysters, taking a road trip, going to a cooking class, and bungee jumping. When couples felt they were learning and growing, they were likely to experience more sexual desire for their mate and greater satisfaction in their relationship—and they were 36 percent more likely to have sex that day.

In a later study, Muise divided couples into three groups. The first group was instructed to seek novelty and challenges, the second was told to seek experiences that made them feel safe and comfortable, and the third was not given instructions. At the end of the weekend, couples who tried novel and challenging activities and those who participated in safe and comfortable pursuits both reported a boost in their relationships. But those engaged in new and exciting pursuits were more attracted to each other and more likely to become intimate. Muise also found that participating in novel activities was not only good for their sex lives, but also for their romantic relationships. Three months later, the couples who did novel activities together were still the happiest and most likely to stay together. The empty nest presents "new opportunities for novelty and growth and to see your partner in a new way," Muise says. "Seize those opportunities to involve the partner and share it with them.

There's lots you can do to reinvigorate your relationship. Renowned biological anthropologist Helen Fisher, an expert on romantic love and consultant for Match.com, says intimacy in a long-term relationship stimulates the dopamine system to trigger optimism and energy, and sparks the oxytocin system, or hormones, to revive feelings of attachment and union.[15] She suggests empty nest couples read to each other and travel by bike, train, plane, and on foot rather than going by car. Fisher recommends couples get emotionally closer by staying in touch during the day, walking arm in arm, holding hands, sitting together on the couch, and falling to sleep in each other's arms.

The Spark of Self-Growth

If you focus on self-growth and do it well, it will rub off on your relationship. If you've always loved watching *The Great British Bake Off* and want to be a great baker, you don't have to "rope your partner in" to have this new hobby strengthen your marriage, Xu says, as long as he doesn't make "snarky remarks, tell you how you are wasting your time, and complain how dirty the kitchen is." New challenges pump you up and make you more fun, which fills the relationship with verve. "It's more fun to interact with someone who is happy and excited and energetic and positive and not in a rut," Xu says.

A person who learns yoga and meditation to reduce stress may become a better partner. Or, if your partner learns to play the guitar or goes on a business trip to Italy, you can benefit from enjoying her new music skills or hearing about her travel. When your friendships and work relationships are stimulating, you have lots to share with a partner. And if you help your partner reach goals, it also boosts the relationship. This is what psychologists call the Michelangelo Phenomenon, in which couples "sculpt" each other toward their desired selves. Like Michelangelo, who said he was releasing sculptures from the rock, you can help your partner chisel themself into who they want to be, Xu says.

Double-Dating

You also can bolster your bond with your partner by going out with another couple. When you go on a double date and talk about serious thoughts and concerns, rather than making small talk, it tends to bring everyone closer and enhance each couple's relationship, says Richard B. Slatcher, an associate professor of social psychology at Wayne State University, who studies marriages and other close relationships.[16] That's what he found when he assigned 60 heterosexual couples to engage in a 45-minute interaction at his lab with another couple they didn't know. One group was asked to answer questions such as, "For what in your life do you feel the most grateful?" or "How close and warm is your family?" He assigned another group to chat about everyday topics, such as, "When was the last time you walked for more than an hour?" and "Describe where you went and what you saw." Slatcher found those who shared deeper emotions and concerns felt closer to the other couple as well as their own romantic partner.[17]

Sharing meaningful conversation can have a lasting effect. Slatcher's study found that a month later, the couples who had thoughtfully shared their concerns felt more like hanging out with the other couple and seemed to be on a path toward real friendship. But the small-talkers weren't interested in connecting again. People who shared deeper thoughts also were more committed to the success of the other couple's relationship and felt closer to their own partners afterward.

Joining with another empty nest couple can add another dimension to an outing. If two couples are playing golf and they all witness one of them get a hole in one, that "doubles the fun," says Geoffrey L. Greif, a professor at the University of Maryland School of Social Work and coauthor of *Two Plus Two: Couples and Their Couple Friendships.*[18] Double-dating also triggers new ideas and can lead to everyone staying healthier.

A few years ago, my husband and I began getting together with Cindy and Michael. Michael, a former fighter pilot who studied rocket science at MIT, shares with my surgeon husband a background in science. And while I had been trying for a decade to get John to shed some weight, Michael had instant credibility regarding the chemistry of calories. While we were together at a restaurant, Michael waved off the bread basket and potato, ordering steak and vegetables and explaining how his low-carb diet helped him drop 20 pounds while maintaining his bon vivant ways. John cut his carbs and lost 12 pounds.

Sharing an evening with another couple can prompt more thoughtful discussions. It may allow a woman to talk to her friend's husband in a "safe, non-sex-charged environment," enabling people of different genders to explore what each other think, Greif says. Double dates also help women, who tend to be more emotionally expressive, to air difficult issues with their mates, who may otherwise avoid them. Men, who often need an activity like golf or a football game to get together, are likely to be pulled into more meaningful dialogues if another woman is present, he says.

Double dates also allow partners to gain awareness because they have a front-row seat at another couple's drama. Empty nesters tend to be more interested than younger couples in bonds they share with others and are more likely to examine their own marriages after spending time with other couples, says Kathleen Holtz Deal, coauthor of *Two Plus Two.* When one half of a couple behaves positively, or negatively, toward the other, the car ride home can reveal insights for the other pair. If the other husband embarrassed his wife, it might prompt one partner to say, "Let's never do that." And if the other couple stood up for each other, it might prompt a spouse to say, "I wish we could do that," Deal says.

THE MAGIC OF WALKING

A healthy marriage requires a lot of work. And sometimes walking is the way to get that work done. While on sabbatical in Switzerland, Slatcher and his wife noticed the Swiss spending lots of time walking and hiking, so they decided to join them, taking long, brisk walks together a few times a week, ignoring cell phones except to track the route. Frequent use of a cell phone is "a barrier to intimacy that makes the person who is trying to talk to the other person feel rejected," he says. Walking is also better for couples than running because it allows time for conversations without huffing and puffing, he says. And walking in nature rather than a man-made environment allows you to relax your mind, reduce stress, improve your mood, and see things from a different perspective.

Walking together at the end of the day is a welcome respite for Jennifer and Nelson Cox, who are both away for work half the week. As Nelson, a corporate pilot and an avid runner, holds leashes for the family's two dogs, his wife, a manager at a credit-reporting agency, tries to keep up with him for three miles down a dirt road near their home in Flower Mound, Texas. "I'm not going to stay home on the couch," she says. Before their two kids left for college, their walks were consumed with talk about homework, tests, and baseball games. But now they find themselves talking more about their careers, weekend plans, and their newest project, decorating an empty nester house they just built. Jennifer says she was pleasantly surprised to discover her husband was so opinionated about the decor. She sees him take the lead on the creative decisions and is delighted their decorator defers to him on color and design. "I like seeing things through his eyes," she says. Jennifer says they are most likely to be in sync when they are side by side: "It's a relaxing stroll down the street," she says. "We're very content."

Nature's Sanctuary

Wandering in nature also works wonders. Instead of visiting urban museums as they did for two decades when their sons were home, Nassim and her husband Cyrus have downshifted into nature, hiking for miles near the Potomac River, along the towpath of the Chesapeake & Ohio Canal. They are unwinding from a year that felt like they were racing down "a highway at 150 miles an hour," as both of them were treated for cancer while they sold the family business and took their last child to college. Now that they have recovered, Nassim revels in hugging a tree at Great Falls Park in Virginia. "It's been standing there for hundreds of years subject to all the elements," she says. "By hugging it, I appreciate it and draw energy from it."

They both sense subtle treasures in nature. They notice smells that come with changing seasons. They hear leaves breaking under their footsteps. They take a sandwich to share with their dog Marchi. "When I am in the park, I feel like I am close to the Creator of so much beauty and order," Nassim says. After coming upon a couple rearranging rocks and dirt to stop erosion, they began taking bulbs to plant. "This place is ours," she says. "What better way to give back? It's another level of connecting. I can call this patch our own. When you are a mother and father you are used to nurturing." Now, they nurture each other, the dog, and the woods. "I feel humbled by the experience of being in nature," she says. "The power, the beauty. I am trying to soak it in."

3

THE DREADED D-WORD: DIVORCE

When the kids leave and duties of daily child-rearing diminish, many empty nesters are reassessing and dissolving their marital unions, part of a trend among older adults known as the "graying of divorce." The divorce rate for people aged 50 and older has doubled, with this segment of the population constituting a growing share of U.S. divorces. By 2015, one in four people getting divorced was 50 or older, up from one in ten in 1990,[1] according to sociologist Susan Brown, co-director of the National Center for Family & Marriage Research at Bowling Green State University.

One reason so many marriages are unraveling is that we are seeking fulfillment in wedlock like never before. In the 1950s, when gender roles were more rigidly defined, it was considered enough for a man to be a good provider and a woman to be a good wife and mother. Now researchers are observing a dramatic increase in marital expectations. People want their spouse to be their best friend, and they want a great sex life, Brown says. Baby boomers, in particular, are focusing on what marriage is doing for them, not what they can do for their marriage. If the marriage isn't fulfilling their expectations, then divorce is an acceptable solution.

The empty nest can also be a grave challenge for a marriage that has been taken for granted. "If the couple doesn't build a solid connection and a solid foundation, not only is the empty nest a confrontation and a trauma, but the fact that they are strangers is a huge wake-up call and very, very disconcerting,"[2] says Marjorie Schulte, a Scottsdale, Arizona, psychotherapist who has counseled hundreds of couples over more than 40 years. "It's like, 'Oh my gosh, who is this?'"

Uncoupling after 50 can take a tremendous toll. It's a major loss that can take you through depression, anger, fear, and loneliness. "It throws you into unknown waters," Schulte says. "But it's also a transition period of real soul-searching and an opportunity for a great deal of growth and evolution."

NO KIDS, NO SPOUSE

Two weeks after Patty dropped her third and last child off at college, her husband left too. "My world was shattered," she says. "I was lost." She struggled to get out of bed and couldn't go down the second-floor steps for a few days. She lost a lot of weight and cried daily for a year and a half. She thought he would return and say it was a mistake. But he didn't.

She never imagined divorce at 50 could happen to her. Attractive and socially graceful, she and her husband "were like the golden couple," she says. The marriage was traditional, with Patty immersing herself in raising three kids, including helping her daughter overcome a reading delay. When it became clear her son was dyslexic, she helped him through homework each night. She was determined he would learn to read well and that he would not feel "lazy and stupid" as she had growing up with an undiagnosed learning issue. She found a specialized school for her son. It was expensive, but Patty strictly managed the family budget, taking pride as she discovered a natural ability to cut costs and build a strong financial future for her family. She says she "stayed out of the rat race" to support her husband's career and the kids, joining the school board and volunteering for the hospital and other charities.

But the marriage was fraying. Her husband Dave logged 80 hours a week as a surgeon, coming home at night to dictate medical notes for an hour or two and fall asleep in his chair. As her kids plugged through school, her husband, a top student himself, demanded ever more academic success. "We were never good enough," Patty says. "Every time we met an expectation, the bar was always lifted higher."

Dave increasingly condescended to her, dashing her confidence and bringing back her demons that she wasn't smart enough. In the last year before he left, she knew he was unhappy, but the phone calls always ended the same way, with him signing off with a perfunctory, "I love you." The relationship "would be great, and then it would be bad," Patty says. Intimacy evaporated. They sought couples' counseling and she recoiled when he said he didn't love her anymore or that he just didn't enjoy her company.

Three years after the divorce, the family has found a new normal. Patty keeps close contact with her kids. She is proud of her dyslexic son, who is thriving in a career in finance. Her daughter is married with kids, and her other son is heading to medical school. She sold the family home and moved to Manhattan to start over again, glad that she managed the family finances well enough that the alimony she received in the divorce allows her to live on her own. "I was like a squirrel with her nuts. We always lived below our means." But Patty still is trying to shake the shell shock. "To this day, I really don't understand what happened," she says. When "your whole world revolved around making sure your spouse is successful and your kids are whole ... and then all that is gone, what is left for you?"

Many empty nest marriages, like Patty's, unravel quietly. Nobody slams the door or shouts. The couples don't fight. But they also don't talk, make love, laugh, or play together. "They don't do any of that stuff they used to do that was so important for the relationship," says Don Cole, clinical director and master trainer with the Gottman Institute.[3] The Seattle-based couples counseling and research center has found that two-thirds of parents experience a downturn in their marriage during the child-rearing years, with divorce rates spiking during the fourteenth, fifteenth, and sixteenth year after nuptials.

During the parenting years, there are disappointments and resentments. You can forget in the heat of battle why you fell in love in the first place. When couples no longer seek and show interest in each other's lives, the union can end in divorce. "Instead of seeing our partner as someone interested in our well-being, we start seeing our partner as selfish," Cole says. "Happy partners is 'I care about you and you care about me. We are committed to each other's needs, not just our own.'"

KID-CENTRIC MARRIAGE

Gray divorce is more likely to happen if a couple hasn't made separate time to nurture their relationship. Many modern-day marriages have been "kid-centric," with couples leading their lives "wedded not to each other, but to the children," Schulte says. Marriages that revolve around the kids and leave little time for a spouse take a toll on marital bliss. Parents often lose themselves if they become overly involved with their kids' sports, or in "over-nurturing" their kids. "You then become second," Schulte says. "And never in life should you be second." That can put an end to marital intimacy.

Michele Weiner-Davis, a marriage therapist in Boulder, Colorado, and author of *Divorce Busting*, says scores of her patients are on the brink of splitting because they have led separate lives, often with one spouse focused on child-rearing and the other as breadwinner. They gradually lose touch and "evolve into very different people than they were in their 20s, 30s and 40s," she says. She recommends that couples put their marriage first for the good of themselves and their kids. "If you don't, there won't be a marriage left," she says.[4]

Married for 41 years and now with two grandchildren, Weiner-Davis says she and her husband Jim, a real estate developer, made it a priority while their kids were young to focus on each other two nights a week, including hiring a babysitter so they could learn to play golf together. Date nights also serve as an example for your kids, teaching them how to have healthy adult relationships, she says. "If you prioritize your marriage, that is a gift for a lifetime," she says. Your kids realize you are "into each other, are good friends, and do things together."

THE ROAD TO GRAY DIVORCE

Both male and female empty nesters who divorce cite "growing apart" as one of the top reasons for the dissolution of their union, according to Jocelyn Crowley, a public policy professor at Rutgers and author of *Gray Divorce: What We Lose and Gain from Mid-Life Splits*. Both men and women also cite adultery and the mental health status of their partner as common reasons for splitting up, according to Crowley's study of forty men and forty women, most of whom had kids older than age 18. Each gender also has particular issues that they say drove the couple asunder. Men often choose to divorce because of money management clashes with their wives and "lingering resentment about the ways the children were raised,"[5] Crowley says.

Women who have weathered gray divorce tend to cite their ex-husbands' infidelity, addictions to drugs, alcohol, and pornography, and emotional and verbal abuse. Crowley found that some women knew their husbands were "serial cheaters but looked the other way because they had kids." When the kids go, many couples feel like there's no longer a reason to tolerate the discord and these long-simmering issues lead to divorce.

Conflicts also surface in the empty nest when women in their 50s and 60s who have taken the "mommy track," or cut back on their careers to raise a family, decide they want to re-enter the workforce full time. That can put them at odds with a male spouse who has been sacrificing family time to be a breadwinner and would like to slow down and look toward retirement.

THE WALK-AWAY-WIFE SYNDROME

Feminism is not just about women;
it's about letting all people lead fuller lives.

                                                                    Jane Fonda

Women often find the empty nest especially rattling. That's because many of them feel deep down that their basic value comes in child-rearing, Schulte says. "If the children come out well, they are successful," she says. "If the child doesn't, they are a failure." But having one's identity wrapped in parenthood is not healthy for the mother or the child, she says. Once children leave home, the empty nest male typically dives into his work and is less involved in the house and in the relationship, Schulte says. "The woman is left not knowing what to do with herself. She then has a challenge of reinventing herself as an individual person who lives life autonomously."

Looking back on the child-raising marathon, many women say they bore the brunt of the child-rearing and that their husbands didn't support their career interests. Once the kids go, marital issues often boil to the surface as many women are bitter and struggling to find a better balance.

Once in the empty nest, men are frequently baffled by their wives' anger and find their spouses "brimming with issues," says David Arp, who together with his wife Claudia has run marriage education seminars in the United States and Europe for more than four and a half decades.[6] Tired of unglamorous household tasks, many empty nester women are more likely than male counterparts to file for divorce. That's what Weiner-Davis refers to as the "Walk-Away-Wife Syndrome." It's common for men to go into their shells like turtles and for women to behave like skunks, spraying angry words, Arp says. Some spouses are like beavers who just work all the time, he says, while others are like chameleons because they adapt to whatever comes, until they can't stand it anymore and walk out. It's often what Arp refers to as "chameleon" wives who tell their stunned husbands: "Hi sweetheart, I filed for divorce today."

LIVING LONGER

Increased longevity also has contributed to higher gray divorce rates. Empty nesters who have made it to 65 can expect to live another 20 years and can find "that's a long time to spend with someone you're not that into anymore," Susan Brown says. Americans are living longer because of a decline in cigarette smoking, a heightened ability to detect and treat medical problems like heart disease and cancer, and improved air and water quality. Today's mid-life and older adult marriages are probably no less happy than they were 25 or 35 years ago, Brown says, but people expect to live longer and figure they may have time for a second act.

The empty nest can lead to an era of doubt, in which one person starts thinking they can't grow into their ideal self with their longtime spouse by their side. "They are at the precipice of the third act and may not be able to grow,"[7] says Northwestern psychologist Eli J. Finkel, author of The *All-or-Nothing Marriage: How the Best Marriages Work*. Over the edge of that cliff is divorce.

MODELING UNHAPPINESS

If you "model" an unhappy marriage with lots of conflict and resentment, you are teaching that to your kids, Schulte says. Our kids are very, very impacted by what we model, more than what we say or do, Schulte says. "Living a happy life is the best model we can give our children."

Chris knew his marriage was doomed when his kids were in elementary school. His wife of more than two decades was manic depressive and didn't get out of bed until 2 p.m. But the self-employed real estate broker was determined to keep his house-hold intact until his kids left. "My obligation was to make sure they were taken care of," he says. "I stayed in the relationship for my kids. Their mother wasn't functional, but I had made a determination I wasn't leaving."

He taught them to cook breakfast and dinner and spent as much time around the house as he could until they both decided to go to community college. Their schedules were full and they found friends at school, which meant their free time no longer meshed with his. "My kids were my emotional anchor because there wasn't anyone else providing that in the household," he says. "When they went to community college, I was lost."

Chris sought escape because he couldn't face coming home to a bad marriage. He'd arrive home after work at 9 or 10 p.m., when the kids were finishing homework. "I played an avoidance game," he says. He played golf four days a week after work and partied with friends, drinking cocktails and eating fast food. His weight ballooned to more than 320 pounds. His golfing buddies worried about his health. "I destroyed myself emotionally," he says. Before long, his behavior had triggered diabetes.

Chris realized he needed to make major changes after his doctor read him the riot act. He stopped drinking, cut sugar, breads, and pasta, and started walking five miles each morning. A therapist convinced him that he was not being selfish by taking care of himself first. While Chris felt he was modeling good habits for his kids by getting up early each morning and working hard in his job, he says he realized "everything else was destructive." Both his kids struggle with weight issues and he is now "trying to teach them a moderate life."

When they left for four-year universities, he filed for divorce and moved to a smaller house, volunteering on weekends at golfing events he loves. "I now feel confident I will be physically healthy enough to walk my daughter down the aisle and to go to my son's graduation," he says. "You can't give from an empty vessel. If you don't take care of yourself, you can't give to others."

STRAYING FROM THE NEST

When the kids leave, couples can face an emotional tsunami, so it's not unusual for spouses to have "encounters," or extramarital affairs. The empty nest can create vulnerability and "an opportunity for people to look for satisfaction and self-soothing by seeking another relationship," Schulte says.

Cathy fell into an extramarital affair once her son left home. She never fathomed that what seemed like a harmless tryst after she became an empty nester could leave her divorced, virtually friendless, eating alone, seeing a therapist, losing weight, and spending lots of time online. She never imagined she would feel like a pariah in a small New England town, like Hester Prynne, who is branded an adulteress in *The Scarlet Letter*. "If someone had said to me two and a half years ago, my life would be like this, I would have said 'no way,'" she says.

At 53, Cathy is struggling to keep a sense of equilibrium. A psychiatric nurse practitioner who treats severely mentally ill patients, she got caught in a downhill spiral after her then-teenaged son started getting in trouble. Her marriage frayed after he fell in with a "total party" crowd. Her union with her husband was further shaken after her son fell out of a party car at midnight, badly breaking his ankle and scraping the right side of his body with road rash, which required three days of hospitalization. She was rattled but thankful. "The kid has nine lives," she says. "He's really lucky."

To this day, when Cathy's phone rings at night, she can't bring herself to answer it, fearing more bad news and trauma. She and her husband sent their son to rehab for a couple of weeks and to an outdoors program for a few months. Cathy couldn't stop questioning her parenting. She couldn't stop wondering what she had done wrong, and whether she had been too focused on her schooling and her career, or if she hadn't been attentive or loving enough.

The nonstop worry over her son took a toll on her marriage. After their son moved out West for college, it became clear that "there was no common goal" any longer with her husband. Her mental health patients unsettled her. "I got so involved in taking care of other people that I lost myself," she says. "My engine was revving all the time. I was exhausted and in complete burnout." She and her husband escaped into a partying crowd and drowned their sorrows in alcohol. After her husband caught Lyme disease and withdrew from their intimate and social life, she went to a holiday gathering without him where she got attention from another man that felt "intoxicating." The new man made her feel beautiful and funny. She eventually became romantically involved with the man, who was also married, and her husband became increasingly suspicious. "I didn't want my marriage to be over, but I felt really stuck," she recalls.

One night when her lover and his wife joined them for dinner, Cathy's husband "lost it," sensing she was having an affair. He packed his bags and moved to his best friend's house, leaving Cathy consumed with shame and guilt. She eventually left the house and moved in with her lover, who had by then left his wife. When her relationship with her new lover began failing, she tried to reconcile with her husband, but he had found another partner.

Cathy regrets that she and her husband never took time to nurture their relationship, especially during her son's high school years and after he left for college. They had drifted apart, emotionally and physically, and hit serious "low points." Once they finalized the divorce, their common circle of friends found out about her affair and shut her out. "When it all came out, I was dead to them," she says. "I lost my entire friend group. . . . This has been the worst experience of my life." Cathy eventually found a new job and moved out West. Her son has finally forgiven her and she's trying to forgive herself.

THE FALL-OUT

> In the social jungle of human existence,
> there is no feeling of being alive without a sense of identity.
>   Erik Erikson

When kids leave home, parents can become "very unmoored" and experience "an enormous disruption to their fundamental sense of self,"[8] says David A. Sbarra, a clinical psychologist and University of Arizona professor who has interviewed hundreds of divorced people. Much of who they are has been shaped by relationships with their children, and their time has been shaped by family obligations. "We have structure and meaning in our life, if only to go to Target after school, which provides an anchor to the day," Sbarra says. Once kids are launched, married couples turn to their spousal relationships and reassess them. Some fail to see their marital relationship is no longer there until they go back looking for it. This can leave them at a gut-wrenching turning point.

Moving toward separation and divorce can hurt your mental and physical health in profound ways. While some suffer relatively few adverse consequences, about 10 to 15 percent of people, especially those who have struggled before, are at risk of falling into a psychological hole, he says. "If you have been depressed in the past, depression can skyrocket after divorce," he says. Some people see their blood pressure rise and face immunological changes, or their bodies are not as able to suppress latent viruses, he says. Divorce also can trigger serious sleep disturbances, which may last for up to three months, he says. Sleep disruptions that last longer can cascade into further health problems. People who divorce after age 50 are also at a greater risk of smoking if they were inclined to smoke earlier in life. Some also "manage" the stress by drinking too much alcohol, Sbarra says.

Divorced men tend to suffer worse health effects. While people in the midst of divorce suffer appetite disruption in general, the diet of divorced baby boomer men, in particular, tends to worsen because their generation often relegated most of the meal planning, food shopping, and preparation to women. Men also tend to have fewer close friend relationships outside marriage, typically just one confidant, while women tend to have more friends, he says.

In her research, Crowley discovered that men often faced a "social gray divorce penalty," as their wives tended to be the ones who kept the social calendar moving and set up dates with other couples. Because their wives also set up times to see their adult children, male divorcees also lost some connection to them, she found. "Men lose all these contacts and find themselves socially isolated," Crowley says. Some men faced an initial loss of connection to their kids that started to mend, while others felt an ongoing loss and extreme social isolation. One man she interviewed had been a member of a church for 30 years, but after his divorce, when he attended his former father-in-law's funeral, he found no one would talk to him. All these factors add up to an increased risk of early death for divorced men, Sbarra says.

NO GOOD TIME FOR DIVORCE

> When two people decide to get a divorce, it isn't a sign that they 'don't understand' one another, but a sign that they have, at last, begun to.
>
> Helen Rowland

People planning to split often try to find the right time to do it. But there is no good time to divorce, says Linda McGhee, a Chevy Chase, Maryland, psychologist whose practice includes kids of divorcing parents. "It's going to have an impact whether your kid is 4, 8, or 38," she says.[9]

But certain times are worse than others, such as when your kid is finishing high school and already facing uncertainty. That's when kids experience a psychological process known as "individuation," or forging a separate identity from their parents. Fledglings preparing to leave are often rebellious and prone to "soiling the nest" so it's easier for them to set off on their own. If you decide to divorce just as a kid is preparing to leave the nest, it's disturbing and confusing and complicates the individuation process, McGhee says. Another terrible time to formally split is when your kid has just left the nest. With so much already in flux, they need the home base to be solid, McGhee says. "And you just told them the home base is being blown to smithereens."

Parents often announce their split when the kids are home for Christmas break, which is also a rough time. When the idea of their parents' divorce is sprung on the kids, it "makes them think what they lived before then was a lie," McGhee contends. "It makes the kid doubt everything that went on before that and makes them feel like it's their fault and that their parents only stayed together because of them."

Older kids today still have more maturing to do because more academic and social demands have been placed on them, slowing down their psychological development, McGhee says. "Their maturation process is slightly delayed," she says. "Your psyche can only do so much work." It's best to hold off on divorce until your kid is adjusted to being away from the nest. "Maybe he needs a year to get his feet under him. . . . One of the best things you can do is keep the rest of the parts stationary. When you make that transition [of divorce], you need to reassure your child nothing is going to change but this."

When you split, your kids need to know they will see both parents regularly and that they are the number one priority. To help them handle the divorce, keep change, and conflict, to a minimum. "If your conflict is low, the children have the best chance," she says.

Honesty is the best policy, but spare your kids the gory details of the discord. You might explain that you've grown apart, don't have much in common, or are making a change because you are not happy together. If you or your spouse have met someone else, you should tell the kids so they can deal with it. Above all, avoid shame, blame, and name-calling, and don't put the kids in a position where they have to choose between one parent and the other.

WOMEN FACE A STEEPER FINANCIAL PENALTY

Divorce is expensive.

I used to joke they were going to call it 'all the money,'
but they changed it to 'alimony.'

Robin Williams

Women, on the other hand, frequently face an economic penalty
in gray divorce. Many have taken time out from the paid labor
force for maternity leaves or to raise children, and when they try
to return to work, they make less money. Women are also frequently occupationally segregated into industries, and positions,
that pay less. They suffer from the "motherhood pay penalty," a
forfeit in their wages compared to childless women that may stem
from employers' biased view that mothers are not committed to
their jobs.

In most cases, women have put less into their savings and retirement accounts. They also have contributed relatively less to the
Social Security system, leaving them with an average of $14,000
compared to $18,000 annually for male counterparts, Crowley
says. "Once she experiences gray divorce, things look really bad for
her" financially, Crowley says, adding that some women try to
compensate by being very frugal, while others must work until
they die. Women's economic disadvantage "really hits home when
they are going through that gray divorce," Crowley says. It's time
to pay the piper."

AVOIDING THE SAME MISTAKES

Once couples have split once, they are less inclined to stick it out if
they are married a second time. Research shows people who are
age 50 and older who are remarried are two and a half times more
likely to split than those who are in first marriages.[10] When people
get married a second time, the available pool of partners is smaller, making it more likely to pick one who is not as good a match,
Brown says. Life in a step-family can also be a "huge strain," one
that creates controversy and is more likely to end in divorce. *The*

Brady Bunch, the 1970s sitcom about a blissfully blended family, was far from typical.

In the wake of a divorce, you should avoid rushing into another relationship. "If initially, after you have split or divorced, you are immediately attracted to someone, run like hell as that's probably the old choice rearing its head, and not because it's great, but because it feels so familiar," Schulte says.

If you don't take stock of what went wrong the first time, you are in danger of a repeat performance. You might see a psychotherapist to help you understand how to change destructive patterns. If you do that, the second marriage is likely to be happier than the first marriage

PREPARING FOR THE EMPTY NEST

People prepare for marriage, childbirth, and retirement but they don't prepare for the empty nest. Without planning for any of these things, it's a bit like stumbling in the dark. You might avoid divorce by:

- Not becoming "wedded" to your kids.
- Renegotiating household roles like cooking and cleaning once the kids leave.
- Wiping the slate clean on previous problems to reignite the emotional connection.

COPING WITH DIVORCE

If divorce is inevitable, you might find a way to make sense of it by explaining to yourself and your partner how the marriage fell apart. "You need a narrative about the experience to protect you from getting into a downward spiral where you get really overinvolved in your experience and get sucked into the vortex of it all," Sbarra says.

You also need to get enough sleep. Compromised sleep can cause a serious health risk when a marriage ends. "We need to get our Zs without knocking ourselves unconscious through drugs and alcohol," Sbarra says. "You've got to figure out a way to sleep like a baby." You also must find a new identity at this phase. Divorce forces certain existential questions that most of us would just as soon avoid, like "Who am I?," "Who are my friends?," and "What should I do with my life?" "Unlike Humpty-Dumpty, we can put our self-concept together," he says.

Reconnecting with activities and people who enhance our sense of self is essential to healing. This kind of redefining who we are drives our overall emotional engine. You must also cultivate a sense of self-compassion, a concept rooted in Buddhism. You've got to treat yourself as you would a close friend and accept inadequacies and failures without getting sucked deeper and deeper in pain. Be self-compassionate and kind to yourself. Give yourself a break. Let emotions pass without wallowing. Experience your divorce as part of a broader, more universal experience.

4

DON'T SUFFOCATE YOUR SPOUSE

Let there be spaces in your togetherness, . . .
Love one another, but make not a bond of love:
Let it be rather a moving sea between the shores of your souls.

Kahlil Gibran

After Lester Bowles Pearson retired as Canadian prime minister in 1968, he began spending lots of time at home with his wife Maryon, who bristled at the situation, declaring there was too much togetherness. "I married him for better or worse, but not for lunch," she quipped. While investing time in your marriage is vital, the relationship can strain if you expect your romantic partner to be your best friend, confidant, career adviser, sounding board, sidekick, and lover. Only in modern times have so many demands been heaped on one's spouse. Today, we look to marriage to "meet our needs for passion and intimacy and to facilitate our voyages of self-discovery and personal growth," says Northwestern University psychologist Eli Finkel, author of *The All-or-Nothing Marriage: How the Best Marriages Work*.[1] That is a job description too vast for just one person. The modern hunger for personal growth, spiritual fulfillment, and authenticity can't be satisfied with one-stop shopping. Expecting so much from a spouse can cause a marriage to collapse like a house of cards.

For thousands of years, marriage was a practical union with husband and wife functioning to meet basic economic needs. Most people lived on farms, expecting their spouse to help produce food, feed the family, and create shelter and clothing. If you were in the middle class, marriage was the route to the right in-laws who could help you raise and borrow money. For the upper classes, matrimony was how you made alliances and consolidated social status. "It was the most important economic and professional decision and you couldn't just make it on the basis of love," says Stephanie Coontz, professor of history and family studies at The Evergreen State College and author of *Marriage, a History: From Obedience to Intimacy or How Love Conquered Marriage*.[2] Coontz describes the shock one man expressed just after the American Revolution when his wife left him "for no better reason than want of love." Intimacy was nice if it happened, but people were fearful that getting too emotionally involved could threaten survival. "You wanted someone who was a good worker and that was more important than just falling madly in love," she says. "People worked *in* their marriages, then didn't work *at* their marriages."

Beginning in the early nineteenth century, spouses sought love and companionship in each other. Life was becoming easier as the agrarian economy was transforming into an industrial one. Steel production, the assembly line, and ships and railroads made goods less expensive and more plentiful. Agricultural advances made food more affordable and abundant, while pasteurization and sanitation lowered mortality rates. There was a strict division of labor: Men were protectors, venturing into the outside world and dealing with cash, commerce, and professional organizations. Women focused on child-rearing, domestic life, and family relationships, and were valued for their ability to nurture. "Love was based on clear-cut gender values and marriage was supposed to outlast love," Coontz says.

In the aftermath of World War II and especially after the boom of the 1950s and 1960s, couples focused on the nuclear family "as the center of fulfillment," Coontz says. A countercultural revolution was eroding traditional marriage. The availability of the birth control pill and the publication of *The Feminine Mystique* by journalist Betty Friedan led to a wave of sexual liberation. Reverend Martin Luther King Jr. prompted Americans to press for civil and individual rights and Harvard psychology professor Timothy Leary urged Americans to explore the meaning of inner life. New research into communications and technology led to an increase in jobs that required more education, Coontz says. This spurred more young men and women to go to college. All these factors ushered in an emphasis on self-discovery and personal growth.

In the last forty years, spouses have been seeking deep friendship, shared interests and activities, and intense communication about feelings from their mates. At the same time, couples have had little one-on-one time because they have been helping their kids develop their full potential in an increasingly competitive economy. With scant time for outside friendships, romantic partners demand more from each other and marriages have become more fragile. "Ironically, the more you just throw yourself into keeping the family going, the more you are cutting yourself off from the infusions of support that will help you keep that family going," Coontz says. When the kids leave, empty nesters often continue this pattern of relative isolation, tethering themselves to their mate. But that can cause you to overlook other important relationships and interests that could advance you spiritually, socially, and emotionally.

Concentrating too much on your empty nest mate to the exclusion of other relationships can be tedious or suffocating. While some couples thrive on tons of together time after the kids go, others grow weary if they are joined at the hip. "It's rare that people could spend a hundred waking hours a week together and enjoy it," Finkel says. "I would urge them to think very carefully about how they can cultivate themselves as individuals, which means the time together is certainly plentiful but not infinite." If your spouse is your sole sidekick and confidant, Finkel says, "the responsibility it places on the marriage is enormous, and many relationships buckle under the strain."

Enhance your empty nest by

- reconnecting with good friends.
- cultivating friendships with like-minded people.
- being open to interactions with people in your daily travels.
- pursuing interests to further develop yourself.

ARE YOU MY EVERYTHING?

People today tend to place an extreme priority on the marital bond to the detriment of other key relationships. The "you are my everything" mentality can make you vulnerable. Relying on your romantic partner for all your social, practical, and emotional support is perilous because circumstances may change, says Liz Spencer, a sociologist in Suffolk, England, and coauthor with Ray Pahl of *Rethinking Friendship: Hidden Solidarities Today.* "If you're totally dependent on a partner, or totally dependent on immediate family, and something happens to that partner or immediate family, you haven't got these other resources," Spencer says. "If you've got a broader repertoire of relationships, including friends, that's a much healthier situation."[3] If you have a wider support group, and the ability to build new friendships and maintain existing ones, there is flexibility and redundancy in your personal community. That's a great insurance policy for emotional well-being.

But when people leave singlehood and enter coupledom, they often spend most of their time with their mate, demoting other relationships to the periphery of their lives. They tend to shrink their inner clique of friendships when a new romantic partner dominates their life. When your attention is wholly centered on a romantic partner, it typically knocks out two close relationships—one family member and one close friend, according to Oxford University professor Robin Dunbar, an anthropologist and evolutionary psychologist.[4]

Single people, on the other hand, tend to have broader and healthier support networks.[5] Singles who live alone are much more likely to spend time with friends, siblings, parents, and co-workers than married people, says psychologist Bella DePaulo, author of *Singled Out: How Singles Are Stereotyped, Stigmatized, and Ignored, and Still Live Happily Ever After.* "Single people have a bigger view of relationships and the world," DePaulo says.[6] "They think differently because their life is not organized around one person." Couples moving in together become more insular and spend less time with friends, DePaulo says. "When your life is humming along, it's fine," she says. "But what happens when you get mad at each other, divorced, or your spouse drops dead?" Your siblings, other relatives, and friends who you have ignored might take you back once your kids leave, but they might not because they feel you threw them away, DePaulo says. Consider which people in your life really matter to you and attend to them. Don't just put them on the back burner and expect them to be there when your kids go to college.

A vibrant social network is key to well-being. Having strong relationships with family, friends, neighbors, or colleagues is a strong predictor of physical and psychological health and increases longevity. Adults get a 50 percent boost in longevity if they have a solid social network, according to a study by Julianne Holt-Lunstad, Timothy Smith, and J. Bradley Layton.[7] Too little social interaction can hurt you and trigger premature death as much as if you are a heavy smoker, an alcoholic, or someone who always skips exercise, and it is twice as harmful as being obese, according to their research, which analyzed results from 148 studies that included a total of 308,849 participants.

Cultivating a robust network of friends and family throughout your life helps you feel responsible for others, gives you a sense of purpose and meaning, and prompts you to take better care of yourself, according to the study. But people often take relationships for granted. "The more we can do as a society to maintain and grow and foster relationships with other people as we age, the better our whole society will be,"[8] Smith says. Loneliness damages the human psyche. Your social network is the key to your psychological and emotional health.

Many of today's empty nesters have failed to build healthy social networks. That's largely because they haven't taken time to build them. Most upper- and middle-class parents have been "intensively involved" in their children's lives in the last 60 years and that trend is continuing now that their kids are adults, says Annette Lareau, a sociology professor at the University of Pennsylvania and author of *Unequal Childhoods: Class, Race, and Family Life*.[9] Middle-class parents tend to continue playing a supportive role and supervise their children as they grow into adults, whereas working-class parents tend to stop once their children are 16 to 18 years old and they feel they are old enough to make major decisions.

Middle-class families tend to enroll their children in lots of organized activities. They usually parent intensively with a style of "concerted cultivation," encouraging their kids to negotiate and discuss issues and question authority, Lareau found. This helps their children carve out middle-class careers, develop a large vocabulary, and feel comfortable in discussions with people in authority.

These days, in addition to coaching and helping with high school homework and college applications, many well-to-do parents are helping their kids apply to law school and decorate apartments. They chat with their kids often by phone and carry around photos of their kids' pets that they call "grandkitties," Lareau says. If they can afford it, they regularly visit their kids who live far away and take grandchildren on vacation. Money permitting, they shell out cash for childcare, pick up the tab for extracurricular activities for grandkids, and pay for schooling. If they live nearby, they are heavily involved in the lives of the next generations. However, this high level of concentration on the next generation, particularly among upper- and middle-class empty nesters, leaves little time for cultivating healthy relationships outside the family, which can strain a marriage.

Working- and lower-class families favor a parenting style Lareau calls "accomplishment of natural growth," in which parents give commands to their kids rather than teaching them to negotiate. They tend to encourage their kids to follow and trust people in positions of authority, and do not structure their kids' activities, instead letting them play on their own. This method prepares children for working-class jobs, teaches them to follow those in positions of authority, and allows them to become independent at a younger age. Because these parents can't afford as many support systems as their higher-income counterparts, they depend more on networks of other adults. Less immersed in directing their kids' lives, they also have more time to cultivate relationships outside the family and end up less isolated than their financially better-off counterparts, Lareau says.

Many empty nesters still place friend relationships on the back burner, much as they did in the years of intensive child-rearing. At the same time, their relationships with their adult children can be strained because the kids take for granted the parents' lifelong attention to developing their talents and skills. Some parents made their kids feel the world revolves around them. These "catered-to" kids can be highly critical of their empty nester parents, as well as inflexible and reluctant to compromise, Lareau says. Blended families face additional empty nest challenges as they juggle money and time with offspring of each spouse, sometimes for as much as 30 to 40 years after remarrying. And many empty nesters are trying to help kids or grandkids with drug problems, mental illness, or special needs. All this emphasis on the next generation leaves them with little time for themselves and their friends.

The challenge is to find "the proper balance between helping our kids achieve in a competitive and less secure economy, while developing ourselves as individuals in a marriage that is based not on gender stereotypes but on real deep friendship," Coontz says. When marriage works well today, "it offers more satisfactions than people of the past would have ever dared to dream." Coontz says. But it takes energy to make it work. It also requires finding the right balance between time for your mate, your offspring, yourself, and the relationships that matter most to you, as there is "an enduring tension" between time for yourself and time for others, Lareau says. Women in particular need to be encouraged to carve out time to pursue their own interests and passions, and to find time for their friends, because they are known to sacrifice what they want for the family.

THE GOLDEN FRIENDS

If you are light on outside relationships because of intensive parenting, one of the easiest ways to connect is by rekindling relationships with old friends. To reconnect, you might

- call a college pal.
- organize a dinner party with friends you haven't seen.
- plan an outing or trip with another couple.
- meet a favorite work colleague for lunch.

Long-term friends are a treasure. Just ask Yvonne, who reconnected with an old friend at a high school reunion, then wove the friend back into her life. Now her pal Patty is a weekly sidekick and her best sounding board. They drive together on weekends to Jones Beach on Long Island, sit in chairs, and talk. Yvonne listens to Patty talk about her father, who has Alzheimer's and doesn't recognize his own daughter, something Patty understands because her mother suffers from dementia. They talk about the alcoholism that has ravaged Patty's extended family. And Patty remembers how Yvonne's mother "checked out emotionally" after her brother died at age 20. They add perspective to each other's lives as they watch waves lap the shore.

Michael, Yvonne's spouse, savors camaraderie and lighthearted fun with his male tennis partners of two decades. A 66-year-old chef who retired and went back to work selling craft beer, Michael reserves weekends for tennis. "I get out to play as often as I can, and it's never enough," he says. He often plays doubles with "the guys" in a nearby park, then they head to a cabana with picnic tables. "We're down here to have fun and play the game," he says. Unlike his wife, he's bored at the beach if he has to stay too long without surfing or playing a ball game. "I would never hold Yvonne back from spending time with her friends," he says. "We both do what we want and we respect each other," Michael says. "We love each other and enjoy each other's company, but it doesn't have to be 24-7."

The differing perspectives, personalities, and experiences of old friends can supplement your relationship with your romantic partner. But many of us have winnowed our social networks, spending less time with friends, siblings, and parents, and being less engaged in civic activities outside the home. Even marriage counselors often fail to consider how the marital relationship is affected by relationships and interactions with other people, Coontz says. [10] A 2017 study shows that when people in middle age and late adulthood socialize more frequently with good friends, they are happier, with fewer reporting symptoms of depression. [11] And it's contagious: Their partners are happier too.

Social science research shows maintaining close friend relationships beyond your romantic partner as you age makes you stronger and better. Midlife well-being of both men and women depends on having a wide circle of friends you see regularly. A 2017 study by William Chopik of Michigan State University of 280,000 people in almost 100 countries found that as we age, friendships become increasingly more important for our well-being. [12]

SCULPTING YOUR MIND AND MOODS

Your mate is also critical to your well-being. Like a sculptor, your romantic partner can help you chip away at your *actual self* to reveal the sculpture, or *authentic self*, inside a raw block of stone. This is known as the Michelangelo Effect, named after the Florentine High Renaissance sculptor. After Michelangelo finished his famous sculpture of David, he announced that he had seen the angel in the marble and carved him to set him free.

If you and your romantic partner perceive each other's ideal self the same way and strive to make that a reality, you both can become healthier, closer, and more satisfied because you are evolving into the people you want to be. However, if you and your mate fail to support or affirm each other, you can sculpt each other in ways that are harmful and bring out the worst. In this situation, friends can help you become your best self.

EMOTIONAL SUPPORT TAKES A VILLAGE

Beyond reconnecting and keeping up with old friends, cultivating a diverse circle of new friends can do wonders for you and your empty nest partner. Research into *emotionships,* or relationships that help us manage our moods, shows that no one person can help moderate every mood, and that not everyone is skilled at handling every emotion. Some people are gifted at motivating, some are adept at comforting, some are good at calming when we are upset or mad, and others are great at celebrating our victories. [13] People with different types of friends who help them moderate different moods report a greater sense of happiness and satisfaction with life. "People who build rich, broad portfolios tend to have greater well-being," according to Elaine Cheung, a psychologist at Northwestern University in Evanston, Illinois, who has spearheaded research in this area and coined the term *emotionships.* "Your spouse may not be able to effectively regulate all your needs," Cheung says. "They may not know the right things to say when something good happens or you are feeling anxious. They might be busy. They might not have the bandwidth to manage all of your different emotions." [14] Having a broad stable of friends with varied skills lightens the load on your mate, providing additional outlets for fun, learning, communing, and connecting.

To create the right portfolio of relationships, Cheung recommends you take stock of the "emotional specialties" of friends and family and locate people to fill the vacancies. While it may sound utilitarian to deliberately cultivate certain types of friendships, it is already what many of us do subconsciously. It's better to be proactive and plan ahead. Many people are on "autopilot mode" and are unaware they lack adequate emotional support until a crisis occurs, Cheung says. "Be more deliberate about thinking about your support network," she recommends. Think hard about who you know who will support you in a difficult goal, or who can listen and offer thoughtful feedback. Perhaps you can find solace by providing a friend with a sounding board and offering compassion. Regular contact with people who are important to you fosters intimacy. Even the anticipation of seeing a good friend can moderate your mood in advance.

While you likely selected your spouse because he or she has traits, skills, and characteristics you admire, you need more than your mate to meet your many emotional needs. The tools we need to see the world clearly, keep our perspective, and learn are distributed in the population among many people. That's why we aren't meant to hole ourselves up on an island. It's why the planet is full of diverse personalities with different experiences, abilities, and insights. Our well-being can be maximized when we have a "village" of people around us with varied emotional skills.

However, not everybody needs a large portfolio of people in their village of emotional supporters, says Margaret Clark, a Yale University professor who studies how people manage emotions. Most of us have a few people we turn to, those we trust, and whom we believe care about us. Some people keep wide social circles and interact with lots of people. But others are most comfortable sticking primarily with few people. "There isn't a one-size-fits-all for sure," Clark says.[15]

Women are more inclined to build networks of emotionally supportive people than men. In a 2010 study funded by the National Science Foundation, Clark asked 108 married couples to report when they expressed emotions such as happiness, sadness, and fear to others. She found that women on the whole expressed a wide variety of emotions to their spouses as well as to friends, while only about half of husbands reported sharing much emotion at all, and those who did tended to express it to their wives. "It was really clear that men don't have the emotional networks" that women do, she says. Clark says that men may be less inclined to share emotions with others because they tend to feel that it reveals vulnerability—and men are less willing to be vulnerable, even with positive emotions. Clark recommends that empty nesters find different people with whom to share different emotions. She also suggests that couples think about their partner's needs and urge them to find relationships that can help them and take pressure off the marriage.

To find close relationships you might

- join a club around an interest or a cause that moves you.
- take a class on a subject you love.
- volunteer to help others and in so doing meet like-minded people.
- join Meetup.com, a global network of local communities that connects people to pursue common interests.

But most importantly, to create close relationships, you must be willing to trust others and take the risk of opening up to them, Clark says. You need to let others know your vulnerabilities and emotions and see how they react. You may need to be resilient, because some people may be slow to respond. Keep in mind that close relationships are not one-way streets. "Listen and be responsive to the other person too," Clark says. "That too is crucial."

You also might build a portfolio of professional relationships to help you navigate the challenges of empty nesting. You might enlist a

- life coach,
- religious counselor,
- yoga teacher,
- personal trainer,
- meditation teacher,
- nutritionist,
- massage therapist, or
- work mentor.

CONFIDANTS YOU ENCOUNTER DAILY

People you come across in your daily travels can bolster your emotional health and often end up sharing your deepest secrets.[16] These are not people you have known long or who you regularly meet. They are not in the inner circle of your four or five closest friends or family members. Rather, they are souls you encounter because you are on common ground: You go to the same places because of shared interests or values. For example, at yoga, you find others who value fitness and learning to live in the moment. At church, you run into others with a similar concern about the afterlife. At a baseball game, you find people who also love the sport. At a chess club, you find others fascinated by strategy. If you form a band or go out to see musicians perform live, you encounter others who share your love for music. In a biking group, you peddle with others who share a passion for endurance, speed, and scenic vistas. When you go to venues connected to your passions and values, you find people who are much like you and who are concerned with what's on your mind. You will find like-minded souls on the way.

Paradoxically, people frequently seek support or solace from random coworkers, neighbors, and people they encounter in common activities. In his book *Someone to Talk To*, Harvard sociologist Mario Luis Small, an expert in personal networks, reveals how people often avoid confiding in close friends and family, as these relationships are fraught with expectations. Instead, more than half the time we confide in acquaintances and near strangers when we need understanding and empathy. When Small launched a study of about three dozen graduate students coping with stress, self-doubt, failure, poor health, and poverty to see who they turned to in times of distress, most named three or four people such as their spouse, mother, best friend, or a good friend from work. But when he asked who they had last engaged about concerns that made them anxious, participants said it was not with someone from their inner sanctum. More than half had confided in "neighbors, friends, professionals, coworkers, and even distant family members they did not feel close to," Small says. They often "confide deeply personal matters to individuals they are not close to, even to those they barely know."

People often avoid tapping their inner circle of relationships, including a spouse, for several reasons. They might avoid discussing marital problems with their mate because they are considering divorce or cheating. If they survived cancer and found a lump, they may not want to worry their closest confidants. They might avoid talking to their mother about a rough relationship with a boyfriend because besides being a friend, a support, and a source of cash, she is also a protector.

People also avoid discussing things they fret about with a romantic partner, sibling, or close friend because they are seeking "cognitive empathy," or a person who has had a similar experience and can truly understand their predicament. For example, if you are struggling to write a book, your spouse may not understand your anxiety, but another writer or editor will. "In some ways, your editor may know more intimate things about you than even the people you are really close to," Small says. "When you are worried about your book, it's not just that you want to cry. You just kind of want to vent. You want to walk through a problem." People seeking cognitive empathy sometimes stumble into listeners. Often, that writer is sitting at a conference and mentions her book to someone nearby who has faced the same struggle.

Relative strangers can provide solace and advice when they have experienced a similar situation. Depending on your circumstances, you might find solace with soldiers returning from duty, victims of violent crimes, military spouses who gave up their career ambitions to trail their partners, parents whose kids have leukemia. You might be sitting on an airplane when a seatmate tells a personal story, and then you reciprocate. "The next thing you know, you are venting about your own life," Small says. Only people who are going through similar situations will really understand your reality. When his first child was born, Small says he got the best advice from a random colleague. When his father died, the most helpful conversation he had was with someone who also had lost their dad. Coontz says interacting with relative strangers is one of the best ways to take pressure off yourself and your spouse. "These kinds of pleasant interactions can increase your well-being for the whole day," Coontz says. "A really good interaction with a stranger at a bus stop can change the space entirely."

Besides reaching out to old friends, finding new ones, and keeping yourself open to meaningful interactions with relative strangers in your daily travels, you also should pursue passions independently from your spouse. As you carve out separate time, you should consider choosing an activity that includes others. Rather than biking alone, you might join a bike club. Instead of running long distances solo, you might consider joining a group of runners, broadening your knowledge and your contacts. If you join a yoga class, connect after *shavasana* with others. We all need to enhance our social networks across the life span to bring out our best. So why not combine social relationships with feeding our passions?

CULTIVATING THE SELF

> There is only one corner of the universe you can be certain of improving, and that's your own self.
>
> Aldous Huxley

Taking time apart to pursue separate interests once the kids leave enhances your empty nest relationship. When we fully develop ourselves and partner with someone similarly complete, it is a far better union than when two partly developed people depend on each other to become whole. If you are discovering new things on your own and feeling "nourished, happy and fulfilled, it presents your partner with a happier, more interesting and more involved spouse," says Marjorie Schulte, the Arizona psychotherapist who specializes in marriage and family counseling.[17]

Going after interests independently is not about being selfish, and it doesn't mean you don't love your mate. Rather, "it helps you be you," says Dr. Elizabeth Lombardo, a psychologist, life coach, and bestselling author of *Better than Perfect: 7 Strategies to Crush Your Inner Critic and Create a Life You Love.* "If your favorite meal is lobster and you have it every day for lunch and dinner, it's not so good," she says.[18] Being your own person isn't about excluding your spouse, Schulte says. "It's about including your mate in your reality while doing what works for you."

Reserving your own time might involve pursuing a sport, engaging in a cultural activity, bird-watching, participating in a book club, playing in a band, or enjoying music. It might be traveling with a friend if you partner hates planes and hotels. Dragging your mate on a camping trip if he hates the outdoors, fears bears, and is mosquito bait can create resentment, anger, and dread. Each partner needs leeway to pursue what they find renewing.

But separate pursuits can require creativity. Caroline, a life coach and author, had juggled graduate school, writing books, and launching a business while raising three kids and was looking forward to her own time in the empty nest. After years of multitasking and caring for others, she wanted to go on mother-daughter weekends and attend yoga workshops. But when she told her husband Haywood she wanted to explore interests that had nothing to do with him, he felt threatened, wondering why she would leave him behind. So Caroline suggested her husband, a former college lacrosse captain, take a "mancation" each year. He took up mountain biking and, before long, had joined a group of men at an annual outing in Park City, Utah, a mecca for the sport with a variety of trails. Now, Haywood's trip with the guys is one of his favorite things.

When our last child left for college, my husband was content to commune with our Great Dane and sink into his armchair reading history. But I require more relationships in my life and figured he did, too. When I heard about a men's book club one night at a party, I connected my husband to the host and he joined a group of men who also love historical fiction. That frees me up to meet a girlfriend to talk about spirituality or writing or literature, which interests me more than history books.

Some empty nesters love their work and can't fathom putting it down, just because their spouse wants to retire. Many people are working well into their 70s these days, feeling restless, worrying about the size of their nest egg, or craving the structure and meaning that a job can provide. Men and women working well past the traditional retirement age is now the hottest demographic in the labor market. Over the next decade, these older workers will be the fastest-growing segment in the workforce, according to the Bureau of Labor Statistics.[19] Workers who are 65 to 74 years old are expected to make up one-third of the labor force by 2022, up from 20 percent in 2002. The percentage of workers aged 75 and older is expected to jump from 5 percent in 2002 to 11 percent in 2022.

WORKING AND THE SELF

Since her kids left home, Margaret Clark, 66, has continued to work as a research psychologist at Yale. She also took on another big responsibility, becoming head of college at Trumbull, a residential quad where 400 undergraduate students live. Clark says she would not have taken on this extra load when her kids were home. But now she and her husband Fred Polner, 69, love hosting students for dinner.

Her husband, a retired lawyer, takes classes that stoke his interest in politics, including a journalism class with *Washington Post* journalist Bob Woodward, whose reporting on the Watergate scandal led to the resignation of Richard Nixon. He likes golf, while Margaret prefers platform tennis and kayaking, so they go their separate ways, coming together to ski, sail, and guide students.

INTERGENERATIONAL RELATIONSHIPS

Relationships with people from another generation can yield great benefits if interests overlap. "They can improve and enhance the quality of everyone's life," says Jon Nussbaum, a Penn State professor and expert on intergenerational friendships.[20] These relationships might be with family members, work colleagues, or friends you find while pursuing a hobby.

An empty nester with a pal from a younger generation is more likely to engage in the community, keep up with contemporary music, try different types of food, and leave the house more often, Nussbaum says. Younger friends tend to be more fluent in technology and familiar with popular culture. A younger adult with an older-generation friend can find a fountain of wisdom on issues like handling the death of a parent or a romantic breakup, surviving a big exam, or saving and investing money. Older friends can help younger ones think more clearly about parent-child relationships or better appreciate the passage of time. Intergenerational friendships "can be the essence of life," he says. They have nothing but "positive physical, psychological, and spiritual benefits."

But Nussbaum says a great intergenerational relationship "ain't going to happen without a lot of work." An open mind is key for bridging natural gaps between generations. The best intergenerational relationships stem from common pursuits or interests.

But stereotypes and age discrimination sometimes put an end to mixed-generation relationships before they develop. Older adults might assume younger ones might drink too much or do drugs, Nussbaum says. "You can't force this" type of intergenerational relationship," Nussbaum says. Sometimes older people turn younger ones away with "painful self-disclosure," such as talking about their health problems. However, with good sense and communication, you can get a clearer view of what's important to another generation and a window into a different world.

Just ask Tara. The 45-year-old mother of a 9-year-old boy found insight and guidance from her closest friend Julie, an empty nester who is fifteen years older. The relationship has been thriving for two decades, ever since Tara was the manager of a coffee shop that Julie and her middle-aged friends frequented. Tara moved beyond Julie's latte order and discovered they had a common passion: discussing the latest books. That's when their connection became "much more than transactional," Tara says. Now they also meet to go to museums, movies, and bars, take golf trips, and hit the beach, and Tara takes Julie to the hipper parts of town. They support each other emotionally. When Tara's father died, Julie was at the hospital. When Julie's sister died, Tara attended the funeral. When Tara's son was born, Julie dispensed useful tips and Tara felt more confident because Julie was a seasoned parent.

Investing in a fuller social life and developing your own interests takes pressure off your spouse and prevents suffocation in an empty-nest marriage. So does cultivating old and new friendships and being open to acquaintances in your travels. If you want your marriage to thrive, you need to invest in it as much as you can, Coontz says, but "that doesn't mean turning it into a two-person institution that excludes the rest of the world."

SEPARATENESS

Elizabeth, 71, and Richard Rubin, 72, a psychotherapist and psychiatrist who have been married for 47 years, use hand gestures to show how to keep an empty nest romantic relationship strong without jeopardizing the self. They interlock fingers to represent a union in which both partners do things in lockstep. When one hand is lifted, the other must move with it. "Some people define that as being really close," Richard says.[21] "But I define that as being fused." He demonstrates his preferred arrangement by taking both hands, separating them by two to three inches and lifting one hand, allowing the other to stay put, while it remains nearby. "You are not confined by the movement of the other hand," Richard says. "Yet you are very much connected."

A healthy cultivation of individual interests is critical. "You have a relationship with yourself that needs to be cultivated the same way your relationship with a person needs to be cultivated," Elizabeth says. "If you lose your sense of self, that harms the relationship." Being dependent "is not sexy," and "doesn't make you attractive to your mate," she says. While dependency may be attractive initially, especially if one mate is a "caretaker" and the other likes to be taken care of, after a while "it gets boring and you feel smothered."[22]

Separateness keeps the relationship fresh, or, as the aphorism goes: Absence makes the heart grow fonder. Whether you go on a girls' or boys' trip, or alone to a retreat, you need to enrich yourself, be independent, and become a better version of yourself, Elizabeth says. "It's a better relationship because you have learned how to be comfortable in your own skin."

Both Rubins explore individual interests, trusting each other fully. A preference for different activities is not a deal-breaker in a relationship, Richard says. He says a sense of humor, common values, curiosity, and political views have a greater bearing on how people get along. "Sharing or not sharing activities is not the major issue," he says . "The activities come and go. You can navigate and negotiate them."[23]

Richard enjoyed scuba diving and playing softball without Elizabeth for years, but now that he is older and prefers a "quieter and more self-reflective" pace, he gardens or hikes on his own. Elizabeth has accepted an invitation to visit a girlfriend in Brazil and plans to go with or without Richard, depending on his work schedule. "There's no question I would go without him," she says. "I am perfectly comfortable. I just don't have it in my head that we have to do everything together."

5

EMPTY NEST BIRDS OF A FEATHER

People tend to shrink their circle of friends when they become empty nesters, pruning those they don't care for much and creating a tighter circle of kindred spirits. When children leave, parents rethink spending free time with mothers and fathers of their kids' friends. They become increasingly aware that time on earth is limited and come to value relationships more than ever. Intentionally or not, they weed their social sphere, leaving it smaller but better. They end up with a greater proportion of emotionally sensitive people in their networks.

Close friends like these are key for health and happiness. If your friends and family soothe and support you, it evokes the most positive emotions of all. However, if they vex and hurt you, it elicits your most negative feelings. "The times you have been the angriest and most disappointed are probably related to relationships," says Laura Carstensen, a Stanford University psychology professor and founding director of Stanford's Center on Longevity.[1] "We are very sensitive to exclusion and disappointment." When kids leave home, good friends "can make a world of difference for our health and well-being," says William Chopik, an assistant professor of psychology at Michigan State University. "It's smart to invest in the friendships that make you happiest."[2]

FRIENDS TODAY, GONE TOMORROW

When kids leave, your parent network can fall away. That was the case for Jeff, a former Olympic ski jumper and father of three athletes, who was accustomed to dashing home from work to join other parents at ski racing, soccer, lacrosse, golf, basketball, and baseball. He and his wife Kathy were surrounded by other parents as they moved from field to field. On weekends, Jeff joined them to smooth snowy ruts on ski hills with rakes or ski edges while Kathy registered kids for races and handed out bibs. They cheered with other moms and dads as their kids Brit, Tira, and Sam flew down the slopes with teammates. In the midst of it all, "the other parents seem like your best friends because you have a common goal," Jeff says. He was so busy with kid activities and running a New Hampshire auto equipment company that he had no hobbies. "You don't have the stamp-collecting community that others have," he says. "I wasn't in a bike-riding club."

After he sent Sam to Bates College, life went too quiet. Jeff dove into his job, which was satisfying on some level, but lacked "any of the social stuff that connects you to a community. You think you are still going to be part of the baseball team or chorus," he says. "But you're not."

His wife Kathy was similarly surprised at how their social circle shrank. Their Connecticut River home had been a mecca for their kids' friends and their parents, who would roast marshmallows over a fire pit and leap into the river from a Tarzan swing. Now they see some ski parents, but it is "a much smaller group than we expected," Kathy says.

Over time they have adjusted. After a couple years of puzzling over how to re-feather the nest, they are building a new social life. Kathy has reached out to younger couples who are hungry to glean tips from seasoned parents. And Jeff is calling old college friends "out of the blue" to reconnect and get together.

FLOCKING TOGETHER

> Make new friends, but keep the old;
> Those are silver, these are gold.
>
> Joseph Parry

Like Jeff, most people find that college friends remain on the closest ring of the friendship circle throughout life, although these relationships are redefined as time goes on. But most relationships on the outer ring of the friendship network tend to disappear, says Rebecca G. Adams, an expert on friendship and professor of gerontology at the University of North Carolina at Greensboro. You simply stop getting together and start drifting apart. "Friendship is a voluntary relationship," Adams says. "It's not like our families that we're stuck with, not like our neighbors who live next door, not like your spouse who you have to get a legal divorce from. All you have to do to stop a friendship is stop interacting."[3] Her research found that friend circles often look very different after five years, as some relationships evaporate and new ones appear.

Friendships need time, energy and effort to survive. "You can't just put them on autopilot," Adams says. Preserving close friendships requires time and energy. Sandy has made a point to keep her girlfriends close, especially when she knew her husband was dying. A widowed 57-year-old mother of four, Sandy now savors memories of her husband Joe making steak and potato suppers for their triplets Chris, Katie, and Joey, and their eldest son Jerry. When Joe became severely ill with pancreatic cancer, her female friends provided a sympathetic ear and a sounding board. When doctors warned Sandy that her husband was failing with an infection, most of her best girlfriends made it to his bedside before he passed away.

If you lose a spouse as Sandy did, or get divorced, switch careers, or retire, your friend circles can become drastically reshuffled, Adams says. Sandy's social life used to revolve around Joe, one of eleven children, whose funeral, attended by 600 people, was a testament to his gregarious nature. Now she has shifted from couples-based to going it solo, often with girlfriends who are also on their own. "It's hard being alone," she says. "You have to be engaged or people forget about you."

In the two years since her husband's death, Sandy has kept in close touch with five girlfriends. "I work my friendships," she says. "I really stay in touch." Now that her kids have left the nest, she updates her friends with texts, and meets them often for a drink or dinner. They trade suggestions for guiding their young adult kids from afar. They take trips together, share laughs, and celebrate birthdays and other special occasions.

Close confidants are particularly important if a woman has lost a partner, gets divorced, or is married to a workaholic or someone who is often away, says Deborah Tannen, an anthropological linguist at Georgetown University and author of *You're the Only One I Can Tell: Inside the Language of Women's Friendships*.[4] Many women have close friends who are gay men, including Tannen, whose best pal is a gay man who is a classical musician. She loves having a close male friend, with whom there's no risk of the tension that can arise with one who could be a sexual partner.

FACE-TO-FACE AND SIDE-BY-SIDE

> The greatest gift of life is friendship, and I have received it.
> Hubert H. Humphrey

While empty nest women usually have face-to-face friendships with other females with whom they share their innermost thoughts and discuss their deepest concerns, men usually get together with guy friends to focus on "side-by-side" activities such as watching a baseball game or playing golf, Adams says. Males tend to spend less time talking intently to each other the way women do, and, unlike women, men more often say their spouse is their closest companion. "Many men don't talk about personal things to their male friends—the wife is the one they tell everything to, the one they feel most comfortable around," Tannen says.

The female tendency to sit and talk with girlfriends starts early. Preschool girls often chat and share secrets, while young boys usually play games or sports with male buddies, Tannen says. This gender divide occurs across many cultures. When the nest empties, women tend to get together to discuss kids, marriages, and future plans. Empty nest men similarly seek same-gender camaraderie, but it's often centered around an activity they didn't have time for when the kids were home. Like Will, most men find it easier to confide in their spouse. A 55-year-old contractor in Virginia, Will says his wife Kirsten is his best friend. Every time she tells him he needs a therapist, he says he's already got one—and that she is his "one and only" counselor. If he's worried about their two sons, Will rarely goes outside the family for suggestions.

Besides talking with his own in-house therapist, Will works out with a co-ed group of friends each morning at 5:30. After deciding a decade ago that he needed to lose weight, he joined a nearby gym, where he has formed bonds with men and women who have common aerobic and anaerobic goals. While his gym mates share a desire to keep fit, they are of varying ages, which Will finds fascinating. While some of his workout friends have toddlers, Will has one kid in college and another who has graduated. He joins his gym group on weekends in friendly rivalry, such as competing in triathlons and obstacle courses that zap you with a light electric shock if you don't move fast enough. "We push each other, we call each other names and have a good time," he says. Like most empty nesters, Will prefers to keep close friends separate from office acquaintances. While the construction business can be "rife with conflict," his workout friends make him laugh and shake off stress.

Will says he loves being an empty nester because he finally has time for himself and he can focus on his bond with his wife. He's also glad to see his sons finding their own paths. David is a firefighter and student at St. Michael's College in Vermont, while Forrest, who just graduated from Tufts University, has moved to Arlington, Virginia. Will loves it when they come home, but is also happy they are just visitors. When their sons leave home again,

Will feels sad for an hour and a half—and then, he says, he is contentedly back to his own life. He feels lucky to have a solid marriage and a good network of friends that he has built over the last 20 years. "If you have got to start from ground zero with your friends, you've got a problem."

FRIENDS ON COMMON GROUND

Empty nesters in particular gravitate toward friends with common values and goals. After their kids left, Will's wife Kirsten found new friends through a common love of philanthropy. Her interest in finding shelter, food, education, and health care for people in need prompted her to join a group of 40 men and women who raise money and distribute grants in the community. They also hope to create a community school with afternoon activities for disadvantaged kids. Kirsten first got involved in philanthropy when her children entered high school and didn't need her as much. She had been part of the PTA, but once her kids got older, she needed more. "I saw on the horizon that I needed to be intentional about how I was going to fill all my hours once the kids were no longer around," Kirsten says. She loves working with like-minded souls. "We care about giving in thoughtful ways and want to put our personal time into solving problems," she says. The beauty of working in a charitable group is that "you have something to talk about other than your kids," she says.

Kirtsen has found new friends of all ages. Some have preschool kids, while others are grandparents. If she has a concern, she discusses it with friends in different generations and gets "a much broader range of experience." And she's found neighborhood friends with young kids who want her advice.

Unlike her husband, Kirsten, 49, seeks advice from friends on personal matters. She might talk about her marriage or meno-pause. "Frankly, you get better conversation from girls," she says. Her empty nest friendships remind her of the conversations she had late at night in college, pouring her heart out. "You get back to that when you have great friends in empty nesting," she says.

IN SICKNESS AND IN HEALTH

Great friends can be a lifeline when your health is at risk. When Jennifer's only child Christian was preparing for final exams during his first semester of freshman year, the last thing she wanted to do was distract him. So when her breast biopsy came up positive for cancer, the 55-year-old former flight attendant buttoned her lip. "I knew because of the close relationship between us that he would feel the stress, and he was under enough stress as it was." Besides, fighting the cancer was up to doctors and, Jennifer says, up to God. "I chose not to tell him until we could see each other face-to-face," she says. "He needed to know I was going to be okay."

Jennifer's husband Randy was reeling from losing his mother, and was focused on his work, designing and building bridges in Florida, so Jennifer didn't want to lean on him too much. Instead, she turned to her girlfriends. "Even though your spouse is your closest relationship, your girlfriends are more in tune with how you feel and what's going on," she says. "Women are more intuitive." They checked in frequently to see how she was handling her upcoming surgery. They listened. They identified with her fears and shared her faith. They joined her husband at the hospital.

It was rough having Christian away from home. As an only child, he had spent much of his time with his parents and had a "born 40" demeanor that made him most comfortable with adults. He was accustomed to going on hikes with his mother and skipping parties to join his parents for dinner. After Christian knew his mother was fighting cancer, he FaceTimed her three or four times a day. She worried that he was worried. For several weeks after the surgery, she was swollen and in pain. "You can't cover it up when you hurt like hell," she says. "You really can't hide it."

The recovery after her double mastectomy was painful for months, and it was physically and emotionally exhausting. "You look at yourself differently," she says. "You just don't feel right. Your body feels different." After regaining stamina, Jennifer began flying north to watch Christian's lacrosse games, confiding in some of the parents of his teammates. Sharing her fears about breast cancer fast-forwarded the connection with these new friends, prompting them to disclose their personal struggles as well. On the heels of an illness came a new a circle of friends.

FRIENDSHIP OF THE GOOD

> There is nothing on this earth more to be prized than true friendship.
>
> Thomas Aquinas

Aristotle divided friendships into three categories: those of utility, those of pleasure, and those "of the good." A friendship of utility is temporary because when it is no longer useful, it ends. You might have a utilitarian friendship with a business partner or classmate. A friendship of pleasure, such as one with a witty parent on the sidelines of high school sports, is also unlikely to survive into the empty nest years because it may end as soon as the pleasure or common activity changes or concludes.

Friendship "of the good" endures because it is real. This genuine friendship is rare and exists for its own sake, not to yield a separate benefit. But such lasting relationships still require time and intimacy to thrive. Human beings intuitively know which friendships are best because they offer the most comfort. People begin pruning their friend networks between age 20 and 30, and continue to weed them throughout adulthood and especially after age 40, Carstensen says. We become increasingly intolerant of those who don't soothe our souls. This winnowing of relationships "is more of a pruning process than a disengagement from life,"

Carstensen says. The friend networks get smaller but have far more soul per square inch.

SHARING THE SAME PATH

Empty nesters often flock toward others whose fledglings have similar paths. Just ask Adams, the North Carolina friendship expert. After her daughter thrived at Oberlin College, went to graduate school, launched a career she loves, and began making more money than she does, Adams lost touch with mothers of her daughter's earliest friends whose children weren't as successful. "They do not want to hear about my problem-free independent child," Adams says. It's been a rougher road for most of the other kids, and their mothers tend to talk about the negatives, Adams says. If your fledglings are thriving, you are most likely to find common ground with other parents whose kids are also doing well. Or, if your fledglings hit a rough patch, you can find empathy and advice from other parents who are in a similar situation.

When accidental friends lose what they had in common, they tend to go separate ways. These are Aristotle's friendships of utility or of pleasure, and they are by definition temporary. Adams also lost touch with the parents from her daughter's high school. Once the kids left, the group disbanded. "All we had in common was raising our kids," she says.

When relationships *do* click over the long haul, these friends tend to have similar personalities and values. And they often share the same education level, race, employment history, and age, Adams says. "We tend to be a lot like our friends," Adams says. Sharing backgrounds and traits makes it easier to identify with each other's needs. If your friend is a fellow empty nester, you are likely to share the same concerns. While you can't call up your daughter to say you are lonely now that she's gone, you can call up a friend in your generation to talk about it. If you lose your husband, it's not your daughter who can comprehend the depth of your feeling; it's more likely to be a contemporary.

Women in particular tend to call long-term friends for emotional support in tough times or times of transition, such as after the last kid leaves. These friends "protect you from day-to-day disasters," Adams says. And those who live far away are most likely to last. They don't annoy you with petty issues like some friends who are right around the corner. A long-term friend who lives far away "doesn't anger you by not showing up on time or getting involved in some dispute at the PTA," Adams says.

BRIDGE OVER TROUBLED WATER

> Walking with a friend in the dark is better than walking alone in the light.
>
> Helen Keller

There's nothing more soothing than close friends to help you through a family crisis. Jean's girlfriends did exactly that. While at the beach in Ocean City, Maryland, Jean became alarmed when she couldn't reach her 19-year-old son Colin by phone. She persuaded her husband Brian to drive straight home, where they contacted their son's friends, who suspected he was in jail. They found a message on their answering machine confirming that he had been arrested with drugs and a gun.

Jean and Brian jumped into action, putting up bail money and hiring a lawyer. They were stunned when their son confessed he was addicted to drugs. "We were so trusting," Jean says. "He had always been such a great kid. His teachers and coaches loved him." But in high school, Colin suffered from Crohn's disease, an autoimmune disorder that affects the digestive system and causes intestinal pain and diarrhea, leaving him isolated and frustrated. He also struggled with dyslexia and ADHD, which made academics daunting. So he had chosen to live at home and work as a pizza delivery guy. Jean, a journalism professor, later discovered that to ease his pain, he had medicated himself with drugs, including heroin. They checked him into a residential treatment center. Addiction experts at the center informed them that their son, like most addicts, was likely to relapse.

Jean was exhausted and overwhelmed. She already had planned a 50th birthday trip to a lake house with four close girl-friends from her childhood. It was scheduled for two weeks after her son's arrest and she knew she needed to go. Her husband went for part of the time and both of them found it soothed their souls to discuss Colin's situation with close friends. They were "completely nonjudgmental and didn't try to give advice," she says. The women got their blood pumping by hiking together. One friend shared the story of her rough relationship with her mother-in-law. Another talked about her young adult's learning disabilities. Jean realized they all were struggling in different ways and "felt completely supported."

Colin's drug addiction took a financial and emotional toll. The cost of his treatment hit $100,000, which required his parents to take out a home equity line of credit. Brian, a blackjack dealer who also runs a roulette wheel in a casino, did his best to take a "businesslike approach" with their son, but he needed to vent and cry. Jean surprised herself at how she was able to keep an even keel. The main breadwinner, she never missed a beat at her university job, which provides the family's health insurance. She couldn't afford to fall off the treadmill.

As is often the case, the crisis left them with little time to focus on their marriage. They had a common goal, which was to keep their son alive. But they disagreed about how to accomplish it. They fought over the cost of different treatment plans, and then would backtrack and insist they needed to spend "whatever it takes." When Colin relapsed, he was suicidal and Jean and Brian were thrown into the urgent situation of finding another rehab program. They worried their son would never shake drugs.

But Jean's girlfriends were there to help them through. They continued hiking and talking on weekends. They discussed what Jean and Brian learned about addiction and family dynamics. Now 23, Colin has been sober for two years and works full time at an addiction center in Arizona. He is helping others break bad habits and his parents are regaining their emotional footing. Jean is proud that her son is using his compassion and brains to save lives and that he's keeping control of his Crohn's disease with IV infusions.

Family therapy and counseling have taught them all better communication skills. They hold lots of little conversations that are "quick check-ins," she says. Colin will call about work and she'll let him vent, affirming his decisions. "I know you will find the best way to handle that," she'll say, or, "sounds reasonable," or "sounds like a great plan." They thank him for staying in touch, for his hard work, and for everything he does to make himself better. She is now her son's sounding board, just as her girlfriends serve that role for her.

FAMILY AND FRIENDS

> If you want to do really important things in life and big things in life, you can't do anything by yourself. And your best teams are your friends and your siblings.
>
> Deepak Chopra

Empty nesters often rediscover their siblings after their kids leave. That's because you have more time and because competition between siblings subsides with age. Women tend to search out their sisters to renew the bond if they haven't kept up with it all along. "If you have sisters, it's not unusual to get closer to them" once your kids go, Tannen says. In researching her book *You Were Always Mom's Favorite! Sisters in Conversation throughout Their Lives*, Tannen found that many sisters had lost touch but gotten back together once their kids left. And while sibling competition may have been "fierce" in youth, the relationship generally evolves into one of mutual support. Reconnecting with brothers and sisters can be a relief and build a bridge from the past to the future. A sibling is "somebody who knows and understands where you came from," Tannen says. "You talk about your parents—they know who you are."

However, as we become older adults, outside friendships are often better than family relationships for boosting health and happiness. "We tend to feel better when we interact with friends than with relatives and spouses," Chopik says. In a study of 271,053 adults in 100 countries, Chopik found that friends are like "a protective environment" and that having close friendships at advanced ages bolsters health and happiness, even more so than good relationships with family.[5] "They give us a unique support," he says. "The good ones are universally positive. Friends are family by choice."

And while marriage can be a source of strong support, it's far from enough. "It's a little unrealistic to expect one person to fill all your needs," Chopik says. Close friends help you handle the ups and downs of life. Single people with great friendships are on a par with happily married people in terms of life satisfaction, and they are happier than married people with bad relationships, his research shows. In a study of 7,481 older adults in the United States, Chopik found that when people have friends who annoy them, they report more chronic illnesses.[6] People who maintain close friendship are happier across the life span, he says.

TREASURING FRIENDSHIP

As people age and realize time is running out, they come to value close relationships more than ever. "The uniquely human ability is appreciation of mortality—or limits on life," says Carstensen. "We know where we stand. We are taking account of how much time we have left." Empty nesters care more about having time with those they love, and making the most of that time. They savor life and relationships more and no longer feel obligated to spend time with people who are not on the same page. "They think, 'I didn't like Bob that much,'" Carstensen says. And Bob falls off the dance card.

Empty nesters thrive when they are engaged with others and feel a part of the community. Life is rougher for those who are isolated and alone. In the African Savanna, wildebeests seek safety in a pack when a lion comes out of the bush. It's the one who is left behind who is in trouble. Of all the predictors of well-being in old age, social integration and friendship top the list.

Section III

Guiding Your Fledglings

6

NOW THAT YOUR KIDS HAVE MOVED OUT

Thirty is the new 20.

Old Adage

Growing up takes a lot longer these days. This generation of young adults is settling on careers, becoming financially independent, and learning to accept personal responsibility later than ever. Young adults now tend to take at least a year or two longer to graduate from college. They also change jobs frequently as they seek careers that pay well and are fulfilling. And they search longer for love, postponing marriage and parenthood until their late 20s. Young adults today are discovering broader possibilities than previous generations and enjoying new freedoms, but they also are facing uncertainty and new fears.

To be sure, some of the trends that are leading to an elongated road to adulthood are the result of broad demographic shifts that have been going on for decades. Young Americans started postponing nuptials in the 1960s, as the invention of the birth control pill led to greater social acceptance of sexual relations between unmarried people in their teens and 20s. More sexual freedom for singles went in tandem with the women's movement, which expanded other options for females. Rather than attending college to find a husband and pursue what some jokingly called an MRS degree, young adult women began pursuing higher education to become lawyers, doctors, and business people. While men accounted for more than 70 percent of college students in the late 1940s, women comprised 56 percent of students on campuses nationwide in 2017–2018, according to the U.S. Department of Education.[1] In 1975, 43 percent of women ages 25–34 were homemakers; by 2016, that share had dropped to just 14 percent.[2]

In addition, advances in technology and machines have created an economy that requires more education and training to snag jobs with higher pay and status. To get good jobs in business, finance, insurance, education, and health, young adults go to school longer and postpone heading to the altar. In 1960, people were apt to be married by age 21. As of 2018, the typical age for marriage in the United States has climbed to 27.4 for women and 29.5 for men.[3]

For all these reasons, this generation of young adults is putting off the portals to adulthood for another six to eight years, says Jeffrey Jensen Arnett, a professor of psychology at Clark University and author of *Emerging Adulthood: The Winding Road from the Late Teens through the Twenties.* Many young Americans these days appear to have adopted Peter Pan's I-don't-want-to-grow-up attitude, rejecting the idea of settling down in their teens and 20s. In particular, those in the middle and upper-middle classes avoid adult obligations because they see marriage, home, and parenthood "not as achievements to be pursued, but as perils to be avoided," Arnett says. Most Americans today believe educational and economic accomplishments are extremely important milestones of adulthood, but they don't think marrying and having children are important markers in becoming an adult, he says.[4] Today's young adults want more time to enjoy independence, spontaneity, and a sense of wide-open possibility. As they fend off adulthood, they think along the lines of the British playwright and screenwriter Tom Stoppard, who wrote: "Maturity is a high price to pay for growing up."[5]

SELF-RELIANCE

The road to adulthood may be longer for this generation, but many well-intentioned middle- and upper-middle-class parents also are unwittingly slowing their kids' journeys. Unlike parents in previous generations, many of today's moms and dads have been highly involved in most every aspect of their children's lives all the way through high school. Many have tapped the full force of their education and drained their bank accounts to grant their offspring advantages in academics, athletics, arts, and social life, knowing that their kids face a tougher economic climate than they did. When their kids are struggling academically, those who can afford it have hired tutors—which can bolster transcripts and increase their children's chances of getting into the best colleges. But all that parental support can create dependence and leave kids less self-reliant once they are on their own. Psychologist Wendy Mogel, author of *The Blessing of a B Minus*, has described kids in this generation as "tea cups" who can shatter easily.[6]

Because so many parents have been hands-on with this generation of young adults, many are fragile and vulnerable, says Monica McGoldrick, a family therapist in Highland Park, New Jersey, and an adjunct faculty member at the Robert Wood Johnson Medical School at Rutgers. "At 18, they leave for college with no adult supervision at a point in life when they are not ready to manage their own lives," she says.[7] While these young adults want to be left alone, many aren't ready to make their own decisions because they have been so intensively guided and highly protected. As they go out in the world, they will likely need help to make the transition. It's a tricky balance, but if you are going to err on one side, it's better to be involved than not involved, Arnett says. Young adults who don't feel their parents are available, or who feel too much on their own, "really have a hard time," he says. "Emerging adults who suffer are the ones whose parents don't care."

ROOM TO GROW

> A wise woman once said to me that there are only two lasting
> bequests we can hope to give our children. One of these she
> said is roots, the other, wings.
>
> Hodding Carter

Teenagers and young adults are much like toddlers in that they
crave their freedom but also need to be reassured that parental
help is within reach. When Monica McGoldrick's son John left for
Northwestern University, she was lucky to have one of her best
friends nearby in Wilmette, Illinois, so she could visit without
intruding on him. Otherwise, she says, she would have been waiting for him around campus, hoping he would give her an extra
hour or two when he wanted to be with his friends. "I would
advise people to have a best friend who lives in the college town,"
she jokes. But short of that, you should keep yourself busy and
focus on connecting to your young adult without being overly in-
vested in his every move. Because her friend was nearby, she
could meet her son for a holiday brunch or a school event like
parents' weekend, and he could leave afterward to see his friends,
guilt free. She understood it could be boring for an 18-year-old to
hang with his mom instead of his new classmates. "You want to
stay connected to your kid, but your kid wants to be free," she
says.

   She learned to step aside on other matters as well. When John
didn't appear lit up by academics the way she was, McGoldrick let
him do his own thing. In the end, it all turned out fine. Like the
lion's share of young adults these days, it took several years for him
to find his passion. Now he makes videos for the National Basketball Association, joining his love of sports with his love of movies.

   Parenting young adults who are not under your roof requires
patience and understanding. You can bolster your bond by

   • letting your kids take the lead on communications.
   • listening more than you lecture.

- allowing them to make their own choices.
- being mindful about money.

LET KIDS MAKE CONTACT

You should allow your newly departed kids to be in charge of communicating with you. Don't text them ten times a day or freak out if you don't hear from them much. You might worry they are skipping classes or staying out half the night, but you need to take a deep breath and let them go it alone, even though it wracks your nerves. Despite his professional expertise and years spent doing research on young adults, Arnett had to brace himself for the "double whammy" departure of his twins Miles and Paris when they went off to college, one to Tufts and the other to Wesleyan University. For their last year together, Arnett and his wife Lene, both textbook writers, decided to take their twins on a "family gap year" at the University of Bordeaux to learn French and travel. The family is close-knit and his kids were never keen on summer camp, so their first year away at school was a big change. Arnett knew there would be a "hole" in their lives with the kids gone, and that he and his wife would "miss them like crazy."

But he's determined to respect their independence, allowing them to be the ones who initiate contact. He wants the parent-child communications to be based more on their needs than his own, and he intends to respect the amount of contact they do and don't want. Arnett says if his kids don't call or text as much as they did in high school, he'll interpret it positively, as evidence that they are thriving. "If they were struggling, they would contact me," he says.

Some parents have success with other approaches, such as sending occasional texts and establishing a regular time to chat when a kid first leaves home. Psychologist Susan W. Hammond of Silver Spring, Maryland, checked in with her son by telephone once a week when he went to college. Hammond texted her son to remind him about routine matters she had taken care of when he was home. She recommends using texts for these basic details and setting up a weekly time to talk on the phone about more serious matters. If a young adult is accustomed to waiting for a designated time to talk to parents, he is more likely to resolve an issue on his own, which builds critical problem-solving skills, she says.[8]

When young adults have space, they also do a better job of accepting responsibility for themselves. They get better at making their own choices, deciding whom to spend time with, being careful with their money, and getting out of bed on time. I tried for a decade and a half to get my son Jack to school on time, but he was frequently five to eight minutes late for his first class. He kept pressing the snooze button on his alarm clock until we were thrown into a last-minute scramble to get him out of the door. I feared he would lose jobs as an adult for being chronically late. One of his favorite teachers, who initially assumed his tardiness was a result of being trapped in traffic, looked up his address and discovered he lived just two blocks from school. She told him he should be the first one in class because of his proximity. But despite his interest in her Spanish class, he simply couldn't get there on time.

When he got to college, he slept through a lacrosse team breakfast and the coach benched him for a game. He was never late again. I am forever grateful to the coach for fixing that hole in my parenting. When your kids leave the nest, they won't always make the right decision. They likely recognize that their parents probably make better decisions. Yet they still want to make the decisions by themselves. You should speak up if there is a serious problem like drug, alcohol, or partner abuse. But short of those extremes, you need to let your fledglings make their own decisions, including the wrong ones.

SKIP THE GUILT

Whatever you do, don't make your kids feel guilty for trying to be more independent. If you are trying to pull your young adults too close when they need space, they will feel conflicted as they try to build a life for themselves. They will be plagued with guilt and worried their parents aren't functioning well without them. They will feel suffocated and frustrated.

You also want to steer clear of the details of your young adult's life, which are bound to worry you. Even if you try to get involved, you're likely to get a sanitized version of reality, one that has been carefully censored to present what your child thinks you want to hear. "They are up to all kinds of things their parents are not going to hear about," Arnett says, recommending that you stay away from the particulars. "Everybody is happier that way."

FIND NEW WAYS TO CONNECT

Easing into the empty nest gradually is never wrong. As her son navigated his first year at the University of Maryland, psychologist Linda McGhee gave him room to grow but made sure she was available if he needed her. Recently, she ordered him a pair of shoes with the University of Maryland insignia on them. Instead of dropping them in the mail, she left work early and drove the 10 miles to campus to deliver the shoes in person. Her son loved them, she says, and sent her a really nice note. She plans to take him to dinner soon, when he finds the time. "I wanted to get my son through the first year," she says.[9]

THE BANK OF MOM AND DAD

Money matters with young adults can be tricky. Today, 60 percent of young adults in their 20s and 30s receive financial help from their parents, according to Kate Levinson, a marriage and family therapist and author of *Emotional Currency: A Woman's Guide to Building a Healthy Relationship with Money*. Empty nest couples frequently clash over whether, or how much, to help support their young adult kids financially. Most parents are stretched to their financial max to help cover college bills and are reevaluating their emotional and financial situations once the kids leave, she says.[10] Many empty nesters also stress over discussing finances with their mate. Conflict arises when some parents want to do all they can to support their kid's career, borrowing money from a home equity line or dipping into their savings, while others insist their young adult should go it alone. Mothers tend to be more financially generous than fathers, using money as a way of caring for fledglings, Levinson says. There's often tension between a desire to protect a couple's financial well-being and that of the adult child, and that friction can make sparks fly. Bridging the gap in financial philosophies requires "deep, honest conversation," but because of a taboo about talking about money, couples tend to avoid the topic.

Money is not just a practical aspect of our lives, it's also "tremendously psychological and emotional," Levinson says. Money is an intimate and touchy topic that triggers strong emotions because handling it involves "needs, vulnerability, power, and uncertainty," she says, and most people fear they are not handling their finances correctly. And money means different things to different people: Each spouse brings to the table their own life experience, family history, gender, and religion, as well as personal and emotional associations with money. Focusing on monetary matters often causes one spouse to consider whether they have value, and if they are too dependent. "It's a very complex dance in a relationship," Levinson says.

It's difficult to have both partners equally engaged in money matters. Cultural biases can dictate that men be breadwinners and make the family's financial decisions. Many baby boomer men grew up with their father in charge of finances, so they want to repeat the pattern. When financial planners attempt to bring both husband and wife to the table for a financial discussion, they often fail because the woman ends up bowing out, Levinson says. "Very few of us want to pay attention to the dollars and cents," she says. "There's a lot of anxiety and fear of making a mistake. It's much easier to say, 'I pay the bills and you take care of the investments. I don't have the bandwidth for so many other details. You take care of it.'" Women have for the most part been trained that they don't have a head for money, she says, adding that even female CFOs of large corporations might not deal with their own family's finances. "Lots of women who are really competent at work run from money discussions in their relationships," she says.

But while working on finances together is tougher, "it's actually the only safe place for a couple to be," she says. Otherwise, one spouse has no idea how much money the couple has or how it's being managed. States Levinson, "You really put yourself at risk if you don't have at least a general sense of the financial circumstances and what the statements are saying."

It's also risky to dole money out too readily to support your young adults. If you want to offer financial support, you should weigh your own needs to make sure you can remain financially healthy now and into retirement. In addition to hurting yourself, giving too much monetary support can hurt your kid. If you provide too much of a fiscal cocoon, it can backfire and prompt your offspring to become lazy. Young adults with too much cash from Mom and Dad can be too comfortable to take risks and work hard. Remember, achieving a middle-class lifestyle is an objective that can take years, developing pluck and character along the way. Being tight on cash can move people to action. "The need for money makes you do hard things you wouldn't necessarily do when you have it," Levinson says.

If you are considering financial support for your young adult,

- discuss the merits and consequences with your spouse.
- do the arithmetic: figure out what you can afford—now and later.
- continue to assess if financial support is helping or hurting your kid.
- consider paying for specific needs rather than opening the spigot.
- don't tie strings to your financial support or use it to manage your young adult.
- create a plan with your young adult and set a finite timeline.

Financial pressure is a motivator, as long as it isn't too extreme. Consider the case of McLean, a 31-year-old Shakespearean actress, who knows she's got to make it on her own. She doesn't take money from her parents because she grew up in a "can-do, work-hard farm house," she says. She works several jobs, including as an understudy at the Folger Theatre in Washington, DC. Constantly scrambling for cash while chasing her dream of starring on Broadway has been grueling, she says, but it has also made her stronger and grittier. To make a better hourly wage, she trained as a ballet barre instructor, which involved several weeks of long hours in workshops. But she also learned a new skill, became fitter, forged bonds with others, and saw her pay rise from $12 an hour to $35. Necessity also has motivated her in her field of acting. "If I am desperate, I have to seek more auditions, and work harder to look the way I should look and sound the way I should sound," she says.

However, too much financial strain also can derail dreams, at least temporarily. As McLean was working to pay off her master's degree in acting from The George Washington University, her car died, throwing an unexpected wrench into her fiscal life. Now she may need to stop acting for a while to dig herself out of a financial hole. The constant stress of earning money outside her career can make it hard to be your own boss. "It's a career where we are always interviewing for the next job, we have to be smart and ambitious enough to be our own boss, as well as maintaining our artistry. It's a lot to juggle." Sometimes, she says, she does wonder if "enough is enough."

Many artists are able to pursue their craft as young adults because they have monetary support from others, such as parents or a spouse. "If you can cut out the whole making-money part," she says, "you have more time to dedicate to your career success." But her way has its benefits. "Until you've experienced real hardship, real pain, real life challenges, you can't understand human nature. And if you don't understand the difficulty of being a human, no one will want to listen to your vapid, one-sided art."

If you do have the means to help out, deciding whether to give a financial boost to your young adult should depend on who they are. As a parent, you want to consider each young adult individually. While one might thrive with extra money from Mom and Dad, others would find that financial help demoralizing. It could undermine their efforts and send the message that the parent doesn't believe the kid can do it on her own. For that child, you are better off closing the account. But if you do decide to dole out money, you must not micromanage it. "You want some accountability but at the same time a minimum of interactions" about the funding, Levinson says. "You want to get out of the 'I'm organizing your life' idea. That's not your place anymore. With an adult child, the kind of dynamic it sets up can be really destructive."

You can learn what is best for your young adult by trying different approaches. If, after two years of cash flow from the Bank of Mom and Dad, the kid is still foundering, then you have to consider whether the well-intentioned funding is working. How do you determine what is right? Step back and see your kid from the perspective of a stranger with emotional distance. Is your young adult failing to take risks or work harder because of your financial help? You don't want to coddle your young adult and remove motivation. Or, if your child is working hard toward an important goal, your assistance might be just the thing to help her reach it. Says Levinson, "No matter what you do, you are probably going to make some mistakes."

If your fledgling is making strides and you are able to continue giving financial support, you need to determine how many years you want to keep investing. Levinson recommends having a heart-to-heart conversation about what's happening and discussing what you both think is best. She suggests that you talk like this: "In six months, honey, I'm feeling I'm going to need to cut back. I'm afraid if it's too easy, it takes a certain edge off for you." Coming up with the right plan for helping your young adult involves serious soul-searching and it's hard to know if you are doing the right thing. You might decide to help support your adult for another year, but you don't want to go on and on without assessing. "That's when you get yourself and the kid in trouble financially and emotionally," Levinson says. "If you are resenting the money, it's not

good for the relationship." Generally, you must go with your intuition and your gut and take care of yourself. For people without
money, it's not a question. "Those kids either sink or swim," she
says. "When there's no money, it's hard." But hard times can also
be a great motivator.

HIGHWAY TO ADULTHOOD

Some kids, especially those whose families aren't financially well
off, must take the superhighway to adulthood instead of the scenic
route. That was Kasey's situation. His single mother Kareline, who
had her first child at 17, grew up living in cars and foster homes.
She was determined to provide better for her three sons, working
as a waitress and housekeeper in Vero Beach, Florida, but her
budget was tight.

As an 11-year-old, Kasey stepped in as the man of the house.
He would wait up until 2 a.m., when his mom returned from her
waitressing shift, to count her tip money and ask which bills they
needed to pay. He got groceries, helped take care of his younger
brother, Jeremiah, and helped with his older brother, Shawn, who
struggled with drugs. "It was always calm and easy to be a mom
with Kasey around," Kareline says. "He always loved me no matter
what."

When Kasey won scholarships to a nearby private school and
later to Florida State University, she was delighted but also devastated he was leaving home. She feared she couldn't balance her
life once he was gone. "I didn't have someone I could talk back
and forth with," she says. "I wasn't sure what steps we should
take." When Kasey graduated from college and headed out West
to find work, she was lost. "I would walk into a crowded room and
feel so alone," she says. She worried when his brothers followed
him to the West Coast, but also was relieved that they could look
out for each other. She's proud Kasey has put his geology degree
to work by selling rocks and minerals at his own shop in Chico,

California, and smiles when she thinks of him hiking in the mountains searching for rocks and polishing them in a tumbler.

Kareline dreams of moving to California to be closer to her kids, but understands they want to make it on their own. So she looks forward to visiting them once or twice a year. Her desire to hike with them in the mountains prompted her to undergo bariatric surgery and lose 80 pounds, delighting them all when she was able to summit a mountain with them. She also has turned her need to nurture elsewhere: She is now raising her nine-year-old niece and eight-year-old nephew, whose mother is unable to care for them and whose father drives trucks, taking him away a week at a time. "Those kids have become mine," she says. She also takes in young adults who have no place to stay. Says Kareline, "I really enjoy being there for all these kids and teenagers. It gives my life purpose."

LETTING GO EARLY

Letting go gradually eases the transition to the empty nest. That's why some parents like Kim and Todd encourage their kids to try their wings early. When their son Dawson was nine, Todd pressed to send him to sleepaway camp in Vermont for a month. Kim was hesitant at first, and before they dropped Dawson off, they both burst into tears. They cried until a savvy young counselor "talked them off the cliff," and promised to call them the following week. The next Tuesday, they got a call reporting that Dawson was thriving. "He doesn't even miss us," Kim told her husband. That summer separation became a tradition, and the four weeks stretched into eight as Dawson found new friends from other cities.

But Kim, director of content at a public radio and TV station in Tallahassee, took flak from friends who kept a tighter leash on their kids in summer. They saw her choice as pawning off her son, while she was determined to keep her only child in summer camps surrounded by other kids. One mother told her, "I provide for my kids to have a wonderful summer so they don't need to go anywhere else." She swallowed the harsh judgment she felt from others, saying she instead "realized I was giving my child a gift, experiencing things in ways that would enrich his life."

The weekslong summer separations helped them all let go emotionally, a little at a time. "Whether we are conscious of it or not, our worlds cycle around our kids," Kim says. "When our kids aren't there anymore, you have to figure what you are going to do with that space." She says she and her husband were able to create a life beyond living with Dawson. "There's a lot about life that's independent of being a parent," she says. When he was gone for long periods at a time in summers, "that gave us a base," Kim says.

Dawson took a gap year after high school, and used the time to travel. First, he headed to Madrid, where he lived with a family and tutored their kids in English. Then he flew to Colombia, working and seeing the country. "He's been breaking us in for a long time for the reality that he's going to form his own person and live his own life," Kim says. She's still sad when she walks into Trader Joe's, where Dawson used to work, and sees his favorite mango sorbet. But the gradual separation helped all of them to adjust to his young adulthood. Now that he's a student across the country at Occidental College, she says, "we miss him and feel this tug, but we are still very engaged in our lives and are not just pining for this child who is not living with us."

The road to adulthood these days tends to be longer and more winding, which often requires patience and assistance on the part of parents. That isn't surprising: Many of today's young adults grew up in an era of intensive, hands-on parenting, and if the scaffolding is removed too quickly, they might crumble or collapse. As this generation of young adults carves out careers, gets a financial footing, and learns to accept personal responsibility later in life, their parents have a lengthier, more complex task in helping them construct the bridge to adulthood. But a longer road to becoming a grown-up is also an opportunity for parents to know our young adults better—if we build the bridge mindfully. It's worth recalling the wisdom of Henry Havelock Ellis, a British psychologist, physician, and social reformer: "All the art of living lies in a fine mingling of letting go and holding on."[11]

7

WHAT YOUNG ADULTS REALLY WANT AND NEED

When I was a boy of 14, my father was so ignorant, I could hardly stand to have the man around. But when I got to be 21, I was astonished at how much he had learnt in seven years.

Mark Twain

Young adults in this generation are keeping closer contact than ever before with Mom and Dad. Once they leave the nest, they use technology such as texting, FaceTime, e-mail, Facebook, and Instagram to maintain ties with their parents. They also keep close the old-fashioned way: by phone. But there's a big difference these days: When we were young adults, we needed to stand in line at a pay phone with a pocketful of quarters to make a long-distance call, while calculating if it was a good use of our limited funds. Now, with the widespread use of cell phones, staying in touch is much cheaper and easier.

Meanwhile, we are part of a larger demographic shift in which young adults are relying longer on their parents' money, advice, and emotional support, often into their late 20s, which can benefit both generations. After young adults leave the nest, one in three boomerangs back for a while for emotional support or to gain a financial footing. This prolonged period of experimentation and self-discovery, in which kids take longer to choose mates and careers, can appear self-indulgent. But as life spans stretch into the ninth decade, today's young adults may be laying the foundation for making fewer mistakes than their parents and preparing themselves to lead happier, more fulfilling lives.

Because young adults and their parents stay in better touch these days, they better understand each other and the relationship tends to be more harmonious than that of previous generations. The bond gets better and stronger when kids leave home at 18 or 19 to go to college, travel, work, or join the military because they are able to make their own decisions about what to eat, how to handle their money, and when to come home without catching flak. Young adults are happier when they are more independent. "Once kids move out, parents are no longer apt to meddle in things kids think is none of their business," says Jeffrey Jensen Arnett, a psychologist at Clark University and author of *Emerging Adulthood: The Winding Road from the Late Teens through the Twenties*. Becoming independent is "a key transition for emerging adults," he says. "When young adults move out, the hierarchy of parents as an authority figure fades away. What remains is mutual affection and attachment they have for each other on the basis of many years of shared experience."[1]

Away from the nest, young adults become less egocentric than they were as teens, and more able to see their parents' point of view. With a little distance, they appreciate how much their parents have contributed to their lives. Most were raised by parents who had fewer kids than the previous generation and were less authoritarian, leading to a closer relationship, he says.

Young adults today are reaching out to their parents: Fifty-five percent report being in contact with them daily or almost every day, 75 percent say they get along better with their parents than they did as adolescents, and only 30 percent complain their parents are more involved in their lives than they want them to be, according to Arnett's research.[2] Overall, today's fledglings see Mom and Dad as an essential source of support, and the emotions they feel for them are among the strongest they have for anyone in their lives.

HELICOPTERING

It's not surprising that young adults these days are so tied to Mom and Dad. Some parents in modern times have become "helicopter" or "lawn-mower" parents, constantly hovering and being overly involved, rather than allowing children to do tasks they are capable of handling alone. In high school or college, a helicopter parent might arrange a kid's class schedule or call a professor about grades. Well-intentioned parents hover because they fear dire consequences if a kid gets a low grade or is cut from a team. Parents may get too involved because they worry about the economy or the job market. Perhaps they think their parents were too laissez-faire and are compensating, or they feel pressure from peers who are hovering if they are not. But being too hands-on with high schoolers or college kids can breed hostility from young adults, who usually crave independence. It also can send a signal to the kids that their parents don't have confidence in them. Attempts to protect a kid from inevitable disappointment or hurt also can remove struggle that is essential to build resilience.

Finding the right balance between parenting teenagers and young adults without smothering them is tricky. The goal is to be supportive without being so enmeshed that we lose perspective. Engaged parenting can bring tremendous benefits to young adults. When they know they are a top priority, they feel loved, accepted, and more confident. They dare to take risks knowing a parent is squarely in their corner. When young adults get the right amount of guidance and support, it can be easier to excel at a faster pace, Arnett says. But suffering and disappointment are inevitable. When young adults stumble or fail, they need to know a parent is available to help them work through it. That can make all the difference.

LOOSENING APRON STRINGS

> A mother is not a person to lean on but a person to make leaning unnecessary.
>
>   Dorothy Canfield Fisher

Grown children benefit tremendously if parents pitch in when they need help, Arnett says. Most emerging adults often want and need their parents' support into their 20s. "The emerging adults who struggle the most are not the ones suffering from the invasion of helicopter parents, but the ones who cannot count on their parents' love and support even when they need them," Arnett says. "When parents offer young adults support on a weekly basis or more often, the grown children report greater life satisfaction and better adjustment," says Karen Fingerman, a professor of human development and family sciences at the University of Texas at Austin, and a leading expert on 18- to 34-year-olds.[3] However, when you offer help, *don't* do so with "strings attached," because that can trigger resentment.

CLOSER WITH MOM AND DAD

This generation of young adults relies more than ever on ties to Mom and Dad. For Tyler, a 23-year-old who was an All-American defensive midfielder on the Yale lacrosse team, the idea of having a wife and kids is "definitely" way down the road. After graduating with a major in ecology and evolutionary biology, he aims to become a physician, perhaps an orthopedic surgeon. But for now, Tyler is living at home in Freeport, Long Island, with his parents and 99-year-old grandfather, commuting two and a half hours a day by train to his job at a Manhattan hospital. He's saving money for med school, hoping to be at the head of his field one day and "be deserving of some recognition for what I am doing," but that is *not* his primary source of motivation.

Rather, he seeks to "be in a position to help underserved people," a goal that is dear to Tyler because earlier generations of his extended family from rural, segregated, Jim Crow Alabama were disadvantaged and struggled with bad health care. As a child, Ty -ler recalls that some of his mother's 14 older siblings smoked cigarettes, including an uncle who died of lung cancer that was discovered in the late stages because he didn't have access to good doctors. Tyler used to worry about his uncle and ask his mother why more couldn't be done for him.

His mother Ernestine, a mortgage underwriter, and his father Mark, who works in employment services for a health care company, did their best to help Tyler, his two brothers, and other relatives who needed assistance, financial or otherwise. Tyler says he feels like he is almost an adult, but he still relies on his parents "quite a bit." For instance, if he needs to get a car loan or to one day take out a mortgage on a house, he will "be on the phone with Mom and Dad." While he always saw his father as "a prominent, authoritative figure" as he was growing up, his relationship has evolved so that he now sees his father as one of his best friends. His mother is "always supportive and telling me I am the best," he says. "She's always trying to pick you up."

Tyler imagines sending his parents on an extravagant trip or buying his mother a nice car once he is out of med school and established as a doctor, even though he knows they are not materialistic people. He continues to view both parents as his role models and says he wants to make them proud. "They have made sacrifices for me and I want to pay it back in the future."

REACHING FOR A DREAM WITH HELP

When parents work with young adults to help them reach a dream, it makes a huge difference for everyone. And it can greatly enhance the family bond, as long as parents don't get too immersed in their kids' lives. Will is grateful that his parents support his goal of hitting the country music charts, even though he feels frustrated at times when they push him to promote himself more. A 25-year-old Nashville singer/songwriter from Plattsburgh, New York, Will almost made it big when NBC scouts selected him to try out for *The Voice*. The network picked up the bill for Will's flights to Los Angeles, as well as his hotel and daily expenses for a month, but he was cut just before he was to appear on national television. Although he struggles to pay bills working as a barista 35 hours a week and is plagued with "second guesses and worries," Will says he is still "in a good spot."

Like many young adults of this generation, Will is closely tied to his parents. His father Bruce, a contractor who builds commercial poultry and dairy barns, and his mother Suzy help him pay for special projects such as recording an album or making music videos. Without their help, the road to stardom would be daunting. He's grateful they paid for his college education at St. Lawrence University, where he played in a band and sang in an a capella group. He understands why his parents and brothers push him to put his songs online. But he wants to develop his singing and songwriting rather than market himself. "I'd rather have my voice speak for itself," he says.

He worries about being a financial burden on his parents but realizes becoming a successful singer/songwriter "takes a lot longer than if I would get an accounting job downtown. . . . The path I've chosen, it's going to be more up and down. I have to work a lot to make ends meet." He seeks stability "financially and relationship-wise" and aims to buy a house one day. But for now it's enough that he has figured out "who I want to surround myself with." He can't fathom abandoning his dream. Says Will, "I don't find anything else that I can wake up thinking about."

Suzy, director of advancement at a Catholic school, says she and Bruce invest in Will's dream but worry about his future because the music business is so competitive and unpredictable. "It's not like buying a car," she says, "It's not tangible. You don't know what the outcome will be."

They stay close to home and limit travel because Bruce owns his own business and is "very hands on," his job is physically demanding, and they care for Suzy's 94-year-old mother. She says they should allow themselves more leisure time now that their boys are grown, but their kids have always been their top priority and "assisting them with their dreams always feels like the right decision." She adds: "I would give them all the money I could if we didn't need to plan for retirement."

Suzy is also concerned about being financially fair as they have two older sons, Jared, a 30-year-old lawyer and Chase, a 28-year-old photographer. "It's hard to think about how to make it even," she says. At the same time, contributing to Will's career makes her happy. "It's saying, 'I believe in your dream and in you,'" she says. "That's the most magical thing. His music."

Like Will, many grown kids in this generation are delaying the traditional trappings of adulthood. This can exasperate parents, most of whom didn't have the luxury of hanging in limbo so long. But therapists say today's young adults are likely to be more centered and fulfilled as they age because they have taken more time to find themselves and carve out an authentic identity. They haven't discarded their dreams and are likely to have fewer regrets.

While young adults seek many forms of support from their parents these days, they often rebel when they discover that the help comes with strings attached. Just ask Hadley, a 20-year-old restaurant manager. She is grateful that her parents have bailed her out at times, but bristles at how they use their support to try to modify her behavior. In high school, her strict, religious parents meant well, she says, but they "had such a tight leash on me it was claustrophobic." They tracked her phone to know where she was and required her to go to church each Sunday. On New Year's Eve, she had to be home before midnight. After they found out she had been intimate with a boyfriend, they put her on "house arrest" for three months and took away television and telephone privileges.

After she dropped out of the University of Tennessee at Chattanooga because she "wasn't feeling it" and didn't want to waste her parents' money, Hadley moved to California and lived with her boyfriend for six months until they broke up. She is glad her parents went to get her and loaned her money to pay the ex-beau back for her car. But when she moved home for a few weeks after the breakup, she clashed with her parents, who used their support "as a weapon against me." She realized "really, really quickly that we were not going to do well with me living with them," as they wanted to know where she was at all times. "They definitely mean well, but they're too protective," she says. Feeling overwhelmed and in need of "space and privacy," Hadley moved out. "I just wanted the freedom to do my own thing."

Now that her restaurant job allows her to support herself, the relationship with her parents is better than ever. She's delighted that she can buy her own car insurance, pay her parents back for her car, and save money for the first time. "It's a nice, independent feeling," she says. These days, she considers her mother to be her best friend, calling or texting daily and seeing her once a week in the restaurant. She says she also has a wonderful relationship with her dad and can't imagine ever living far away from them again. Says Hadley, "Everything has taken a turn for the better."

GROWING PAINS

But things can take a turn for the worse if a kid comes back from college with new ideas and finds a lack of understanding at home. For Ricardo, a college sophomore, returning home on holidays to his family in Gaithersburg, Maryland, is frustrating. Ricardo worries about economic oppression faced by disadvantaged students and wants his parents to share his passion for social justice, as many of his fellow students do. He admires his mother and father, both first-generation college graduates who work for nonprofits, and feels they "have done a really great job of instilling good values" in him by helping others in need. "They definitely have shaped what I am passionate about and what I am interested in," he says. He credits his upbringing—and the time the family spent living in Guatemala, Ethiopia, and Mozambique, where his parents worked for nonprofits—with giving him "a different lens when I navigate day-to-day things."

His parents nudged him to apply for a college scholarship, which provides him with a mentor, financial aid, and help finding employment. At college, he works three jobs: at a preschool, a high school, and the college athletic center, swiping people in and helping athletes get equipment. His scholarship covers $50,000 a year, and his parents took out a $7,000 loan, an amount he will match.

However, things changed after he studied sexuality in college. Ricardo was introduced to the concept of "heteronormativity," the idea that heterosexuality is normal and the rest isn't, and he began questioning his own orientation. As he was growing up, the word "gay" was used as a sign of weakness, while at college, homosexuality is accepted. He has tried to tell his parents that things are more complicated than gender binary, the assertion that there are only two genders—male and female—but his parents don't understand. Ricardo knows that his father's brother is gay and that the family has hidden it. "When I went back home, it was very, very hard because my parents haven't received the same information and education that I have." He sometimes challenges comments that family members make about sexuality and, he says, it has "caused a lot of problems."

Those family clashes worsened when Ricardo, a tall, handsome soccer player in high school, returned home at age 20 wearing nail polish. His father, who grew up in Guatemala, in a culture in which masculinity dominates, was horrified. To make matters worse, both he and his father are opinionated and stubborn. So when Ricardo went home "doing things people perceived to be more feminine," and no longer emitting the "jock-ie, sporty vibe," his parents were shocked. His friends and his 17-year-old brother's friends would call him derogatory words like "fag." Even though they were joking, it hurt. "It is, and was, very difficult," he says. "I don't know how to navigate and adjust to all these things I am learning."

Now Ricardo feels like he has to be "fake" about who he is. "It's not to say that if I came out gay, they wouldn't love or accept me," he says. "But it would be very difficult. It's definitely something that will take time for them to really be comfortable with. Now it's difficult going home."

STILL A KID

While stretching their wings, most young adults crave connection with a parent, even if it's just a text or a fast phone call. For Elinor, a 22-year-old senior in college who is studying to be a history teacher, dialing up her dad every day or FaceTiming with him once a week is centering. "I just like knowing he's there," she says. "If I am stressed or having a bad day, I know I can call my dad. It's nice to have someone who is removed from where you are." They chat about her two younger brothers and news from home. They talk about high school, when she had to "grow up a little bit faster than everyone else."

Her mother was fighting mental illness and lived elsewhere, and Elinor had to shore up her siblings, babysit when other teen- agers went to parties, and swallow her resentment at being sad- dled with household tasks. She made sure her younger brothers showered and brushed their teeth, and plugged her ears doing homework as they argued and wrestled. She also became a sound- ing board for her father, who was contemplating divorce. "I could tell it was hard for him," she says. "He was lonely. We only had each other in high school."

She wanted to help, but when her dad would grouse about her mother, it shook her up. "I don't want to be put in the middle," she says. "It's not my place." She felt guilty disengaging, but she couldn't do it anymore. "His wife was my mother, too," she says. Elinor worked on getting her father to understand he needed to lean on someone else, which initially was hard for him. She sug- gested he see a therapist. Now they talk instead about Elinor's plans to become a teacher.

She appreciates that he never tells her what to do, but instead listens to help her figure it out on her own.

NO TIME FOR THE SCENIC ROUTE

Some young adults buckle down earlier out of necessity. To stay financially afloat, Marie, a 22-year-old senior at Macalester College in Saint Paul, Minnesota, waited tables and bartended 15 hours a week. A cross-country runner and track and field athlete, she was trained to focus. Marie knew she had to earn money immediately after graduation to start to pay off her large student loans. And, she says she didn't need more time to find herself because she had been at a liberal arts college, which gave her an opportunity to explore ideas. So she leveraged her major in economics and secured a job as a financial adviser in Philadelphia. "It's not necessary that I find my dream job now," she says. She plans to study for the LSAT and head to law school in a year. She is at ease living on her own, having rented apartments, fetched groceries, and generally fended for herself since she left home after high school.

Growing up a "latchkey kid" in Brookfield, Illinois, with a father who was out of the picture and a mother who worked full-time doing taxes for an alternative energy company, she says she was "always kind of used to having to take care of myself, which was fine." As a teen, she ate "random things" instead of sitting down for a family dinner, but was never resentful, as she felt her single mom was doing her best. She appreciates that her mother is on her side, adding that "some people don't even have one parent who is very supportive."

Maria expects she and her mother always will remain "extremely close." She texts her mother every couple of days and talks to her every two weeks as she juggles her busy schedule, but knows her mother understands. Marie brims with gratitude, saying her mom is "always very selfless when it comes to me."

BLAZING A PATH—WITH BACKING

Lots of young adults draw their parents closer once they find their footing. Anna, a twiggy 26-year-old business owner and Instagram "influencer" with 13,000 followers, says she and her parents became more attached after she finished high school and went to Iowa State. She says they always knew she was a creative "wild child" who would blaze her own path. When she wanted to launch a T-shirt line in East Nashville, her dad, who works for a technology company, drove down from suburban Chicago with his toolbox and built the interior of her store. And when she needed money to launch it, her parents gave her a loan. "They believed in me," she says. They wanted to know how much money she needed to avoid bankruptcy and eating ramen noodles at every meal. If she needs a plane ticket to fly home, they'll pay for part of it. "The shop is completely me," she says. "My rent is completely me. But if my car is totaled, they would help me." While she hated high school, Anna has carved out a niche she loves with a blog where she models and styles trendy clothes and accessories. "I've grown up and I think I'm finally doing something that I like," she says. "It helps when I'm happy and my parents know that I am."

Anna is amused when her 62-year-old father, who is getting ready to retire, offers her out-of-date business advice, like suggesting that she put an ad in the newspaper. And she laughs at his "old school ways," such as when he tried to help her write a business e-mail. She says his style is formal and middle-aged, while Anna's generation responds to a tone that is casual, brassy, and flip.

She's tight with her mother and calls her frequently. Yet when it comes to her social life, it's her girlfriends who get the real scoop. "I love my mom being my best friend, but I think personally there should be a separation of information," she says. "You don't need to tell them everything." Anna censors her personal stories so they "can worry less."

Anna is far from alone in editing her experiences for her parents. Young adults are well aware that standards, social norms, and behavior have shifted. While some middle-aged people cringe at online dating services, which can appear dangerous to those of us who dated pre-Internet, many millennials wouldn't do it any other way. "Skipping the gory details can be better for everybody," Arnett says.

HALF KID, HALF ADULT

Young adults tend to vacillate between feeling on the high end of childhood and the low end of adulthood. Most of them are going through a prolonged period of identity exploration, instability, and self-focus, feeling in-between, with an optimistic sense of possibilities. They are less certain about the future than full-fledged adults, but also more optimistic. Teens and young adults both search for their identity, however, young adults move through this stage with more intensity and a heightened sense of urgency. As they enter their later 20s, these grown children are aware that the stakes are high and that they are approaching the age 30 milestone. Arnett's research shows that nearly all young adults, some 96 percent, agree with the statement, "I am very sure that someday I will get where I want to be in life." But they also face feelings of frustration and ambivalence. Sixty percent said they felt both like grown-ups and not-quite-grown-ups. They are looking for support from more experienced adults—in particular, their parents.

Evan, a 25-year-old Nashville tattoo artist with his own studio, says he feels that he "flops back and forth" between being a kid and a grown-up. "In a lot of ways, I feel a lot more grown-up than when I was 18," he says. "I'm a lot more emotionally mature. But when Evan is "doing taxes and things like that," he says he feels like he still has the mental capacity of an 18-year-old.

As a child, Evan loved to draw. When he first went to college, he dabbled in printmaking and painting and declared a studio art major. However, he decided the fine art world wasn't for him and became obsessed with tattooing. "I was thinking about it in the shower," he says. He pitched his parents on the idea of an apprenticeship, creating a business plan to show them how he could make good money as a tattoo artist. His father, an artist, and his mother, a teacher who is inclined toward the visual arts, agreed to let him live at home for a year so he could get the required training. They weren't upset when he decided to leave college because, he says, "they always trusted me to make my own decisions." Evan says he and his parents "are quiet, don't raise our voices, freak out, or get angry." Living with them, he still felt like a kid, but unlike in high school, he tried to be respectful, and became "more true and open" with them.

Once Evan built up his tattoo business and felt financially secure, he reached for another milestone: He bought a house. His income was steady, but he didn't have much credit history and the bank wouldn't give him a loan. So his parents cosigned the loan. He pays the mortgage himself, and is "super grateful" his parents agreed to help him so he could build equity. "I now understand the value of being at a point of financial success where you can springboard your kids into something more reliable," he says. The property he owns "is better than something I would have gotten" without their help. Evan says he is surrounded by friends who reject jobs that could earn good money. "They don't want to settle, but they don't know what their passion is," he says. "They don't know how to apply their creativity to something that's lucrative, so they end up in this limbo phase in their 20s." His friends say they can't do as well financially as their parents. "No one is really thinking of retirement in the realm of realistic possibilities," he says. He predicts a lot of his friends will be working service-related jobs indefinitely.

Like many young adults, Evan has evolved emotionally because of his close relationship with his parents. These days, he rarely quarrels with his parents. If he does, he likes to resolve it "then and there." He says he really enjoys spending time with his mother and father and that he often goes with them on walks for an hour or two or out for coffee.

In their late 20s, young adults are more likely to strike the right balance with their parents. They want help in certain areas and need independence in others— such as their social and romantic lives. Karsen, a 27-year-old entrepreneur, values her father's experience as an owner of sports bars, taverns, and eateries in Arizona, and consults him frequently on questions of "adulting," like figuring out taxes, finding a new business space, or strategizing to take her company to the next step. She consults her mother on creative matters.

It's not lost on Karsen that young adults in her generation are getting married later than their parents did. When Karsen's mother was her age, she already had two kids and a husband. "I'm 27 and don't have a boyfriend," she says. "Kids are *way* in my future." In the 1970s, a couple might get married at 25 and be divorced a few years later. However, today, "that same couple would be more likely to simply live together for a few years, then head their separate ways when things go south," says John J. Zogby, a pollster. "On one hand, a divorce is a far more disruptive and messy life event than simply moving out of your partner's apartment," Zogby says. "In that sense, you have to applaud the wisdom of today's twenty- and thirty-somethings for taking their time before tying the knot."[4]

As Karsen sifts through "the virtual tech" dating world like Tinder and Bumble or meets a man on Instagram, she doesn't expect her parents to understand, so she shields them from specifics. She doesn't want judgment. "When my mom or dad judges me, it is the most hurtful thing," she says. "One of my least favorite things is disappointing my parents." She says some topics are right for her parents, while others belong in the realm of her peers.

BRIDGE TO ADULTHOOD

Young adults have tasks to complete before crossing the bridge into adulthood. They must learn how to meet their own basic needs, such as safety, food, shelter, human connection, and love. They must build self-reliance and independence. "The decade from 20 to 30 is jam-packed with developmental tasks, including finding a way out of your parental home and starting to care for and nurture yourself," says Jennifer L. Tanner, a developmental psychologist at Rutgers University who specializes in mental health and family studies. "They must become their own parents."[5]

But Tanner says many young adults are waiting perilously long to find a partner. Young people in large cities like Los Angeles, San Francisco, and New York are spending six, seven, or more years longer than their parents on the search for the perfect spouse. Many are opting out of marriage and don't have romantic partners. "In your late 20s, you have a biological clock and they are ignoring it," Tanner says. However, most Americans are eventually tying the knot. In the 1970s, 80 percent of Americans were married by age 30; today it's only at age 45 that 80 percent of Americans are married. "There are a lot of things you can redo," she says. "But if you miss the window of partnering and reproduction, that is very difficult." Tanner says young women are "more tied to the biological clock" and more likely to miss out because of an "elongated transition to adulthood." At 26 or 27, you should think about "growing up," she says. "You can't spend too much time finding yourself."

She advises young adults to "feed their souls" rather than focusing on status and money. Kids who move most successfully and happily into adulthood know who they are and invest in themselves, she says. Many young adults today will live well into their 80s or even 90s. If young adults seriously ponder their values and goals and come to understand what brings them meaning and joy, they will find long-term fulfillment as they create their own nests.

AGE 30 LOOMS LARGE

At 25 years old, Aaron is just starting to focus seriously on his future. He is well aware that age 30—the modern marker of adulthood—is not far away. His father, an obstetrics and gynecological surgeon, followed a pretty straight path at this stage of life. But

Aaron's has more twists, turns, and uncertainty. Creative, cerebral, and intense, he is inclined to "flip between a lot of the arts." He studied film at New York University, then became a singer and bass player in a band, working in a restaurant to make enough money to live.

But as he gets older, Aaron is reaching the end of his savings and getting tired of living on "meager means." Sometimes he discovers that his mother has put money on his credit card, like the time he spent too much on Christmas and before he knew it, was about $2,000 in the hole. He wants to solve his financial problems by himself and is looking into a new career direction that is "more reasonable" and lucrative, but also creative and entrepreneurial. Says Aaron, "Now it's to the point where I need to figure stuff out more."

8

OBSTACLES IN THE WAY

You are only as happy as your least happy child.

Old Adage

Although the umbilical cord is cut, emotions continue to flow back and forth between parent and child forever. When a newborn baby cries, it can trigger the mother's body to release oxytocin, the "cuddle hormone" that helps her bond with the child. When a toddler stumbles, both parents can feel the pain. And when young adults leave the nest and struggle, parents tend to mirror their emotions, becoming anxious and distressed. The effect of our kids' emotions on us as parents continues to be visceral.

If our young adults seem successful and happy, we believe we raised them well. But when they fail or are unhappy, which is inevitable in life, we may feel impotent and at fault. It doesn't matter what is causing the unhappiness. The problem might stem from running with a partying crowd or from outside events, such as becoming the victim of a crime. It might be a broken heart, a disability, a learning issue, a tough transition to college, a young adult's divorce, or an injury. But whatever it is, mothers and fathers suffer alongside their kids, according to Karen Fingerman, a professor of human development and family sciences at the University of Texas at Austin. Her research shows that the old adage is true: the well-being of middle-aged parents is directly related to that of their least happy child.[1]

Even if parents have other children who are thriving, if one is unhappy, so are the parents. In a study of 633 adults between the ages of 40 and 60, Fingerman asked parents to report on their kids' successes and problems over the past two years, the quality of the parent-child relationship, and their own well-being. She discovered that having just one child who was experiencing hardship and unhappiness damaged the well-being of the parents. It didn't matter if siblings were thriving. Parents still identified with the struggling child. Having just one kid with problems "is going to make your mood worse and cause psychological distress for the parent," Fingerman says.[2]

Even when young adults are far from the nest, parents feel their pain. Thanks to modern technology, we are able to know all about their lives and virtually witness their struggles. "The impact on parents of kids having problems is instantaneous," Fingerman says. "Even if the kid isn't living with you, they are texting you. There is an immediate effect." Kids are also more apt to off-load miseries to a parent than report good news. For many parents, stories of woe trigger sadness.

TROUBLE LEARNING

Learning issues can make a fledgling suffer. Just ask Peter, a varsity basketball and baseball player at a Los Angeles boarding school, who appeared to have it all. But Peter struggled with attention deficit disorder and got low Bs and Cs on his report card while his friends earned As. He also did poorly on standardized tests.

Unlike many of his classmates, who formed a long line outside the nurse's office to get a daily dose of Adderall to help them focus, Peter didn't want to take the drug. His mother Susan, a 58-year-old yoga instructor, says she and her husband, an investment banker, "got on his back to do better" and boost his grades. But he wasn't driven to succeed academically, and the competition at school stressed him out.

When college admissions decisions arrived, Peter was devastated. While his friends slapped Berkeley and UCLA stickers on their cars, Peter ended up at a small, mid-tier liberal arts college. While others hugged each other, he was crushed. In the fall, when he and his friends went their separate ways to college, he was still upset.

Drugs looked like a good way out. Peter took his first hit of marijuana freshman year, telling his parents much later that he felt relaxed, like "something switched," and that "all of a sudden I felt like I could breathe." He began smoking marijuana more to feel better, but that left him badly behind in classes. He decided to take Adderall to speed up, falling into a dangerous cycle of smoking marijuana to stay calm, swallowing Adderall to speed up and do homework, then smoking pot again.

Toggling between drugs took a toll. When his parents visited, he had circles under his eyes and was physically "wrecked" and jumpy, Susan says. "We just knew something was wrong." They told themselves he was just having a tough time in school, "probably partying too much," Susan says.

Peter transferred to the University of Maryland and rushed a fraternity, but he was sick of school and dragging himself through the motions. His parents checked his grades online and found he was almost flunking out. His dad drove to his dorm and found Peter in bed, packed him up, withdrew him from college, and took him home. Then they took him to a drug addiction specialist and discovered their son was abusing Adderall.

There was a domino effect on the parents. Susan was anxious and depressed as she worried about her son. She fought with her husband, which happens routinely when a young adult is stumbling. Her husband accused her of being too soft; he wanted to take away Peter's car and money. He would hand Peter $20 and wonder if he was spending it on food or pot, demanding that his son "man up." Susan cried and offered Peter a warm place to stay at the end of the day as he did odd jobs.

Susan worried about what it would all mean for her other two sons, who were watching Peter flail. He lied to his father, enraging him and triggering anger in his mother. She couldn't sleep and wandered around the house at night, disappointed and embarrassed that her son had a substance abuse issue and couldn't finish college. "It took me about two years to acknowledge that I had a son who was not perfect," she confesses. At the same time, she was glad he was owning up to his addiction. "More than anything, I had compassion for him," she says. "I knew he was feeling bad for letting us down."

Peter wanted help and agreed to get on a plane to a 90-day wilderness program. During family therapy there, Peter learned to accept himself, and his parents understood that his attention issues and his father's high expectations had created anxiety and that Peter had turned to drugs to deal with it. His therapist explained that Peter was highly sensitive and felt like a failure because he didn't meet his parents' expectations. Peter says a high-achieving student "is not who I am." His attention issues make academics frightening rather than enlightening. While his father hopes he will return and finish college someday, Peter fears he might relapse into drugs again if the pressure ratchets up too much.

For a while, Peter worked with disabled veterans in Utah, helping them bike, water ski, and do ropes courses. Now 28, he manages a coffee-roasting business and shop. He's succeeding in sales and says he is drug- and anxiety-free. Susan has regained her own balance as her son is finding his way.

As Peter's parents saw, one unhappy child is enough to devastate parents, no matter how their other children might be faring. Parents are sensitive to positive and negative events in their kids' lives because it reflects on their own achievements in parenting. "Parents have a distinct investment in grown children reflecting decades of child-rearing," Fingerman says. When she began her research, she thought children who were flourishing might offset the problems caused by their siblings who are struggling. "We had expected that a successful child might mitigate the negative impact of having a child who suffers problems. We thought the successful child might give the parent something positive to focus on. But parents still seem to suffer whenever one of their grown children does."

Parents may internalize a struggling kid's distress, be ashamed that their relationship with their grown child is suffering, or become upset because their kid's problem is placing excessive demands on them. "Any one or all of these factors may contribute to parental worry and depression," Fingerman says.

DESCENT INTO DRUGS

Drug addiction can devastate young adults—and their parents. Burt initially learned that his daughter Gracie was addicted when she was 23 and called to announce she was hooked on opioids. She told him she had tried drugs in high school and became severely dependent on them in college. "It was a total shock," says the 63-year-old Kentucky entrepreneur. "At the time I didn't realize how bad it was. I knew about as much as the average person who has never dealt with that kind of issue—which was nothing."

It started unbeknownst to her parents when Gracie walked into a high school party as a freshman and the host's mother offered her a choice of vodka or whiskey. The woman also handed her the opioid pain medication Percocet, saying it wouldn't show up on a breathalyzer if she was stopped by police. Gracie says the drugs and alcohol calmed her anxiety. "I felt so maladapted to life," she says. "I was ill-equipped to relate to peers. I felt like an alien." She dressed "weird," with lots of black, darkened her hair, and wore dark nail color. She lived in a "one-stoplight town" and loved the "rush of getting away with something." Like many kids from rural areas, she was able to find more secluded territory to experiment with drugs, alcohol, and sex.

Then an avalanche of trauma hit. While at church camp, Gracie learned that her best girlfriend Rachel and her mother had been shot and killed in a murder-suicide by her friend's stepfather.

Gracie went numb, started drinking more, and was raped by a football player. She didn't tell her parents about the assault, struggled with an eating disorder, and cut her skin. She escaped into Percocet and became dependent on it.

Gracie went to college at age 17, joined a sorority, and appeared to be thriving. "For the first couple years, it was great," she says. She "put on a happy girl face," while at night she drank and smoked pot. Junior year, she traveled to see concerts, doing "party drugs," including cocaine and Ecstasy. One night, she swallowed a capsule that contained meth, quickly became addicted, and rapidly lost "a crazy amount of weight."

Caught snorting in a bathroom, Gracie lost her job. She began pushing meth and discovered she had "no off button." She was using drugs daily but still managed to graduate at age 20. Gracie dated a new guy who introduced her to heroin. She snorted it through a straw and was hungry for more. Her parents didn't have a clue.

Her health slipped. She moved to a new city but spent money her parents gave her to relocate to buy more drugs. "They didn't know where the money was going, and I didn't have an answer for them."

Gracie didn't want to distress her parents but knew the drugs were destroying her. She knew her mother Teresa had been struggling with empty nest blues since Gracie's younger sister left home. Gracie tried to handle the addiction by herself, limiting her drug use to drinking and smoking pot, but she couldn't. Whenever she went back home, she got "insanely sick," lying on the couch and explaining that she was working long hours and that her boss was demanding.

When Gracie told her dad about her addiction, he and Teresa were shocked. But they sprang into action and brought her home for five days. She was in withdrawal when she arrived, her father says. She lied and was oddly irrational. "She was barely human," he says. "She was like someone I didn't know."

At home, Gracie "tried to detox and lost my mind," she says. "I was seeing and hearing things and having insane flashbacks." Burt dove into the Internet, discovering a sprawling industry in addiction treatment. He and his wife pledged to spend everything they had to get Gracie off drugs and were determined the crisis would not strain their marriage. They settled on a rehab center in Malibu, California, where Gracie agreed to go if she wasn't forced to stay longer than 30 days.

Gracie drove to California to the rehab, buying drugs to keep her on an even keel on the trip. Once she was settled, she initially blamed her parents for her addiction, but then realized it was her fault. Struggling with guilt, she "flipped" after a few months at rehab and ran away with a boyfriend who was also getting treatment there. They checked into a hotel where she begged him to shoot heroin into her veins, launching a downward spiral into more drugs and alcohol.

Her parents, at wit's end, told Gracie if she relapsed again she would be on her own. "I finally realized there was nobody I could turn to," she says. Determined to kick her bad habits, she split with her junkie boyfriend and headed to Alcoholics Anonymous, remaining in rehab for six months, then living at transitional places for months after that. Now she is pursuing a master's degree in marriage and family counseling at Antioch University in Los Angeles. She is specializing in addiction and recovery, speaks at drug addiction meetings, and is puzzled that people find her compelling. She aims to work in rehab and eventually open her own practice.

Like many parents whose kids abuse drugs and alcohol, Burt blamed himself. They had homeschooled Gracie until the second half of eighth grade and, while he knew she despised it, they thought she was learning more than she would in a traditional school and that she would be far less likely to do drugs. But Gracie felt isolated and complained that her social life was stunted. When she went to school with other kids, they made fun of her and picked on her, he recalls.

Burt viewed her rebellion in high school as a typical teenage rejection of parental authority. A retired Air Force captain, he "wrote it off as 'grow up, toughen up.'" She continued to be angry and rebellious later in college. "She went through a phase where I just couldn't talk to her," he says. "I couldn't connect with her as a teenager no matter how much I tried."

Now Burt faces "a lot of anxiety, fear, and constant worry." He feels terror each time the telephone rings, worried that he will hear that his daughter Gracie has died of an overdose. He says the addiction treatment "just about bankrupted" the family, exhausting Burt and Teresa's retirement savings. Instead of retiring, Teresa still works full-time at a job she finds "dry and high stress." However, he says they don't blame Gracie. "It's just what happened," he says. Gracie is grateful her parents are supportive. "I see a lot of my friends who are in recovery and their parents want nothing to do with them or vice versa," she says.

Now the family does family therapy sessions over the Internet. Gracie says her parents always have lived a clean lifestyle and never could have comprehended how she was living. "My mom has never had a speeding ticket in her life," Gracie says. Now 26, she says her parents "thought I was going to be married by now." She is embarrassed "about the ways I messed up."

When a kid like Gracie goes offtrack, it can derail the parents as well. But it's important to keep your own equilibrium as you support your young adult as best you can. If you collapse, it can further hurt your child. Take deep breaths, chill, and keep yourself centered.

If you face a crisis with your young adult, first evaluate what kind of help is needed, which might involve consulting a psychiatrist, therapist, or learning specialist, says Michael D. Kaplan, a clinical professor at the Yale School of Medicine. Some kids will accept assistance, while others fend it off. The ultimate goal is to assist them in helping themselves become financially, socially, and emotionally independent, so they can take care of themselves and you can back away, Kaplan says. Once they are 18, "they go to their side of the football field and you are not the quarterback anymore," he says. "You become more of a bystander, less of a participant."[3]

Often, what appears in the eyes of a young adult to be an overwhelming obstacle is just a small bump in the road. If your kid tells you he got too drunk, slept with the wrong person, got a C minus, or angered the boss, listen, but don't jump in with advice right away, Kaplan says. "Don't meet their level of agitation, because that will just make it worse," Kaplan says. "Lower it down and listen. Let them work it out." And don't take what you hear at face value, he says. "Most problems go away pretty quickly. Most things are small bumps you just have to let the kid handle. Ride it through with patience, patience, patience."

SHADES OF ADDICTION

> No one is immune from addiction; it afflicts people of all ages, races, classes, and professions.
>
> Patrick J. Kennedy

Some situations require professional help, such as addiction, which comes in many forms, including video games. When Rav returned to San Jose from accepted students' day at Carnegie Mellon University, his parents Sita and Jim got their first hint. After years of teachers' complaints that he was too quiet in class, Rav told his parents he had asked a question at his first college gathering. Intrigued as to what in the curriculum had so piqued his interest, they inquired what the question was. He said he had asked if there was a place to rent a car in case he wanted to go to a gaming tournament. His parents immediately reminded him he was going to college to study. Says Sita, "It was a clue in retrospect."

When Rav returned home for spring break, his mother knew he had papers to write but he played video games nonstop. He had been a dutiful A student in high school and she was worried. But she buttoned her lip because he was in college. "You don't see him much and you don't want to sour the relationship," she says.

The next clue came when Jim, an auditor who learned frugality growing up, noticed several food charges—$8 here, $6 there—on his son's college debit card, which puzzled him because they had paid for the meal plan. He called his son for an explanation. Rav admitted he had been sleeping until 11 a.m. and missing morning meals and classes because he was up all night competing in video game tournaments. He confessed he had received a D on a midterm he had walked into fully unprepared.

His parents were sick. "It freaked us out," Sita says. "It was such a bad start, a waste of money and of time." They pressed Rav further, and felt even more concerned when he told them he figured if he got good enough at the video games, he would have more friends. "I could tell them I made the platinum round and I would be able to impress people," he said. Sita was saddened that her son was motivated by a simple desire to be liked and respected. "All this was wrapped up in a kid who was struggling to adjust to college," she says. "He was creating an identity with it."

In high school, his friends had been top scholars who took the toughest classes and competed for grades. But in college, he was adrift. He had lost his "bragging rights," and didn't know who he was. He wasn't on the varsity sailing team and he wasn't an expert pianist or an a cappella singer. He figured he could be a great gamer. He could learn tricks and shortcuts. He was dogged. He could stay up all night and improve his "levels."

Young adults who get hooked on video games are usually struggling with psychological issues and see the technology as a way to cope and a form of escapism, says Edward Spector, a Bethesda, Maryland, psychologist who specializes in video game addiction.[4] Spector has built a gaming computer, and has an Xbox, a Wii, and hundreds of video games in his office to help him relate to his patients. He says that depression, anxiety, shyness, autism, attention deficit hyperactivity disorder, and obsessive-compulsive disorder are some of the most common issues that can draw teens into technology in an unhealthy way. Too much technology can lead to lost sleep, crashed grades, and strained relationships.

The most common scenario is a 19-year-old male college student who has failed out because of uncontrolled use of the Internet or video games, Spector says. Many young adults who are addicted to video games live a nocturnal existence. Some appear in his office at 9 a.m. without having slept. They often shower infrequently and come in the same clothes they have worn for days. Many flunk out of college and move back home, finding themselves even more socially isolated. Spector says addicted gamers need to get away from their video game lives and get back to real life.

Parents also feel like failures when a kid struggles as Rav did. "Somehow you failed to pass along coping tools," Sita says. "There was a part that was incomplete. You didn't send off a whole person." She says they had always pressed Rav on academics, but not on building friendships. It pained her that Rav was lonely and thought gaming was the solution. She worried he would flunk out. She feared his poor preparation and missed classes had created gaping holes in his learning that would backfire in higher-level classes. She worried the woes would cascade and he'd never get a job.

There had been years of sacrifice he didn't appear to appreciate. She had bought discount clothes and postponed haircuts to save tuition money. Once Rav admitted his addiction, they dipped into retirement savings to pay for counseling. "We raised him with the idea that we were going to send him to college," she says. "You invest so much money and so much time you think they can't ever blow it and they do."

Three years later, after counseling and lot of discussions with his parents, Rav had a strong senior year, graduated, and got a good job as a computer coder for a Boston software company. Sita worries he might lose control of the gaming again, but they've all learned to take a breath. "It was a gradual process of us learning to take a step back from his life and him learning to tie his own shoes," she says. Now, Sita says, they've learned to accept "there are going to be bumps in life." The experience, she says, has allowed them all to be imperfect. "It sort of softened life a little bit and made it less scary."

SERIOUS ILLNESS

When a young adult suffers from serious illness, it's like a hurricane threatening to topple the nest. And it can take a lot of restraint to allow that young adult enough space to live their own life. But Tera, whose daughter Peyton is in remission with stage IV ovarian cancer, is determined to do exactly that. At 18, Peyton has spent the past year in chemotherapy, in surgery, and in the hospital fighting a strain of the disease that usually strikes women decades older. Well aware she faces a lifelong battle with the disease, the willowy, wide-eyed beauty is pursuing her dream to be a model, which started when she was spotted by a scout at a concert in Denver.

The first warnings surfaced when she was almost 16. Peyton felt back pain and thought it might be a pulled muscle. She was in pain, but doctors found nothing. While on vacation with family friends, she started throwing up and was diagnosed with ovarian cysts. Peyton passed out in the shower and later noticed bumps on her rib cage. On her birthday, doctors at Children's Hospital in Denver diagnosed a severe and rare case of ovarian cancer. They installed a port to deliver medicine directly into her system and blasted her with chemo. Her 5-foot 9-inch frame dropped from 115 pounds to 87. She stayed in the hospital for six months and underwent surgery and a new type of chemotherapy. Before long, she was declared cancer free. But the cancer has since returned.

Because Peyton was hospitalized and undergoing treatment during much of high school, she decided to get her GED instead of repeating classes. "This is her life and her journey, and she needs to live it and go for it," her mother says. "I'm still very, very involved. But my job is now to be in the background supporting her. It's not about me."

Determined to follow her passion despite cancer, Peyton lives with five young models in an apartment near her modeling agency in Los Angeles. Her mother says it's remarkable how happy and animated her daughter is when she's working: "It's life altering. When you put her in front of the camera, she's in the zone. She just listens to the photographer. She nails it." Peyton won't hide her surgical scar in photo shoots, and does not want airbrushing to erase the port that delivers her chemotherapy. She aspires to be a Victoria's Secret model and show the world that "scars are sexy." Tera, who manages real estate in Florida, keeps close touch with her daughter. She hears sadness in her daughter's voice over the phone at times, but knows Peyton is determined to model and remain hopeful.

Because of the cancer, Tera and Peyton are more like best friends than mother and daughter. "It's given us an opportunity to bond like very few teen daughters and their mothers do," Tera says. Having her daughter in another city can be tough, but Tera says she wants her daughter to live life to the fullest. "I love watching her fly," she says. They remain optimistic despite long odds: The cancer has spread through the bloodstream and lymph glands. But Tera channels her background as a physical therapist to keep her emotions in check. "If she saw me break, she couldn't be strong." Peyton plans to head to New York City next year to become a runway model, and Tera is determined to give her the space she wants to live and explore.

The misfortune has opened new doors. Peyton has been on-site on a movie set in Toronto, advising the director of the film *Life in a Year* about a young female character who is diagnosed with ovarian cancer. Tera struggled to watch it, because the character dies in the film. Through the shock and suffering, Tera says she has become much more spiritual and thankful and has learned to live life with kindness in her heart. And, Tera says, Peyton is determined to show others "how beautiful imperfection is."

DEPLOYED

Military service can require strength and faith from a young adult and but particularly from a parent. Now that her son Jacob has completed boot camp with the U.S. Marine Corps at Camp Pendleton in California and is about to be deployed as a helicopter crew chief, Andrea is asking God to bring him back alive. "I am 100 percent worried that something might happen to him," she says. She burst into tears when he moved his stuff out of her house the summer after his senior year in high school and drove his minivan out West. She worries he will see active duty, return injured, and suffer PTSD. "It's very hard knowing this is all for real," she says. At the same time, she is proud that her 21-year-old son "has a very grown-up attitude about the fact that you don't always get out alive" when you are in the military. "I think he realizes that he could possibly give his life to serve his country," she says. "He's an old soul and he's brave to think that way."

Jacob was a model teen who grew up fast after his father abandoned the family, Andrea says. A longtime Boy Scout and varsity basketball and soccer player in high school, Jacob rejected drugs and alcohol. Instead of doing a two-year mission like most of his Mormon brethren, Jacob wanted to serve in the Marines. While he considered college, he chose to enlist because money was tight. Andrea, a dental hygienist and mother of five, explains that he "was not wanting to tax me" financially. "I feel like he's very protective of me," she says. "It was a noble thing" to enlist in the military, she says. "He wanted to be independent because his dad wasn't there."

She is proud that her son has taken responsible steps toward adulthood. As a boy who had "no father influence, he kind of did it on his own," she says. "He carved his own way with his fingernails without any leadership from his father." He supports himself and his new wife Emma, and hopes to go to school on the GI Bill after completing military service.

Jacob has been named head of his platoon and will be posted in South Korea. Andrea says she is banking on her faith to help her handle the anxiety of Jacob's deployment. "I will be praying for strength because you can't have fear and faith at the same time."

GROWING UP WITH PAIN

Sometimes parents must endure agonizing trials when a child suffers, but later discover that these painful experiences can yield spiritual growth, connection, and understanding. Liza endured a childhood of what seemed like "medieval torture," says her mother Marcia. Born a dwarf, Liza would probably not grow taller than 3 foot 8 inches—not enough to reach a light switch. So Liza and her parents decided to pursue limb-lengthening procedures. Doctors performed more than 25 surgeries, using drills to decompress the vertebra at the base of her skull and installing metal "tinkertoys" known as *fixators*. They broke bones in her arms, and six bones in her legs—three different times. Magnetic rods inserted in the shaft of her femurs and tibias lengthened Liza's limbs until she "grew" to almost five feet tall.

Besides the physical pain, there was also emotional pain that waxed and waned. It was easiest for other kids to accept Liza early in elementary school. Her mother recalls a wide-eyed classmate advising Liza, "Don't you like to eat vegetables and fruits? You need to eat more of them so you will grow." But later years were tough for Liza and her mother. Marcia says it "wasn't cool for some high school kids to have a friend who was a dwarf," adding that her daughter "spent a lot of time with me," for lack of a friend group. Liza would have sleepovers but would end up crawling under the covers and crying because the girls did not include her in their fun. Marcia worried about her child leaving the nest because she was "more socially inexperienced" than many of her classmates and constantly recovering from all the limb-lengthening and neurological procedures.

But she finished high school and was ready for the next step. It took a lot of strength and faith for Marcia to leave her third and last child Liza at Virginia Tech for freshman year. She noticed other students doing a double take after seeing her daughter's shortened arms and fingers. "I wanted to glare back at them," Marcia says, adding "How rude can you be to stare?" Driving back home in the car, Marcia worried if the other kids would accept Liza. She wondered if her daughter would meet friends who would judge her before they got to know her, as they had in high school. But Liza was eager to be a college student. After her first week at school, she called her parents, ecstatic. "It's the first time in my life I said, 'Hi, my name is Liza' and they acknowledged me." Now, Liza is finishing a five-year program to become a teacher of kindergarteners and first and second graders.

Liza has moved past the pain, embracing dwarfism and striving to educate others about it. She wants to be a role model for other young people with her condition, achondroplasia, and has discovered that her classmates are wonderfully accepting of others with differences. Liza is relentlessly upbeat. When people asked her about dwarfism when she was a child, she told them, "I'm just a regular girl who is short." Now she says, "Being short statured has its challenges, but I'm proud of the things I've accomplished and the person I am today."

Marcia has also come to terms with her daughter's suffering and even feels grateful for the experience, which she says has changed the whole family profoundly, making Liza, her two siblings, her husband, and herself more resilient and sensitive to others. "What we realized with this whole journey is that there are so many people who are going through more," Marcia says. "There are some children who have serious illnesses and don't survive. But we got through our challenges. It was difficult, and the end result is extremely rewarding. I wouldn't trade anything for our journey."

A HAVEN IN A HEARTLESS WORLD

The joint journey and mutual dependence between parent and child continues into young adulthood and beyond. "It isn't like you drop them off and then go off to a party," says Steven Zarit, distinguished professor emeritus in human development and family studies at Penn State University. "You don't go from being a hands-on parent one day to having no contact the next. . . . They come back sometimes for good things and when they are in need."[5] In the words of historian Christopher Lasch, the family continues to be "a haven in a heartless world."[6]

Parents today provide emotional and sometimes financial support to their kids throughout their lives. Mutual support "flows back and forth between parents and kids," Zarit says. When young adults blossom, parents can almost feel it. And when they struggle, it takes a toll. "We can still see our children as babies whom we protected and cared for and as young children when the whole world was a possibility for them," he says. "To see them hurt makes us feel bad." However, when things go south with young adults, most parents learn to cope and make the best out of a bad situation, he says. In times of trouble, Zarit says, there is usually a period of upset, "and then a gradual rebuilding of one's life."

9

THE NEST THAT NEVER EMPTIES

HI, MOM! I'M HOME!

More than 24 million young adults in the United States, or about one in three, are living with their parents. Surprisingly, in 2014, for the first time in more than 130 years, adults ages 18 to 34 were slightly more likely to be living in their parents' home than they were to be living with a spouse or a partner in their own household, according to the Pew Research Center.[1] These young adults who are doubling up with Mom and Dad are known mockingly as the "boomerang generation," "growing-ups," and "failed fledglings."

But this phenomenon, once viewed with disappointment, anxiety, and shame, is becoming increasingly acceptable and part of an economic revolution that appears to be here to stay. This boomerang trend has been building for three decades but accelerated during the Great Recession of 2007 to 2009, as a weak economy and an anemic job market sent droves of young people home for a financial security blanket. As the economy has continued to recover, millennials are still remaining in the nest, saving money to pay off steeper-than-ever college loans, launch businesses, learn a skill, go to graduate school, or just save money.

Immigration is another factor. Two-generation households in this country are increasing in step with an influx of Latino and Asian American young adults, whose cultures value family cohesion and have a strong tradition of staying home until marriage. Living rent free in a childhood bedroom to focus on long-term goals is a rational choice in an era when young adults no longer can count on doing economically better than their parents. Achieving financial independence is much harder for many of today's young adults, who face steeper housing costs and a job market that requires more education and skill than their parents needed when they came of age. Many are saddled with high student debt, working in low-paying jobs, and struggling to pay the bills. They are postponing marriage and putting off becoming parents as they try to gain a foothold.

But despite the harsher economic climate, young adults are upbeat as they sift through career options. Many have discovered that living with parents can create an opportunity to develop a closer relationship and smooth over misunderstandings from the turbulent teen years. Many remain there for longer stretches than previous generations. Don't be surprised if you need to help your young adult come up with a plan for becoming independent. As a parent, you don't want to drain your savings to make retiring difficult or impossible. Manage this phase so it does not evolve into the Mom and Dad Motel.

A LATER LAUNCH

The boomerang phenomenon brings to mind the 2006 comedy *Failure to Launch*, in which the charming but immature main character, Tripp, postpones traditional milestones of adulthood and settles in with his parents, taking advantage of his mother's laundry service and home-cooked meals and cavorting with like-minded buddies. Tension rises and zaniness ensues after his fed-up parents hire a young woman to lure their 35-year-old son out of the nest.[2]

But today's boomerang generation is far from the film's comedically exaggerated characters. Despite mounting education costs, more people in their 20s are going to school longer than ever before because the nation has shifted into a knowledge-based economy that requires more training. And it's taking longer to get that cap and gown. Only half of those who enter a four-year college have graduated six years later. "There are going to be a lot of bumps in the road," as young adults drop out of school to raise money to cover college costs or go through part-time while holding a job, says Jeffrey Jensen Arnett, a psychologist and leading expert on young "emerging" adults. [3]

Young adults born in the late 1980s and early 1990s entered the workforce amid gloomy economic trends and that's still affecting them. Recent economic shifts have taken a particularly heavy toll on young adults without a college diploma, who are returning home because they can't find a job, earn a decent wage, or afford to rent in an economy with a declining number of well-paying blue-collar jobs, says Andrew J. Cherlin, a sociologist at Johns Hopkins University. "Working-class kids are taking a long time to become adults partly because they can't find the right kind of jobs," he says. [4]

High school graduates today have a much tougher time than their parents gaining a financial foothold. In the 1970s and early 1980s, "you could have a high school degree and get a job that paid a middle-class wage or put you on the path to a middle-class wage," says Laryssa Mykyta, an assistant professor of sociology and demography at the University of Texas Rio Grande Valley. But with the movement of blue-collar manufacturing jobs overseas, "That's no longer possible," she says. "Young adults who aren't going to college aren't stepping up into the middle-class lifestyle that their parents had. Their economic security is threatened." [5]

A LEG UP

Without a college degree, it's hard to afford living independently. When Maddy graduated from high school at age 18, she tried college for a semester, but found it wasn't for her. Instead, she wanted to put her childhood training in ballet, jazz, hip hop, acrobatics, and contemporary dance to work as a professional dancer. But there was no way to afford that on her own. She moved in with her father and stepmother on Long Island for three years to study dance in New York City, while performing with a semiprofessional dance company and at conventions. Living with them "was a no-brainer," she says.

But after clashing with her stepmother, she moved in with her mother Yvonne. Maddy was 20, and the move helped her understand the challenges her mother had faced when she was younger. As a child, Maddy recalls her mother being stressed out and busy most of the time, cleaning the kitchen sink and shower, picking up clutter, and dusting after coming home from work. She now realizes that her mom had worked long hours "to pay bills and not lose our house." She no longer feels "deprived of a normal childhood" because her mother couldn't organize playdates as stay-at-home moms had. Instead, she is grateful that after living at home for three years, she was able to save $7,500 to sublet an apartment and pursue her dream of dancing professionally. Yvonne says she didn't charge her daughter rent or expect her to help with other expenses because Maddy didn't go to college—her dance training was her preparation for adulthood.

Now 26 and living in Los Angeles, Maddy struggled at first to make ends meet, working a minimum-wage job as a barista and then a waitress. These days she is doing better, making more money teaching private piano lessons and dance classes. "I have found a way to integrate what I love into paying the bills and it feels very good and very rewarding," she says. "I am lucky to have the skills I have." She says her financial burden is bearable because she doesn't have student loans. But the teaching jobs she takes to pay the bills sometimes conflict with auditions.

She calls her mother and father every day or two. They talk about her friendships, work, dancing, drama with roommates, goals, and finances. "My parents are available and accessible," she says. "My friends are really busy and I can't just unload on them all day." Like many millennials, Maddy considers her parents her go-to people. "They are the ones I call right away." In sharp contrast to her thinking during her high school years, Maddy now believes her parents "are full of wisdom" and, she says, they know her better than anyone else does.

INVESTING IN THEMSELVES

Living independently is more financially feasible for millennials with a four-year college degree. But many are going home after graduation to invest in themselves and improve career prospects. Many are finding that to get a very good job they need post-college training, so they live with their parents to save for graduate school and other programs. "They are using their 20s to better themselves," Cherlin says.

If a young adult in the 1960s had dallied like this on the road to adulthood, he or she would have been viewed as "someone who didn't have a hold on life," Cherlin says. Back then, you could learn on the job. But today, it is normal for 20-somethings to take time to explore their future, switch careers a few times, and not jump straight into the next step of adulthood the way their parents or grandparents did.

Young adults prefer to live independently so they can run their own lives without parental commentary and make their own choices about what to eat, what to wear, and what time to come home at night. But unless they have gone into engineering, medicine, or another high-paying field, it's challenging to make a substantial salary at a time when rental costs in metropolitan areas have skyrocketed.

GOODBYE TO CHICKEN FEATHERS

Moving in with Mom and Dad can also make dollars, cents, and *sense* while a young adult is making a career change. Just ask Harry, a 29-year-old college graduate with a degree in agriculture and business who found himself up to his ears in chicken feathers. At first, Harry was pleased to have a job as a supervisor at a chicken plant in Arkansas. He was stationed on the front line of the slaughtering operation, a fast-paced environment in which birds were placed in a water bath, then stunned and knocked unconscious before a blade chopped off their heads. "It was a pretty eye-opening experience," he says.

But after two years on the job, "I didn't see myself staying in the chicken industry," he says. "I couldn't deal with the dirt and the dust and the smell." He investigated a poultry-free career, landing a job near his parents' house at a bottling plant that is similarly fast-paced but "a lot different than with chickens."

Because he didn't have time to scout for an apartment before his new job started, he moved back home. "I was getting my feet back under me," he says, adding that he did not expect living with his parents would be "a long-term thing." His mother Jennifer was thrilled to have him around as a young adult, admitting, "I wanted him back in the area selfishly."

Once Harry moved back in, his mother no longer imposed a curfew on him as she had in high school. "I didn't have any problem with him coming in and out," she says. "I didn't ask him any questions." And Harry adopted grown-up habits. Instead of hunkering down in his room with his door shut and watching TV as he did as a teen, he watched the news after work with his mother, who says it was great to have this time with her son. He was careful to keep his stuff straightened up, and he would call his mom on his way home from work to ask what he could pick up at the grocery store. He says he had new respect for his mother, and a "better appreciation for what she did every day."

On weekends, he helped his dad outside. He did yard work, cut down a tree, and stained the fence. He fetched heavy stones from the woods, loaded them onto a tractor, and helped his father, who is a teacher, build a patio. When his parents wanted a hardwood floor, he ripped up carpets and used his relocation stipend to lend his parents money for supplies. When the garage door broke, he paid to fix it. "He would do anything to help you out," says his mother, a nurse's aide. Harry was proud to chip in. "When I was in high school, they were the ones who helped me out if I needed extra money," he says. "When I moved back, I helped them out."

Harry says he and his parents "didn't have any clash points," and that he was "not in any hurry to get out of there." But after a year and a half at home, he decided to move in with his girlfriend in her new place. He says he knows his mother misses him now that he's moved out, but "it's part of growing up and being on my own."

AN ECONOMIC BOOST AT HOME

Compound interest is the eighth wonder of the world.
Albert Einstein

Many young adults find the transition from school to the working world far more daunting than going from home to college. When Alexa graduated from Ohio State, she found a great job just three miles from her family's home outside Cleveland. Her savings, built up from working two jobs each summer, plus waitressing and retail jobs during college, were running on fumes. "It's not like I was rolling in money," she says. She didn't have any close friends nearby and dreaded living alone. And she was reluctant to shell out money for a rental, especially because she was likely to go home for dinner every night to visit her parents. At age 22, she moved back in with her mother and father.

Alexa didn't want her parents to think she was taking advantage of their generosity. She was grateful they're "not the taking type." She didn't pay rent, and they didn't ask her to chip in for electricity or water, either. She took her mother's grocery list off the fridge twice a month and returned with bags of food "just to help out." Despite shelling out about $100 each time, she was still "totally making out." Because she considers herself a "terrible cook," she washed and folded her own laundry, as she had since she was 14, and did laundry for the rest of the family in exchange for meals her mother and sister made for her.

The only tension that arose was over tidiness. While Alexa describes herself as "a very clean person," it wasn't enough for her parents. "It's a little bit hard to keep clean to their standards," she says. "You are afraid to mess something up." She says her mother takes off work the day before the housekeeper comes to pre-clean it, and her father requires her to stash her shoes in the garage before coming into the house. While she is grateful that he bought her a car in college, she was frustrated that when she came home, he vacuumed the interior each Sunday. "We would get into bad fights about how clean my car was and start screaming at each other," she recalls.

However, she is delighted that her father taught her that "the sooner you start saving, the easier it's going to be." He runs a company that does asphalt paving and her mother is an office manager, so they don't earn "enormous salaries," Alexa says. But they do have a good relationship with money. She also started reading about investment trends and money management in college. "I knew as soon as I had money, I wanted to invest," she says.

Moving home enabled her to build up a $30,000 nest egg that she has invested in mutual funds, and to start a $20,000 retirement fund. At age 26, she has watched the money grow over four years. She always admired how her uncle, a woodshop teacher with a modest salary, lived at home until age 30, saving his money and investing it well. Now he owns a big house with his own woodshop and 10 acres of property. She also watched her grandfather live frugally. After spending his career working in a factory, he retired at age 55 and takes regular trips to Italy. When Alexa moved into an apartment in Cleveland with a roommate after three years at home, she continued her frugal ways by taking the bus to work each day for $5 instead of driving and paying $6.50 for parking.

She took flak from peers about living at home but says it was well worth it. Residing as an adult with her parents transformed the relationship that had been strained during teen years, when she "couldn't stand them and couldn't wait to get away." She chalks up the former conflict to her own immaturity. "Now I have such an appreciation for them. I respect them so much, as they are by far the best two people I know."

Like Alexa, many young adults become closer to their parents while living at home for a spell. Two generations under one roof can be emotionally healthier, says Karen Fingerman, professor of human development and family sciences at the University of Texas at Austin. She says strong kin support is critical on the road to adulthood. "Grown children can get advice from parents who have good advice to give," she says. That support can be a lifeline, especially now that fewer young adults are finding long-term partners. Unlike in the1970s and 1980s, when young adults separated from parents, became autonomous, and were more likely to have a romantic partner, many young adults today don't have a mate, or are waiting longer to commit, which can make their parents "the most important people in their lives," Fingerman says.[6]

THE STIGMA FADES

Millennials boomerang back for a multitude of reasons in addition to these economic and educational reasons. Living arrangements with multiple roommates frequently disintegrate. Some young adults grapple with a physical illness or mental health problem, such as anxiety. Single mothers also are moving in with their own parents because they need help with childcare and other household jobs. Other young adults move in with parents because they have landed employment that doesn't begin for several months, have lost a job, or want to find a new one.

And as more and more young adults move back home, the less stigmatized it becomes. Young adults returning to live with parents used to be commonly criticized as "losers" who ruined their parents' empty nest by coming home "when they should have been charging ahead," says Frances Goldscheider, a longtime family demographer at Brown University. When she asked her students in the early 1980s if any of them would consider returning home after graduation, "they looked at me as if I had fallen from the moon," she says. "My students wouldn't have dreamed of being there."[7] Only one student raised her hand to confess she was planning to live with her parents until she got married, which is common in her Latino culture.

Since then, young adults have seen increasingly more of their siblings and peers moving in with Mom and Dad. Doubling up for a while seems to work well for both generations. Many young people living in their family homes are defraying the cost of living for their parents, with 48 percent reporting that they are paying rent, according to a Pew study.[8] A 30-year-old living in a two-generation household might cook for parents, kick in rent money, and do domestic chores, Mykyta says. "Interdependence isn't a bad thing, as long as the young adult continues to mature."

Overall, parents see more benefits than burdens to these two-generation living arrangements, with 61 percent of them describing life with a young adult in the house as positive and strengthening their relationship, according to Arnett. Kids like it too. According to the Pew Research Center, 78 percent of young adults said they were satisfied living with their parents.[9] Surveys of Americans of all ages show that the top criteria for being considered an adult are accepting responsibility for yourself, making independent decisions, and achieving financial independence. "Moving out," Arnett says, "is not on the list."

TIME-OUT TO THINK

Living in harmony with the younger generation requires good management. When their daughter Lydia graduated from college unsure about her next step, Peggy and Kirk invited her to stay with them in New York City as she figured it out. Peggy admits she felt some trepidation after four years with no kids at home, having found "a pretty good rhythm and a pretty good life." They also were planning to retire to Wyoming in a year so they knew it would be a short-term arrangement. "It's a big change to have anyone living with you and turning it from a very relaxed and intimate duo to a trio," she says. She also knew Lydia was nervous about coming home after college.

Peggy had watched several of her middle-aged peers "freaking out" when their kids returned after college, upset because their highly organized, kid-free homes were now messy and full of stuff. She decided to manage the situation preemptively. Peggy and Kirk held a "roommate meeting" to set up house rules with Lydia, including policies for emptying the dishwasher, cooking, and cleaning up. Being "really matter-of-fact and direct" worked well, Peggy says.

Peggy and Kirk told Lydia her many boxes and cartons belonged in her bedroom, and recommended she close the door. They knew Lydia wasn't ready to give away books, papers, and other reminders of her college years, but they also didn't want to run into those piles daily. Kirk knew his daughter loved to bake late at night, so he made sure the kitchen was stocked with ingredients. He was delighted to find fresh muffins on the table, "the evidence of a midnight baker," but gently reminded her that he didn't want to wake up and "have to wade through flour to get to the coffee pot."

They also knew Lydia was anxious about her next move, realizing she was putting a lot of pressure on herself. "She was a bit at loose ends and not happy" that she was not yet on a career track, Peggy says. In college, Lydia had pushed herself hard academically and run all four years on the cross country and track teams. "When she got home, she needed to know we loved her and that we would help her," Peggy says. They made a concerted effort to talk about subjects other than Lydia's search for a job and a career and were careful not to bring it up too often.

As she was mulling career options, Lydia found a part-time job as an assistant coach of a high school cross country team, and she

hired herself out as a running coach for adults. She started studying for the LSAT. When her parents were packing up to retire to
Wyoming, she summoned the courage to switch coasts and got a
sales job at a tech start-up in San Francisco.

Looking back, with Lydia now headed to law school, Peggy
describes the seven months Lydia "boomeranged" back to their
Manhattan apartment as perhaps their "most successful parenting
interlude." Peggy says they focused on giving "unconditional love
and no criticism." It was like having a 22-year-old girlfriend at
home, Peggy says, as they were "past real teenage crisis moments,"
which have become "a hazy memory." Kirk calls the time together
magical. "It was really a great time of being with Lydia and helping
her think about the big questions in life," he says.

Peggy advises her friends with returning young adults to just
enjoy it. "It's going to be so short-lived," she says. "Look at it as an
unbelievable gift that you will have this time with a child who is so
special to you." Kirk says he sees the role of a parent with a young
adult back home to be "100 percent supportive" as they figure out
the next step. Peggy discovered that after a few years as empty
nesters, she and Kirk were much more "synched up" and better at
"staying a couple and being parents to her."

PUTTING OFF THE ALTAR

If I get married, I want to be very married.

Audrey Hepburn

Young adults today are not hurrying to the altar. Unlike in the
1950s and 1960s, when "you had to get married in your early 20s
or you were considered mentally ill," being unmarried is now acceptable, says Cherlin, author of *The Marriage-Go-Round: The
State of Marriage and the Family in America Today*. While "marriage used to be the first step into adulthood, now it's often the
last," Cherlin says. "Among young adults there is a sense that one
doesn't get married until everything else in your personal life is

going well. They don't feel the need to get married in order to live with someone or have kids," Cherlin says.

These days, just 10 percent of Americans aged 18 and older say having a spouse and a child is "extremely important in becoming an adult," says Jonathan Vespa, a demographer for the Census Bureau.[10] Economic security is a higher priority. "Most Americans told us that being gainfully employed and being done with school comes first, and then family life comes second," Vespa says. And only one quarter of Americans today say "not living in your parents' household" is a marker of adulthood, he says.

Both young men and young women are postponing nuptials. In the 1950s, most women were married by 21 and most men by 22; today the first marriage occurs at nearly 28 for females and 30 for males. And just as young men are more apt to be older when they get involved in a committed romantic relationship, they also are more likely to live with parents: 35 percent of male millennials live with Mom and Dad, compared to 28 percent of young women, according to Richard Fry, a senior economist at the Pew Research Center who analyzes Census Bureau data.[11]

Longer life expectancies may be a factor in young adults putting off marriage. While Americans anticipated living into their 70s in the 1980s[12] life expectancy is now about 80. As younger people envision a longer life span, it makes demographic sense that they also extend the time they take to find a mate, Vespa says.

Young adults are discovering that living at home under the childhood roof "is a good way to save money and take time to find someone you want to be with," Cherlin says, adding that young adults now view marriage as the "capstone, or the last brick we put in place."

At age 26, Maddy isn't happy that she is still single. She doesn't want to have her first child at age 40, but she hasn't been in a serious relationship since high school. "I don't want to rush into anything," she says. "I am not going to settle for the next person I date." She admits she is gun-shy in the wake of her parents' divorce. She questions whether humans are supposed to be monogamous. "I don't know if it's natural to have the same mate your whole life," she says.

Maddy says her father is her "ideal guy," and that she will not settle for a man who doesn't do his part in being a full hands-on dad and husband. "You can't be that guy who sits on the couch because I won't have it," she says. She says she'll move in with a potential mate before marriage to make sure she has a man who will do his own dishes and laundry. Her current boyfriend has so far cleared the first hurdle: He lives at home with his parents and takes on a lot of responsibility in the house. "That's one reason I am talking to him," she says. "He's worthy of my time."

Goldscheider suggests that fewer young women are interested in matrimony these days because they seek men who want to "get involved around the house and there are not nearly as many guys who are willing to do it." Uneven distribution of domestic work drives young couples asunder. About three-quarters of young adults live together before tying the knot, but Goldscheider says a young woman is more likely to leave if her male partner believes the household should be governed by traditional gender roles.

THE VOCATIONAL PATH

While most high school students want to go to college, many don't because of rising tuition costs and because they can't afford it. For many, the debt burden that comes with a college diploma isn't worth it. Although attending a four-year college can mean the difference between working with your head and working with your hands, many families grapple with the decision because the mortar board no longer guarantees a good job.

For kids whose parents didn't go to college, jumping through college admissions hoops—taking the SAT or ACT, getting recommendations, filling out applications, and writing essays—can appear daunting, especially without role models and help from parents, teachers, and tutors. They may feel the American dream of a college education is out of reach. For young adults who don't follow the path to a four-year college, technical schools, an apprenticeship, the military, a two-year degree at a local college, or the workforce can be a better option.

But going without a college degree takes a toll. The pay gap between people who have four-year college degrees and those without them is bigger than ever. According to the National Center for Education Statistics, in 2017 the median earnings of young adults with a bachelor's degree was $51,800, or 62 percent higher than the $32,000 median earnings of young adults who had only completed high school.[13] Median earnings of young adults with a master's degree or higher were $60,000, about 20 percent higher than those with a bachelor's degree. This pattern of higher earnings for more education held for young men and women, as well as white, black, Hispanic, and Asian young adults.

For young men without a college degree, times are particularly difficult. Over the past 55 years, it's gotten tougher to hold a job and earn a decent wage, Fry says, adding that wages of young men without a college degree "have really taken a drubbing." More young men are falling to the bottom of the income ladder. In 1975, only 25 percent of men aged 25 to 34 had incomes of less than $30,00 per year, but by 2016, that had risen to 41 percent (both in 2015 dollars), according to Fingerman. They often end up living with their parents because they can't afford to live independently.

Young adults in metro areas in the Northeast, where housing costs tend to be steeper, are more likely to stay in the family home, while fewer in the less expensive South live with their parents. In 2013, the median stretch of time spent living under the family roof was more than three years, up six months from what it was in 2005, according to Pew research based on credit card data.[14] According to the Bureau of Labor Statistics, 90 percent of young adults who have boomeranged back into their family homes move back out by age 27.[15]

A NUDGE OUT OF THE NEST

When young adults are able to move out, but don't, some parents nudge them out of the nest. Mike and Claire created such a welcoming environment at home that their son Luke, a Niagara Falls firefighter, had no desire to leave. "We made it so easy for him to stay," Mike says. Luke loved to watch TV and relax at home after work. His parents worried he wasn't mixing enough with peers, and they felt he needed to be on his own to grow. Luke often came home after work with a few 20-something friends who crashed on the couch.

The parent-child relationship felt frozen in time. It further frayed when Luke would walk in the door and forget to say hello to his parents. They'd have petty arguments over mowing the lawn and shoveling the walk. "It felt too much like we were still in elementary school or high school," Mike says. But they couldn't bring themselves to kick their son out. Mike and Claire took a dramatic step: They sold the house and bought a smaller place in Buffalo, where Luke couldn't live because his job requires him to stay in Niagara Falls.

Claire says it was heartbreaking for Luke and his sister to bid their childhood bedrooms goodbye, but it was time. "Change is painful, even though the change is something you need to go through," she says.

Now Luke is happy in his own place. Mike and Claire have relocated and met other middle-aged empty nesters who meet at restaurants, go to yoga class, and attend book club meetings. "I miss having my son around," Mike says. "But we have a much better relationship now because there is a little separation. When we were living together we never were able to move from a father-son to a more equal relationship. Sharing a home kept us in a parent-child dynamic that we couldn't really break out of."

FINDING "BOOMMATES"

> One of the oldest human needs is to have someone who won-
> ders where you are when you don't come home at night.
>
> Margaret Mead

Some empty nesters and retirees are taking in young adults as "boommates" to help defray their housing costs. The practice, more common in other countries, has been getting a boost in the United States from empty nest baby boomers—and with good reason. In the 100 largest metro areas, Americans 53 and older have about 3.6 million unoccupied rooms in their homes, according to the real estate firm Trulia.[16] Advocates for multigenerational housing say renting out a room could help older adults supplement their income and offset their living expenses, while providing affordable housing for budget-strapped millennials. To match older adults who have extra space with younger adults who need a place to live, apps such as Nesterly have sprung up.

For empty nesters and others with more house than they need, sharing a home can cut housing costs in half at a time when the cost of supporting oneself is more than the average Social Security payment, according to Annamarie Pluhar, author of *Sharing Housing: A Guidebook to Finding and Keeping Good Housemates.*[17] If you are a baby boomer sharing your home with a millennial, you might benefit from help with taking out the trash, walking the dog, and carrying groceries, which can all allow an older person to live longer in their own home. Renting a room from an older adult can save a young one $14,000 a year in housing costs now that rents have risen 25 to 48 percent in the past several years, according to David Weidner, managing editor for economic research at Trulia.[18]

Most people seek shared housing to save money, Pluhar says. But they stay in shared housing because they discover there are "significant benefits including companionship and help," she says. "We as human beings are not meant to live alone. We are meant to be connected. We have lived in tribes for millennia. Our very being is dependent on being interdependent." Shared housing leads to "levels of intimacy, connectedness and healthfulness," she says.

Pluhar has lived in shared housing throughout her life. When she was a child, and her father was a graduate student, a family friend lived with them. As a teen, during a difficult financial time, her parents rented out a room to help pay the bills. She lived in group homes during and after college, then bought a house in Silver Spring, Maryland, with four bedrooms so she could have housemates.

For young adults who don't want to boomerang back to their childhood room to avoid unhealthy patterns, living in another multigenerational home is a way to take advantage of adult wisdom. "Living with somebody who is not your parent can teach you new patterns, new ways of relating, and new ways of thinking about being in a close relationship," Pluhar says.

BOOMERANGS ABROAD

Americans are far from alone. Young adults are boomeranging home around the world. In Italy, Spain, and Japan, where it is difficult to find housing, many young adults remain with their parents well into their 40s, often staying single and not having kids, says Katherine Newman, a professor of sociology at the University of Massachusetts Amherst and author of *The Accordion Family: Boomerang Kids, Anxious Parents, and the Private Toll of Global Competition.*[19]

In Europe, almost half, or 48 percent, of 18- to 34-year-olds lived with their parents in 2014, according to data from the European Union's 28 countries compiled by the Pew Research Center. More than two-thirds of young Italian adults, or nearly 7.4 million 18- to 34-year-olds, live at home with their parents, making the country the butt of jokes about the stereotypical *mammone*, or Peter Pan–like children who never grow up.[20] In 2010, then–cabinet minister Renato Brunetta even proposed banning adults over 18 from living with their parents, "to deal with the culture of mummy's boys and big babies."[21] Brunetta made the suggestion on a radio show where he conceded his mother had made his bed until he left home at age 30.

However, in a few countries, including Sweden and Denmark—where the government owns nearly one-third of rentals, picks up most housing costs for young adults, offers educational stipends for students, and doles out generous unemployment benefits—young people rarely remain under the family roof. Some leave home as early as 16 to go to high school elsewhere, with the government picking up the tab.

REENTERING THE NEST

When young adults come home, many parents are anxious about the reentry. If you have a kid who boomerangs back to his or her childhood room, you can manage this time without falling into familiar old patterns that stir tension.

- Hold a meeting to discuss sharing household chores, such as preparing meals, vacuuming, and fetching groceries. Explain that everyone must pitch in.
- Communicate directly, be assertive, and don't expect your children to show up for dinner. Request no loud music or parties unless everybody's on board.
- Help your young adult come up with a constructive plan to move toward a self-sufficient future.
- Suggest your young adult pay full or partial rent. This contributes to the household and can help a young adult learn to budget, plan ahead, and develop maturity.
- Understand that some young adults may need more time to be launched. Older kids with learning issues, mood swings, anger management problems, or social anxiety may require a longer nesting period to address these issues, as well as therapy and/or medication.

- Resist the impulse to "baby" your young adult. Unless your young adult is mentally ill or has a serious illness, it's best to discuss the time horizon for the home stay, which can affect other major decisions, such as whether or when to sell the family home.
- Discuss the living situation every few months.

Family assistance can be a two-way street. Once you are in your 70s and 80s, you may need support from your kids. Perhaps it makes sense in your 40s, 50s, and 60s to help your kids get a foothold. Newman advises parents and society in general to stop fretting and moralizing over young adults "lingering" in their parents' homes. "It's a perfectly reasonable for families to band together for mutual support and help young adults gain the credentials they need without ringing up much debt," she says. "This is a reasonable response by families to difficult economic circumstances."[22]

It can be trying if your young adult doesn't appear to be moving forward with a plan toward the future. But if they are engaging in behavior that will help them in the long run, such as studying, working, and saving money, or doing internships or a low-paid work experience that is a bridge to a career, parents who support them "are making a rational, reasonable, and honorable investment in the next generation," Newman says. "We should lay off the hand-wringing about whether or not we are coddling people." Living at home for a spell should not be a source of shame or belittlement, she says. "Families have always stepped up to help the next generation get where they want to go."

Section IV

Words of Wisdom

10

WORDS FROM THE WISE

Those only are happy who have their minds fixed on some
object other than their own happiness; on the happiness of
others, on the improvement of mankind, even on some art or
pursuit.

John Stuart Mill

The empty nest ushers in a new phase of freedom, but it also
brings an unsettling sense that time is running out and an urgent
feeling that we need to make the most of it. There stirs deep
inside us a nostalgia for earlier times as our minds edit out the
stress of child-rearing and launching a career. Our friends and
family face challenges, fight illness, and pass away, and our search
for meaning intensifies.

Yet parents whose kids have left years and decades ago often
have discovered that this can be one of the best and most meaningful phases of life. Seasoned empty nesters find fulfillment in
many ways but along common lines: by finding a sense of belonging through building human relationships, finding a purpose, serving something larger than the self, and experiencing transcendence.

A NEW SEARCH FOR MEANING

Few pursuits in life provide a more powerful source of meaning than raising children. Yet parenthood is stressful, requiring sacrifice, energy, patience, and a casting aside of the self. Good parenting necessarily involves postponing your own rest and relaxation. The demands of raising kids can be so all-consuming they can sabotage happiness in the short run.

When the kids leave and the load lightens, it's tempting to make up for lost time by following the advice of Greek philosopher Aristippus, who argued in favor of *hedonia*, or a feel-good approach to life. Hedonic pursuits are aimed at pleasure, enjoyment, relaxation, and comfort. That might include shopping, vacationing, drinking, eating sweets, sleeping late, and generally having fun. But researchers are finding that pursuing pleasure does not necessarily lead to life satisfaction.

More and more psychologists today are drawing a distinction between a happy life and a meaningful life. According to Martin E. P. Seligman, a positive psychologist at the University of Pennsylvania and author of *Authentic Happiness: Using the New Positive Psychology to Realize Your Potential for Lasting Fulfillment*, getting the most out of life requires being positive, engaging in activities that bring transcendence or flow, staying connected to friends and family, and "using your signature strengths in the service of something that you believe is larger than you are."[1] Meaningful pursuits include fighting for a cause, studying something new, or volunteering to help others.

True well-being is not about satisfying your own needs and desires or accumulating wealth and other trappings of success, which can leave you anxious and adrift, says Emily Esfahani Smith, author of *The Power of Meaning: Finding Fulfillment in a World Obsessed with Happiness*. "Chasing happiness can make people *unhappy*," Smith says. "Even though life is getting objectively better by nearly every conceivable standard, more people feel hopeless, depressed, and alone," Smith says, citing the rising suicide rate around the world and in America, where it recently hit a 30-

year high. Despair and emptiness stem not from a lack of happiness, but from a lack of meaning, she says. "Happiness comes and goes," Smith says, "but meaning gives you something to hold on to."[2]

While many empty nesters and retirees treat this phase of life like a permanent vacation, that approach "ends up feeling kind of empty," Smith says. She recommends that empty nesters find well-being by "turning down the volume on yourself and connecting to something beyond." When the kids leave, "there is a vacuum that can create a crisis of meaning and identity," she says. "You need to fill that bucket with something else to restore a sense of meaning."

A SENSE OF BELONGING

> The need for connection and community is primal, as fundamental as the need for air, water, and food.
>
> Dean Ornish

Empty nesters with strong social ties and a goal of serving others are most likely to find fulfillment. Just ask Martina, an 84-year-old widow whose four kids are in their 50s. The former fifth-grade teacher rarely feels lonely. After her kids grew up and her husband Bruce began losing his vision, forcing him to retire from managing a car dealership and car wash, they concentrated on cultivating social connections near their home in Bradford, Vermont. They signed up for bus trips to Pennsylvania, Missouri, Michigan, Tennessee, Arizona, and Canada, even touring Hawaii by coach.

With Bruce's eyesight worsening, he enjoyed listening to tour guides. And, eager to interact with fellow travelers but wary of any pity, he often tried to conceal his lack of sight. "He was embarrassed by it and didn't want anyone to know," Martina says. "He didn't want sympathy." She did her part by describing in detail scenes outside the window—such as buffalos or the Grand Canyon. And he kept his hand on her shoulder when he walked. "It was a game, helping him keep the cover," she says. Their favorite part of the trips was finding friends, which delighted Bruce.

After Bruce died, Martina reached out to connect with others in their small community. She volunteers often for her church, managing church investments and compiling a parish prayer list for friends and loved ones in need. She teams with a younger friend on the cemetery association who shares her interest in restoring gravestones of Revolutionary War soldiers. They go together to look for gravestones that have tipped, cracked, or fallen. Martina sings in the church choir and at the senior center. She takes classes in Bible study and is writing a memoir. She's a docent for the historical society and treasurer of the retired teachers' association. "I care about the town and want to contribute," she says. She is baffled when friends tell her they feel alone. "I'm not ever lonely because I have so many contacts," she says. "I enjoy doing things with people I don't necessarily know well because I get to know them."

BELONGING TO KIN

Forging strong bonds with family also bolsters well-being in the empty nest. For Tin, a 72-year-old great grandmother from Vietnam who lives in Virginia, the empty nest is overflowing with grandkids. Now that her own kids are adults and absorbed in careers, she cares for her eight grandchildren, who range in age from 8 months to 12 years. She makes meals and presides daily over her son Kenny's household, which bustles with his kids, nieces, and nephews, while he and his wife Trish run their nail salon.

Tin says she rarely feels tired and is never sad, except when her grandchildren leave on vacation. She is firm in her mission to help them grow up with strength and good health and says she doesn't need lofty pursuits to feel fulfilled. She savors the passage of time rather than fretting about it. "I don't care about the time that is past," she says. "Naturally, the people are young and then get old."

She knows her grandkids, like her kids, will "grow up and fly away," but feels grateful she can share their lives.

REVELING IN RELATIONSHIPS

The love of family and the admiration of friends is much more important than wealth and privilege.

Charles Kuralt

Sometimes a crisis reminds us of the value of close relationships. Kathy realized how much her friends and family mattered after her last son left for college and she suffered a life-threatening injury. She was painting a ceiling at home when a blood vessel ruptured, causing a stroke that paralyzed her right side and left her unable to walk. Surgery and months of toggling between the hospital and a rehab center left her dependent on others as she fought her way out of a wheelchair.

But the injury and its aftermath jolted Kathy, 62, and her husband Vincent, 65, into realizing they wanted to live each day with relationships as their highest priority. "We realized how much the people in our lives mattered to us, more than all the things and careers and all the rest of it because they were there in our time of need," Vincent says. Their kids, parents, siblings, cousins, nieces, nephews, aunts, uncles, and friends rallied, visiting Kathy and bringing meals. When she wasn't able to leave the rehab center for Thanksgiving, 20 relatives teamed up to deliver it to her. "Everybody pitched in to help," she says. "If you don't have an event like this that really tests things, you don't really see how important those relationships are."

The injury also prompted Kathy and Vincent to simplify their lives to focus more on others. They sped up the sale of their Victorian home in Millburn, New Jersey, and moved to a cottage on the shore. Their beach location is an attractive getaway for their sons Ryan, 31, and Brendan, 29, who they see often. As they watch Kathy navigate with a walker or a cane, her sons are now more sensitive to disabilities. "If they hadn't had this experience, they couldn't possibly relate," she says. When Kathy and Vincent go out in public, moving slowly because of Kathy's poor balance, they have noticed a new level of kindness and empathy. Says Vincent, "When there are these crazy challenges, it can make you much more connected to the people around you."

When people form lasting, intimate bonds with others, they feel part of a larger tribe. But we live in an age of social isolation: More than one-third of Americans aged 45 and older say they are lonely, according to a national survey by the AARP.[3] Lonely adults are less likely to be involved in activities that build a social network, such as going to religious services, volunteering, joining a community group, or spending time on a hobby. They are more likely to spend their time sleeping, eating, watching television, and sitting in front of a computer screen. And they are more inclined to use drugs and alcohol. Loneliness compromises the immune system and makes people less likely to flourish, according to the AARP. Researcher Lisa Jaremka at Ohio State University found that loneliness has the potential to trigger recurrence of the herpes virus and lead to increased levels of inflammation associated with heart disease, Type 2 diabetes, arthritis, and Alzheimer's. Being without close personal relations can also accelerate aging, she says. If you have lost touch with people you care about, it's time to reach out.[4]

FINDING PURPOSE

> The purpose of human life is to serve, and to show compassion and the will to help others.
>
> Albert Schweitzer

You can find a new sense of purpose after your kids leave by working toward an attainable goal that means something to you and helps others or advances a larger cause. A purpose might be curbing poverty or improving education in a large or small way. It might be supporting someone who is disabled, elderly, or ill. It might be learning a new skill, launching a new career, or writing a book. Purpose might mean working to end racial or gender discrimination, fighting for human rights, or improving the environment—globally or locally.

Finding purpose requires having a passion and serving something larger than yourself. "The happiest people do have a sense of purpose," says Caroline Adams Miller, a positive psychology expert and coauthor with Michael B. Frisch of *Creating Your Best Life: The Ultimate Life List Guide.* "They don't wake up to make themselves better, faster, and stronger. They wake up because they have an interest in making the world better, not just for themselves. If what you are doing isn't infused with passion from the marrow of your bones, it will be very hard to muster the stick-to-itiveness to get through it."[5]

Living purposefully in the empty nest requires knowing yourself and understanding your strengths, passions, and values. "People have to turn inward to figure out how to best lead their lives," says Rebecca Schlegel, a psychologist at Texas A&M University who runs a lab that examines issues of the "true self," identity, coping, well-being, and meaning in life. Her research focuses on existential questions such as "What does it all mean?" Schlegel says happiness and a life well lived are achieved when living "in accordance with one's true self." Knowing your true self is the first step in finding a path that aligns with your values and skills, she says. There's an existential crisis when the kids go because suddenly you don't know who you are. During child-rearing years, your identity as a parent can be all-consuming and you don't often have to think about who you are. "Self-definition is kind of provided for you," she says. "A big piece of the puzzle is there." When the kids leave, it can generate concern about self and identity. "The compass you were using isn't quite there anymore," Schlegel says. "Freedom is exciting, but it poses a little bit of an existential threat."[6]

Finding out where you can best focus your energy at this stage involves trying lots of activities—the same approach we take with young kids by exposing them to many things to see what fits, Schlegel says. "You've got to put yourself out there and try on different things to see where you find feelings of authenticity," she says.

When the feeling is authentic, you feel a sense of flow, a combination of engagement and excitement and a loss of the self. You find a kind of transcendence, escape ruminative patterns, and "get in the groove," she says. People find flow in many pursuits, including writing, teaching, photography, exercise, yoga, meditation, rock climbing, making crafts, cooking, and volunteering. If you are able to meld your talent and expertise and engage in an activity you perceive as giving back or morally good, you are likely to arrive at a "feeling of rightness that gets you out of overthinking," Schlegel says. "That is the sweet spot for authenticity."

GIFTS THAT GIVE BACK

Many people find purpose by devoting themselves to a cause. Eleven years after the last of their five children left the nest, Julie, 59, and Steve, 62, are stepping down as university professors to focus on improving schooling for orphans in remote villages in Uganda.

Earlier in their careers, they'd spent decades working as researchers in East Africa and found themselves haunted by images of children digging for food in gardens to earn money to pay for a day at school. And when their last child was a high school senior, they took a hard look at themselves and their values. They had always been driven by a mission to educate others and knew it wouldn't be enough to sit on a beach or just play golf. "The biggest mistake people make is accumulating money thinking that if they have enough, they'll be happy," Steve says. "We can't imagine in retirement that we would become different people with different goals. We have dedicated our lives to students and it was inconceivable to us that we would want to change that as empty nesters and into retirement."

They identified their priorities: spending quality time with their kids and grandkids and leaving a legacy of service. They created True Africa, a nonprofit that finds sponsors to provide tuition, classrooms, desks, uniforms, school supplies, lunch, goats, medical care, mosquito nests, and water systems for vulnerable kids.

Now two of their daughters are board members and four grandchildren are fund-raising, with hopes of joining them in Uganda next year. The plan is to work in rural schools and with village elders toward building one brick and cement-floored dorm or teaching quarters each year. "This is an integral part of our lives," Julie says. "The role of our family is critical in everything we are doing in our empty nest era." They plan to lead the nonprofit for another decade, then hand over the reins to the next generations.

Their Africa project has filled another purpose: helping their offspring step out of their own needs and challenges. "It creates much more of an empathetic and whole person as an adult," Steve says. "They become much more outwardly focused, much more of a citizen of society and the world." Their kids and grandkids have been able to "better calibrate what they really have and how it can best be used," Steve says. Focusing on helping others "helps you emotionally and intellectually and personally," he says. "It gives you a sense that you are useful to others and those in need." Says Julie: "This has become a core thread in our family culture."

They also reap rewards themselves. Every year, Steve and Julie return to Uganda and see kids they helped graduating from vocational school and universities. "You see how much can be accomplished with so little," Steve says. They have learned a new sense of optimism from the Ugandans, who have much less than most Americans yet appear more hopeful, he says. "It's discouraging to come home and find pessimism in a location where we have so much and appreciate it so little."

Altruistic projects like this provide purpose, connect us with others, expand our social awareness, provide new perspectives, and promote deeper feelings of compassion, according to Timothy

Smith, a professor of clinical and health psychology at the University of Utah. "Although we intuitively believe that focusing on ourselves will make us happy, research has consistently shown that the less we focus on ourselves, the happier we tend to feel," Smith says. "We feel happiest when engaged in meaningful relationships and meaningful activities."[7]

Striving for meaning rather than seeking fun or entertainment leads to fewer negative moods and better long-term psychological health, according to a 2010 study by psychologists Veronika Huta of the University of Ottawa and Richard Ryan of the University of Rochester.[8] Their study's participants who aimed to be happy by engaging in purely fun activities reported more positive feelings and fewer negative vibes right after the experiment. But three months later, their happy mood had faded. In contrast, participants who strived for meaning—by helping others, forgiving a friend, thinking about values, or studying—felt less happy right after the experiment, yet three months later, said they felt more inspired and part of something greater than themselves.[9]

A SECOND CAREER

> Realize when you are "middle aged" you have a chance for a whole second career, another love, another life.
>
> Sharon Stone

Sometimes the path to a second act can be a winding one. After his four daughters became self-supporting and he parted ways with his wife, Cam simplified his life and found new purpose. He is determined to use his time as well as he can because he feels he's living on borrowed time. After two heart attacks, a stroke, and a pulmonary embolism, and having lived a decade longer than any male in his family tree, Cam never expected to reach age 60. "Tomorrow might be the day for me," he says, adding, "I'm really quite fine with that. I don't have this terrible longing to live another 5, 10, 20, 30, 40 years. I am not morose. I am very much at peace with it."

But that doesn't mean he is living a life of leisure. After decades of running his family's car dealership, expanding it, and launching a successful technology business, Cam was exhausted and ready for a change. He was tired of meeting sales targets, brokering deals, and facing too much stress. He had paid off his mortgage and his kids were launched, so he sold his business and bought a house in Canada on an island, with no cell service, an hour and a half northwest of Montreal, where he could relax, go on raft trips, and watch the waves. "I just really wanted to do nothing," he says.

But Cam was restless. He had always been fascinated by story-telling and film. When a movie producer friend came to visit and suggested they partner to make inexpensive, independent films in Hollywood, Cam didn't hesitate. He packed up his motorcycle, drove to Los Angeles, and moved into a one-room apartment. Now he revels in searching for scripts, learning how to improve them, and scouting for actors, locations, props, and investors. He organizes production, investigates film festivals, and builds teams as he did in his earlier business life. And he continues to learn by working with a writer and director, describing the relationship as that of a "comrade in arms working to solve little questions and problems together." The whole adventure is "not about the crowning achievement," or winning an Academy Award, Cam says. Instead, he finds satisfaction and purpose "in all aspects of the process."

HARNESSING PASSION TO FIND PURPOSE

As parents with kids at home, we can become so accustomed to ignoring our own needs and passions, it can be hard to unearth them. When the children leave, we are jolted into wondering what we're supposed to do next. Answering that question can trigger stress. But remember, the right amount of stress is a great motivator, says Elizabeth Lombardo, a Chicago psychologist and author of *Better than Perfect: 7 Strategies to Crush Your Inner Critic and Create a Life You Love.* Too little stress can lead to complacency and lack of action. Too much stress can lead to avoidance and procrastination. But the right amount, known as optimal stress, gets you moving in the right direction. Lombardo suggests viewing your search for purpose as an adventure, instead of seeing it as work that is overwhelming or anxiety producing. Don't worry if the next step isn't clear, Lombardo says. "De-stress on that. It's part of the process to discover what it is."[10]

To find purpose, here are HappiNest suggestions:

- *Revisit your past to recall what lit you up.* Remember your childhood dreams. Was there a subject in high school or college that captivated you? Do you want to create a charity, start a business, become a speaker, learn to swim?
- *Listen to yourself.* Don't engage in an activity just because your friends do. Let your internal GPS guide you.
- *Make a list of things you are good at and that make you come alive.* What are your top talents and skills? Where do you add the greatest value? What are you most curious about? What triggers your emotions? How can you connect to others by further developing your interests?
- *Consider a cause that moves you.* Is there an injustice that outrages you? Damage to the environment? Child trafficking? How can you play a part in correcting it?
- *Connect to something that's bigger than you are.* What can you do to benefit others or the world? The more you help others get what they want, the more you will get what you want.
- *Write your own obituary.* What do you list near the top? What will you regret if you don't accomplish it? Figure out what you would do if you weren't afraid to do it.

Once you identify a new empty nest purpose, fear can block you from taking the next step. Even when human beings are unhappy where they are, they often avoid wading into new situations because they fear failure and find it easier to be in the known, says Margie Warrell, an Australian motivational speaker and author of *Brave: 50 Everyday Acts of Courage to Thrive in Work, Love and Life*. But that can lead to regret. "When you are an empty nester, if you stay in the confines of what's comfortable, you miss out on opportunities to explore new horizons," she says.[11] We turn away from challenges because the human brain tricks us into believing it's better to avoid risk and play it safe.

In his best-selling book, *Thinking Fast and Slow*, psychologist Daniel Kahneman, winner of the Nobel Prize in Economics, notes that people tend to overestimate the likelihood that things will go wrong if they take a risk. We seize on what could go wrong rather than what might go right. "The brains of humans and other animals contain a mechanism that is designed to give priority to bad news," Kahneman says.[12] Rather than taking a risk and facing the possibility of regret, we tend to stick with the status quo.

We don't just think about what could go wrong. We also tend to imagine the worst possible outcome, also known as *catastrophizing*. And human beings tend to discount the cost of inaction and playing it safe. Because of this blindness to the cost of remaining in the status quo, many people convince themselves that their circumstances will improve over time by doing nothing. "Doing more of what is not working in the hope that it will work at some point is just wishful thinking," Warrell says. "The unconscious bias we have toward sticking with the familiar can prevent us from taking the very actions that would move us toward our dreams." Warrell says life rewards brave action. "Fear regret more than failure," she says. "We have to be really, really careful to separate out the fears that are serving us and those that are holding us back and fueling our self-doubt."

We can rewire our brains to chase passion, overcome obstacles, and find adventure. "The more you do something, the more comfortable it becomes," Lombardo says. She likens taking a risk to putting a foot in a hot tub. "If you have the mind-set that it's too uncomfortable, you are likely to avoid taking the plunge. But if you wade in with an open mind and get comfortable with being uncomfortable, your body eventually acclimates. If you have a passion or a purpose, it keeps you young, motivated, and energized. When you have that energy and excitement, that's your reason for being here." Taking active steps and following passions can open portals. Doors open to new opportunities, innovative ideas, and unique experiences you might never find if you play it safe.

Take these steps to reach empty nest goals:

- *Find role models who inspire you.* Include people in your life who have similar goals or are ahead of you in achieving them. Find people who have qualities, values, or character traits you most want to emulate, Miller says. "If you put yourself out there in the right direction and surround yourself with people who believe in your ability to succeed, you will thrive."
- *Break down your goals into small, manageable experiences.* Take one step at a time. It's less intimidating and builds momentum.
- *Announce your empty nest goals to others who can hold you accountable.* Find people who won't let you off the hook, Miller says. You might meet weekly or monthly so you can hold each other accountable. You need only look as far as Weight Watchers and Alcoholics Anonymous to see how effective group accountability can be.
- *Try new things every other week.* That might mean volunteering, taking a class, or sketching a business plan.
- *Don't let age define you.* While we can lose the full force of some abilities when we are empty nest age, we actually become more effective overall because of the emotional and social skills we develop over a lifetime.

LEGACY OF SERVICE

The best way to find yourself is to lose yourself in the service of others.

Mahatma Gandhi

For Paul, contentment always has come from serving others. When he was a teenager, he noticed a man without a coat on a bitter cold winter day and didn't hesitate to offer the man his own. "Something in me just wanted to serve without expectation of getting anything back," says Paul, a recently retired father of four grown kids and grandfather of three. His career developed out of his concern for the well-being of others. A federal employee for decades, he started at the bottom rung and worked his way up to leading a team of fourteen, helping employees improve their physical, mental, and spiritual state. He created wellness programs and oversaw employee counseling, childcare subsidies, occupational safety, and fitness at the Department of Defense. He set up quiet rooms for employees facing tough times to give them a place to meditate or take a break. Paul was a man on a mission: "I was making people whole."

That larger purpose was critical to getting him through the four to five hours he spent driving to and from work each day. "You have to find a reason to come to work and it can't be because you want a bigger paycheck," he says. "It's got to be a higher meaning because that's going to keep you going during the tough times." After he had a mini-stroke at home in 2015, Paul decided that 38 years of work for the government was enough. "Okay Lord, you don't have to send me any more smoke signals to let me know it's time," he said.

Since retiring, Paul has focused on ministering to people in need around his hometown of Hagerstown, Maryland. He offers company and advice and sometimes officiates at weddings. "We don't carry bibles and preach on the corner," he says, "but we do make ourselves available." He says he knows he was meant to invest in relationships. He and his wife, Sandra, recently came across a neighbor who was struggling with alcoholism. They listened to him, befriended him, and took him back to the church. When the man died, Paul officiated at the funeral. "We really need to stay in the moment, because sometimes the moment is all you have," he says. "You can't miss the opportunity to serve." He's gratified that his emphasis on helping others has left a legacy of service among his four adult children, who are a doctor, teacher, administrator of a nonprofit, and director of strength and conditioning for a school. "They all have this desire to serve," he says.

Paul's wife beat back fear in the empty nest to help herself, her kids, and other people's children reach their potential. Sandra is opening doors for the next generation, just as a pivotal teacher did for her. When she was a girl, her father, who had joined the Air Force out of high school, discouraged her from going to college, saying he wasn't going to help pay for it. She had wanted to become a lawyer, but her father said that wasn't a job for a woman. Sandra had been pulled out of an all-black school in tenth grade and bused to a primarily white one in an upper-middle-class suburb outside Indianapolis. She suffered from culture shock, missed her old friends, and struggled adjusting to such a different culture.

However, a teacher who heard her deliver a speech in high school changed her life by praising her effort and helping her get a scholarship. "I didn't know anything about college," she says. "I never had anyone sit down and tell me what it was." With that help, she attended Indiana State University. While she didn't graduate, Sandra later devoted herself to raising and schooling her own children. When the empty nest loomed, she was determined to banish the "negativity" she felt about school and finish her college degree.

At age 50, she took her grandson with her to orientation after enrolling at Hood College in Frederick, Maryland, two hours from home. When she arrived, she felt old and overweight and wanted to quit, but she persevered. "It was a milestone for me," she says. As part of her bachelor's degree in sociology, she founded Pearls for Girls, a community group in a housing development, to mentor 8- to 18-year-olds whose parents lived in poverty. She led group conversations about social conflicts, schoolwork, and dreams. She took snacks, taught the girls to make cornbread, and reminded them to comb their hair and dress in respectable clothes. "I was doing for them what I had done for my own girls," she says. She told them they needed to do better in school and required they read as a condition of remaining in the group. She photocopied chapters in books and led discussions that intrigued them. When she wondered if anyone was taking her messages to heart, she heard them mentoring each other with her words. She saw some of them go to college.

And Sandra got something in return for giving back: "I didn't have time to sit around and think about myself and the fact that my children were moving on without me," she says. "I was able to put all of that time and energy into something larger than myself." When she got a part-time job at a methadone clinic to earn money to buy her books, another door opened. While she doubted she had what it takes to help people addicted to opiates, she has found a rewarding career as a substance abuse counselor. The career found her, Sandra says. "I think if you make yourself available, the thing you need will find you."

Sandra's experience illustrates how a person's concern and commitment to helping future generations bolsters well-being. *Generative* adults, according to the famous twentieth-century psychologist Erik Erikson, take care of people in future generations by contributing something worthwhile for the long run. In so doing, they thrive themselves.[13]

Because devoting yourself to future generations is hard work, people tell themselves positive and redemptive stories to sustain them in their efforts, says Dan P. McAdams, a psychology professor and director of the Foley Center for the Study of Lives at Northwestern University. "They tend to tell these very redemptive stories about their lives," often about overcoming adversity, McAdams says.[14] Middle-aged adults who devote themselves to helping future generations tell narratives about themselves that are more positive and optimistic, with happier endings.

TRANSCENDING THE SELF

> I kind of entered a flow state. I've been there before while
> climbing. You are not thinking ahead. You are just thinking
> about what is in front of you each second.
>
> Aron Ralston

We also find meaning in the empty nest through transcendent
experiences that wash away our sense of self and make us feel
more connected to others and the world. Such experiences exist
on a spectrum of intensity, according to David Yaden, a researcher
and expert on transcendence at the University of Pennsylvania.[15]
On the low end of the spectrum is a state of flow, in which petty
concerns and anxieties evaporate. You might find a state of flow
engaging in challenging tasks such as skiing, knitting, model building, gardening, reading, or writing. In this subtle form of transcendence, you may lose yourself in time and not notice that hours
have passed.

A deeper form of transcendence, known as awe, can be triggered in different ways. Standing on the edge of the Grand Canyon or hiking up a mountain and looking down could prompt
perceptual awe. You might experience *conceptual awe* by viewing
a 10,000-year-old artifact at a museum or listening to a TED Talk
about a brilliant idea. All of these transcendent experiences act
like a reset button, refreshing your mind, broadening your perspective, and bolstering your well-being, Yaden says. He suggests
that transcendent experiences, where you feel "overwhelmed with
connectedness," can be especially helpful for empty nesters who
feel a greater sense of isolation or aloneness with the kids away.

However, passive activities like watching television or scrolling
through social media do not trigger transcendent experiences.
That's because "they don't require a lot of focus, aren't challenging, and there isn't enough engagement with something vast,"
Yaden says. Watching a television program about the Grand Canyon won't trigger the same kind of awe as standing at a scenic
overlook. Seeing a social media post about a natural history mu-

seum is no substitute for being there, he says. Rather, getting out of the house and seeing the real thing is the best way to reinvigorate the self. Being in front of something awe-inspiring allows you to see the world from a broader perspective and lift the fog. Yaden says he walks down to a river daily, which allows him to feel "part of a greater whole." He distinguishes this communing with nature from a hedonic getaway such as going to get a donut. Transcendent experiences, he says, "melt the boundaries between yourself and everyone else."

Rosemary Sword, 63, finds transcendent beauty by hiking up volcano craters near her home in Maui. "Finding joy in the moment is what helps us to take the next step," says Sword, a coauthor with psychologist Philip G. Zimbardo of *Living & Loving Better with Time Perspective Therapy: Healing from the Past, Embracing the Present, Creating an Ideal Future.* "It's really important to focus on the moment throughout the day so we are not stuck in the past or overly planning for the future. It can be as simple as noticing a color that brings us joy, or a flower, or the sky."16

When the last of her four children left for college and her husband Rick died of stomach cancer, Sword found herself alone for the first time in decades. The plans she and her husband had made to continue researching and counseling people suffering from trauma were dashed. Instead, she fell into grief and depression. She didn't want to burden her kids, so she turned inward and wallowed in self-pity. "I had to slap myself to get out of it," she says.

Before he died, Rick gave her the best advice: He challenged her to write another book. "He was giving me tasks to carry on and keep me busy," she says. "I got busy, even though I was super depressed." Now she is back on track and plans to write well into her golden years, which she must do for financial reasons, but also because she feels an emotional need to be productive. "When we suffer loss—whatever it is—a hole is left in our lives," Sword says. "We have a choice to fill that hole with something."

She knew the best approach was to look forward instead of into the past. She finds flow and joy and meaning in her writing. Sword also finds transcendence through art, which she has dabbled in since she was a child. She loves to paint small acrylic pieces— usually landscapes and pets. "When we are depressed, it's like we are looking backwards," she says. "It's paramount to realize that's what you are doing and to turn around and face your future."

FINDING FLOW THROUGH INTERESTS

Bonnie finds a state of flow by tapping into her longtime hobbies. That helped her get past the fear she felt when her last child Nathan left home for the Air Force 17 years ago. She was scared his aircraft might crash or he would be injured while working in the belly of a plane as an in-flight refueler. She prayed that her son and his buddies would be safe. And she missed staying home with her three kids, reading to them, baking, and growing flowers and produce, which she sold them from a farm stand in West Hartford, Vermont, by her home. After spending 90 percent of her time helping her husband and kids, she felt lost without them.

"It took me a while to adjust to the fact that the kids were all gone," Bonnie says. "It hit me between the eyes. I was crushed. I really felt empty." She decided to put her passions to work. After decades of baking, she stumbled on a new career demonstrating how to bake cookies, cakes, pies, and breads at a flour company, which eventually sent her around the country as an instructor. Yet she still felt "not all that happy," she says. "That's when I saw how entwined my life was as a mom and a caregiver," she says. "I realized I had to reinvent myself other than just what I had at my job."

She signed up to help third and fourth graders read. "I felt like I needed to give back to the school system that my kids had enjoyed," she says. She also aims to train others at a food bank or shelter to make whole grain, nutritious breads.

For Bonnie's husband John, a 67-year-old former lineman for a power company, purpose and joy come from hands-on projects. John spent his career climbing telephone poles 60 feet in the air to repair blown electrical fuses. After his kids were on their own and he retired, he scrolled back in time to when he was a teenager who loved hot rod cars. He bought a 1965 Plymouth and started on a scavenger hunt, hunting down used replacement parts to rebuild the engine. The car became a work of art he sculpted for four or five hours each evening. "I am the kind of guy who likes to keep busy," he says. "I don't like to sit around."

Once his muscle car was finished, he moved onto a larger goal: designing and building a small house an hour away on a lake in Goshen, New Hampshire, for himself and his wife. "It's something I always thought about doing," he says. For seven years, he painstakingly planned and oversaw the project. "I've always liked design and art," he says. "It was unbelievable to go from a design on paper to standing inside the house. It was better than what I had imagined."

NO TIME FOR REGRETS

> I'd rather regret the things I've done than regret the things I haven't done.
>
> Lucille Ball

If you identify genuine interests and pursue them, you won't regret it. Regrets are about opportunities you let slip through your fingers. They are about what you backed off doing out of fear or anxiety. They are about seeking sanctuary in the status quo. For many people, one of the biggest fears is FOMO—the fear of missing out. You don't want to be nearing death, haunted with regrets over what you might have done.

In her book, *The Top Five Regrets of the Dying*, palliative care nurse Bronnie Ware shares what she learned from her patients, a powerful reminder of how fleeting life can be. When faced with mortality, Ware's patients had epiphanies, including "I wish I'd had the courage to live a life true to myself, not the life others expected of me."[17] Ware writes that fear of change had them pretending to others, and to themselves, that they were content.

A NEW SEASON

The empty nest is a time to celebrate and discover. "It's time to explore introspectively as well as outside of ourselves" says Dean Ahlberg, an empty nester and senior minister at the First Church of Christ, Congregational in Redding, Connecticut. "As you venture into new endeavors, you will connect with others and feel your life matters all along the way. You are simply redirecting energy in a new way. It's time to get reacquainted with spontaneity, to re-center our own lives and gifts, and to seek opportunities to continue our growth as children of God."[18]

WORDS OF WISDOM FROM SEASONED EMPTY NESTERS:

- Prioritize relationships. "When you are young, you are focused on the future, but looking back, the things that matter the most are the relationships you build throughout your life," says Vincent, a former high school teacher and banker.
- Keep busy by volunteering. "I love life," says Pie, who retired from her job at the National Portrait Gallery then returned as a volunteer, riding the subway there until she turned 80. "I don't want to miss anything." She also volunteers at a food bank.
- Don't plan to retire. Retire to do what you planned. "The biggest mistake people make is accumulating money thinking that if they have enough, they'll be happy," says Steve, a professor. "Rather than retiring to spend time on yourself, aim to do more good for others and model that for your offspring."

- Build in ways to help with other people's children, says Alfred, a former journalist who welcomed his sons' young adult friends to stay in a spare room for months as they pursued graduate degrees and launched careers. In return, they served as house and pet sitters.
- Double up on pets. "Pets make a difference," says Alfred, who has always filled the empty nest with at least one dog and one cat.
- Surround yourself with others. "Get out of the house," says Paul, a retired federal worker. "Don't just hang around the house and be alone with your thoughts."
- Be part of something bigger than yourself. "Somebody is always going to need you," Paul says. "You may want to play golf all the time, but that's not living if you don't find a way to give of yourself. Look for the good you can do."
- Get involved in improving the environment or the lives of others. "Help out at a park, clean up the highway, help at an animal shelter, or train a therapy dog," says Rosemary, the therapist in Maui. "The more it can be for the benefit of all, the better. Help someone else other than just yourself."
- Go back in time and find what you were passionate about. "At some point in your life you were passionate about something and that passion can be rekindled," says Rosemary Sword. "Reconnect with it."

11

LESSONS LEARNED

It is not in the pursuit of happiness that we find fulfillment, it is in the happiness of pursuit.

Denis Waitley

When I started this journey to discover how this generation of empty nesters can find fulfillment after the kids leave, I never imagined how complex it could be. I now know we are trudging through new territory without a road map in a world that is vastly different from that of our parents. On one hand, we have far more opportunities than people in previous generations. We can find information in a flash on the Internet; connect to people across the planet by phone, e-mail, text, or social media; work remotely; make instant purchases with credit cards; and travel to more places more efficiently.

But we also have more obligations and less time. Our kids are taking longer to finish school, settle on careers, and become independent, requiring more parental support in their 20s and even 30s. Our parents are living longer and needing us more. Helping family on both ends of the age spectrum is demanding and prompts many empty nesters to dip into savings and postpone retirement. Meanwhile, as technology has eased our lives, it also has carved out a landscape that is distracting and ever changing.

Creating a *HappiNest* takes hard work, and it's different for everyone. As I have researched this topic and interviewed more than 300 people, including psychologists, sociologists, young adults, and empty nesters, I have discovered that this is a time of transition, revitalization, and repurpose. To thrive, you must act in concert with your values and pursue what is most critical and meaningful to you.

FARTHER, NOT FURTHER, AWAY

Don't despair because the kids are gone, thinking your work as a parent is over. They might be farther away, but they still need your guidance—just less frequently and through technology instead of face-to-face. As they flutter their wings, take a deep breath and let them go. But remember, the ties you have built are woven into their safety net.

If you cling to their feathers, you will weigh them down. Whether your fledglings have gone to college, graduate school, the military, or to live or work elsewhere, you must let them take the lead on communications. If you hear radio silence for several days, don't call for an update, because that is for you, not for them. They need to make decisions on their own. They will stay up too late. They might drink too much, eat wrong, or spend foolishly and run out of money. They might skip classes or arrive late at work. They will have relationships that will cause heartbreak, anger, and frustration. They will stumble and fall in ways you can't anticipate. And they will censor much of what they tell you anyway, which is probably good. If you know too much, you might judge through the lens of your own generation. Of course, if you see signs of mental illness, physical abuse, or drug problems, it's your responsibility to intervene. Otherwise, you must allow your offspring to experiment, learn, and discover.

LISTEN. DON'T LECTURE.

We have two ears and one mouth so that we can listen twice as
much as we speak.

Epictetus

From time to time, your young adults will parachute in for advice
from Mom or Dad. That's when it's wise to listen and resist the
impulse to be the puppeteer, which you may have done while
parenting a young teen. However, now it is important not to direct
the show, but rather to assist your young adults in finding the
solutions inside them. You may sense distress when they discover
a romantic partner is deceitful or unkind, but you must resist the
instinct to tear the offender to shreds—as much as you might be
tempted to do so. Young adult relationships are by definition vola-
tile. If you eviscerate your child's partner, that partner might come
back on the scene and lock you outside the theater, or your child
could end up marrying this partner and remembering your words
long afterward. Prompt your child to weigh behavior on both
sides. Walk them through how they might have handled themselves differently. You might share your own mistakes.

Even though your offspring may be smarter, stronger, taller,
more attractive, and more talented than you are, emotional development is chronological and stems from experience. You can lecture all you want, but it's better to save your breath. Step into the
ring as an assistant. You are the aide-de-camp—no longer the
leader.

REVOLVING DOOR BLUES

Just when you think you've found empty nest equilibrium—days,
weeks, months after your last kid leaves—they come back for a
weekend, holiday, or summer vacation. It's a jolt because you have
been gliding in a different gear. Instead of serving meals before
the homework drill, you pour a bowl of cereal or open a box of

takeout. But when your young adults return, it's like they are frozen in time and expect to find life as it was before.

They arrive with childhood habits—and a new attitude. Accustomed to newfound freedom, they might roll in at 2 a.m., while you must rise a few hours later. You may find food glued to dishes, towels on the floor, dirty T-shirts on the stairs. You may have excused them from chores in high school to allow more time for sports, studies, and extra curriculars—and now you have a kid who expects too much from Mom and Dad.

But don't become the staff when the kids come home. Draft house rules and call a meeting to divide the load. Seek suggestions and find common ground. Maybe you can handle a late-night return, but you require text updates. Perhaps you take turns making evening meals. You might leave a note by the kitchen sink saying how you want to see your reflection at the bottom. You will be doing them and their future housemates a favor.

And then, just as you get the rhythm right, it's time for them to leave again. The blues envelope you, the passage of time weighs heavily upon your heart, and for a while its déjà vu all over again. You mourn the childhood days in your rearview mirror. But don't fret, brood, isolate yourself, or stalk your kids as they adjust to the exit. Reach out to a friend who shares your situation, and go for a walk, run, cup of coffee, or glass of wine. Invite others over for dinner. Your contemporaries are most able to help you sort through this mother of all transitions.

If your young adult boomerangs back, don't despair. It's not uncommon for young adults to come home for weeks, months, or even a few years to get a financial foothold or decide what to do next. For longer stays like this, you might charge your young adult rent or ask for help fetching groceries and paying bills. Think of the boomerang phase as a chance to know your child as an adult. But make sure they have a plan for moving ahead and eventually out. Don't let the nest become a permanent residence or drain your retirement savings.

THE BANK OF MOM AND DAD

As young adults take the scenic route from adolescence to adulthood, parents are increasingly picking up the tab. Many empty nesters are subsidizing their young adults well into their 30s to pay for housing, education, everyday expenses, and travel costs. Parents also stretch themselves to the limit to give their kids clothing, cars, and help with down payments. But if you give your kids too much, you can remove the hunger and blunt initiative. Weigh your priorities and retirement plans and determine how much you want to help — if at all. Set boundaries and make a policy. Too much generosity can strain the parent-child relationship as both sides strive for independence.

A VARIETY OF NESTS

The empty nest years are different for all of us. Some fledglings soar, while others never leave. Most are somewhere in between. Some struggle with addiction or psychological or developmental disabilities, while others face financial hardship, become victims of a crime, or are stricken with illness. Some need time out to figure out the next step or to save money to return to school or relocate. Happiness comes and goes with our own challenges and the welfare of our offspring. Life is fluid and we can't control fate. But we can manage our response to whatever happens and take steps to make life as pleasant, enjoyable, and fulfilling as possible by planning ahead, educating ourselves, and cultivating a wealth of human relationships.

FRIENDS OF A FEATHER

There is nothing on this earth more to be prized than true friendship.

Thomas Aquinas

Relationships become increasingly important as we age and our desire for power, social standing, and material things diminishes in favor of human connection, harmony, and spirituality. Before I came to understand this myself, my father Harry made me aware of it. He described attending reunions at Dartmouth's Tuck School of Business in which just-graduated classmates in their 20s returned wearing their best "bib and tucker," bent on impressing each other with big-name clients or employers. At later reunions, they regaled each other with accomplishments such as landing a big job as a CEO or director of marketing or snagging a coveted international job.

By the time these classmates had hit the six-decade mark, they were "beginning to coast and anticipate retirement," my dad told me. These relationships had changed from competitive to companionate. "They were very relaxed, loquacious, and not competitive," he said. "They had met their life's objectives." They were no longer working on big projects. They were less distracted and were "coming in for a landing."

Now in his mid-80s, my father says he and his contemporaries are not at all competitive. Instead they trade stories, valuing friendship and each other's company more than ever.

Maintaining the right friendships and finding new ones requires energy and putting yourself on the line, just like being a suitor. But it's well worth it. Longtime friends dating back to college or high school tend to endure through the life span, remaining in the inner circle. These are people you can count on and whom you call in a crisis like my friend Colleen, who brings me endless comfort, joy, and connection. If they live far away, they are more likely to last because you don't have conflicts over small, everyday issues, like showing up late. Time together is the glue that binds relationships and it pays off: Studies show that close friendships and social integration are top predictors of well-being as we age.

To find new empty nest friends, pursue what you love. That's where you will find like-minded individuals. That might mean joining a biking group, taking a painting or photography class, bird-watching, attending a church-related activity, or volunteering at a school or charity. When you chase an authentic interest with others, you fall in with people with similar passions and values. I have always loved photography, which entertains me for hours and connects me with others. I am convinced that photographing young adults makes them feel like celebrities and helps them excel and win. When I capture an athlete crossing a finish line or passing a ball, or a parent on the sideline, I pass it along, creating connection through my art. When I shoot sports with other photographers, we share tips on how to cover the field. I admit I might not always understand the strategy of the games, but I know I've got the big picture.

Cultivating a diverse circle of friends with different strengths can open many new doors. Take stock of what you are trying to do and scout around for who is doing it well. Do you wish you were more organized? A better speaker? More positive? Better able to look beyond yourself and bolster others? Braver? The best way to become your best self at this stage is by reaching out to others who have mastered the qualities or skills you hope to acquire. When you surround yourself with people who embody what you value, there is a social contagion that helps you succeed. Trust others and communicate your vulnerabilities and emotions. Listen and be responsive to the other person.

As I have toiled to finish this book, I have reached out to others who have written several books. From them, I have learned invaluable information and found inspiration. I have shared my fears and discussed roadblocks. They have identified with my struggle and helped me regain perspective, offering tips for which I am forever grateful. And they say they have found new energy and inspiration in return.

DOUBLE-DATING

Friendship also works well two by two. If you have a mate, connecting with another couple can provide twice the insight. When couples double-date, sharing emotions and concerns rather than making small talk, it brings everyone closer and enhances each couple's romantic relationship. And empty nesters, by virtue of their age and experience, tend to be more interested than younger couples in building emotional ties. They also are more likely to learn new interpersonal skills, examine their own marriage, and become more self-aware after witnessing an interaction between another couple. As we become older adults, friendships like these are more likely than family relationships to boost health and happiness. Close friends are family by choice, providing a unique and powerful form of emotional support.

We have common ground with Susan and Robin, a couple whose kids grew up with ours for nearly two decades and who are both physicians as my husband John is. We're able to offer each other advice and share complaints when it comes to dealing with issues like kids' career paths, or how to run the Bank of Mom and Dad. The conversation often tends toward medicine or sciences, a different range of topics for me. The subjects that surface enable me to see a side of my husband I don't see when we go out alone.

We've recently found a close community of parents who join us on weekends to watch our sons play college lacrosse. It's like being students ourselves as we approach 60, but so much better: We've got wisps of gray hair, but a lot more soul. We're on the same side and find common ground in many ways. As we haul food and drinks for our pregame tailgates, celebrate victory or soothe each other in defeat, we are well aware at the end of each game that time flows by like a river. There is a tacit understanding that it's important to treasure and savor each moment.

CLOSE ENCOUNTERS

Another source of solace and human connection is far from obvious: It's the near strangers you come across in your daily travels. Research shows that people often divulge their deepest secrets to people they barely know. You might stumble across an empathetic soul in a supermarket, at a conference, or on an airplane. It might be only a quick interaction, a knowing glance. But if you engage others with eye contact or a question, you can find astonishing stories, mutual understanding, connection, and joy.

TOXIC RELATIONSHIPS

While creating bright interactions is enlightening, pruning toxic relationships is key to a healthy empty nest. When we are young, we are far more likely to tolerate dissonant relationships. But after we finish the child-rearing marathon and realize our time on Earth is running short, we become less interested in consorting with clashing personalities. Those who vex you also hurt your health.

You needn't keep company with naysayers who cut down or cast doubt on your dreams to justify why they don't chase their own. Weed out your friend roster to prune those who aggravate rather than inspire. Let go of people who leave you drained or create unpleasant distractions that hinder you from moving ahead or enjoying time with those you love. As people age into retirement and beyond, they tend to shrink their friend circles. But there's no reason to wait. You don't need to make waves. Just loosen the rope that binds that friendship boat and let it float away.

REDISCOVERING EXTENDED FAMILY

The empty nest is prime time to reconnect with siblings who have drifted away. Family relationships can be fraught with frustration stemming from rivalries, perceived injustices, and favoritism. Bridging those gaps can require patience, maturity, and understanding that you have developed over the years. But there's no one who shares your genes and personal history like your brothers and sisters do.

We also can learn profound lessons from siblings. My older sister Mary Anne, who has fought multiple sclerosis for a quarter of a century, has taught all of us how to accept what we cannot change and live with positivity and joy. My mother says Mary Anne has taught her that "in spite of disability, one can enjoy life and smile in the present."

My younger brothers Mike, Jim, and Joe, all two-time Olympians and national champions in ski jumping and Nordic combined skiing, live in Vermont and Utah, while I spend my life as a journalist in cities. Mike, an engineer who once went farther on a ski-flying jump than anyone else in the world, is getting a grasp on the writing life now that his teenage daughter Greta is leaning toward literature. Joe, who cross-country ski raced until his eyes froze over on his road to the Olympics and later ran 250-kilometer races across the Gobi, Sahara, Atacama, and Antarctica deserts, is now immersed in child-rearing. Jim, a visionary and off-the-charts entrepreneur, is immersed in a global battle to cure Parkinson's disease for himself and others. In the scramble to achieve and raise families, we drifted apart. But now we are seeing our different journeys weave together in the tapestry of time.

We started with a spiritual leg up from our mother Barb. She was so involved in meeting our needs as kids that she nearly collapsed when the last of her five children left. Looking back at a spell of empty nest depression she suffered, she says she realizes what she lacked back then: an ability to savor the present.

Now, in her mid-80s, she has learned to stay in the "now" about 80 percent of the time. After my older sister was diagnosed with multiple sclerosis, Barb suffered for years, seeking medical care and big-picture answers. She studied holistic health and learned to practice imagery, a stress management technique that involves using your imagination to picture a person, place, or time that makes you feel relaxed, peaceful, and happy. That helped her sleep, remain calm, and live in the present. Just as she was finding equilibrium, Jim was diagnosed with Parkinson's and she became so stressed that her hair started thinning.

She dove deeper into spirituality and taught herself to "push out the past." She says she has managed to banish worries and fear of the future for herself and those she loves. "Now when I open the door, I hear birds, crickets, a neighbor's doggie, and I love it," she says. She appreciates "every flower, tree, sunset, and blade of grass." Even driving the car is pleasant, she says, because she enjoys "being aware of this beautiful place called Earth."

DON'T SUFFOCATE

Relationships with extended family and friends beyond your marriage are critical to preserving your empty nest union. A marriage can strain if you expect your mate to be your best friend, romantic partner, confidant, career adviser, sounding board, and lover. The modern thirst for personal growth and fulfillment simply can't be satisfied by one person. And in an era when life often has revolved around kids, marriages have become more fragile. Late-life decoupling, also known as "gray divorce," is becoming ever more common. If you tether yourself to your mate, remaining in relative isolation, you can suffocate each other and overlook other relationships that help you evolve spiritually, socially, and emotionally. Maintain a healthy circle of friends to take pressure off your spouse and broaden your views.

YOUR KEY RELATIONSHIP

Your most critical relationship is your primary partner. Content couples usually motivate each other to be healthier, exercise more, set goals, and feel responsible for each other. Maintaining a romantic relationship keeps you closer to your mate—and to life in general. But if you clash constantly with your mate, it is a daily reminder that you are failing. The frustration you feel can lead to sleep disruption and overeating. It chips away at your confidence and energy and casts a long shadow over your soul. Marital problems can trigger or worsen anxiety: Research shows that women were six times more likely to be clinically depressed if their husbands were unfaithful or their marriages were struggling. If you've put your spouse on the back burner when the kids were home, you will need to invest yourself in reinvigorating the relationship.

One of the best ways to add spark to your romantic relationship is by finding novelty together. Participating in novel activities increases blood flow to areas of the brain rich in dopamine, the feel-good neurotransmitter. When you engage in a new, challenging, and exciting activity with a partner, you associate the sense of joy and exhilaration it generates with them, sparking romance and intimacy. Intimacy in a long-term relationship stimulates the dopamine system to trigger optimism and energy, and it sparks hormones to revive feelings of attachment.

Finding novelty needn't be time-consuming, expensive, or complicated. You might wander through a new part of the city, cook a different cuisine together, try a new activity like learning to ballroom dance or bowl, or take an art class or a short trip to a new place. You can read to each other; travel by bike, train, plane, and on foot rather than by car; and walk arm in arm or sit together on a couch. Taking long walks, especially in nature, is also a great way to strengthen an empty nest union. Unlike jogging, it allows time to talk, which brings you together and bolsters your mood.

AN EMPTY NEST ROAD TRIP

After our third child left for college, I refused to return to an empty house, but a long or exotic trip was out of the question. We packed up the car, pointed the GPS north, and drove to Montreal. My husband John dusted off French phrases from his high school days and we walked for miles, identifying architectural styles and reminiscing about college art history courses. We sat at a café and found feelings of freedom buried after a quarter of a century of child-rearing. We remembered why we fell in love in the first place. After losing several friends to heart attacks, suicide, and cancer, we both feel a more urgent need to savor time and use it well.

GOING IT SOLO

If you find yourself single in the empty nest, you are far from alone. This generation has seen an unprecedented explosion of over-50 divorce. In many cases, when the kids leave, so does the magic. After nearly two decades of supervising their kids' education, extracurriculars, and social events, many people find they have little in common. At the same time, longer life expectancy means an adult in their 40s or 50s can expect to live another 20, 30, or 40 years, and that's a long time to live if you aren't on the same page with your mate. If you find yourself single at this transition, don't despair! Cultivate human relationships, focus on finding your strengths and passions, and act on them.

PASSION AND PURPOSE

Having a purpose is more important in long-term health and happiness than wealth or education. Pursuing passions infuses you with excitement and energy, which spreads to your family and friends. If you lack passionate pursuits, recall your childhood interests before others told you what you should become. That's how you discover the empty nest version of your authentic self.

As I was growing up, I found magic and transcendence as a figure skater. I lost myself as I tried to jump higher, spin faster, interpret music more artfully, and move more gracefully. In the rink, I found others who shared my goals. When I became a journalist in the Capitol, I would imagine the marble hallways were ice and feel the same joy moving down the corridors in search of interviews. As a six-year-old, I had spent hours in my room penning fairy tales with magic markers. Two decades later, I found a similar satisfaction shaping news stories. Sitting elbow to elbow with other journalists in the Senate Press Gallery, I found a roomful of like-minded souls and a community that helped me transcend the stress of daily deadlines.

As an empty nester, I have found other ways to tap the passions of my youth. Instead of lacing my skates, I go before dawn each day to a Barre 3, a ballet barre class in Spring Valley, Washington, DC, where we move to music in unison, pushing ourselves to our physical limits and strengthening our muscles and psyches. I find flow there as I once did on ice, but I don't risk breaking my bones. My barre class has brought me into a community of mostly younger women who juggle parenthood and careers and ask me for advice. Though our common love of music and movement, we have discovered the joys of intergenerational friendship.

Watching these young people navigate their first careers doesn't make me feel old: It spurs me on to launch a second or third career and allows me to appreciate the advantages I have with decades of life experience.

Neuroscientists have found that while our "fluid intelligence," or innate ability to solve problems or figure things out, dips and we process information more slowly in our 40s, 50s, and 60s, we more than make up for it in "crystallized intelligence," which stems from knowledge and experience. I've also experienced firsthand how we can keep our brains humming by challenging ourselves to learn, read, socialize, and further develop in other ways.

SELF-IMPROVING

Focusing your energy on improving yourself or gaining a new skill is a great way to find fulfillment. When my last kid left, I faced a fear that has dogged me for decades. I enrolled in the Capitol Speakers Club, founded in the White House by Bess Truman to train women to become public speakers at a time when few had a voice.

During my first speech, I stammered. My eyes fled from the audience, my gaze glued to the paper in front of me. It didn't help that I had forgotten reading glasses and couldn't see the words I had typed. The women were of all ages, with varied backgrounds and different goals. But over the course of two months, we all choked, tripped over lines, and made myriad mistakes until we came together in a final performance, bonding like soldiers in the same foxhole. We weren't accidentally compatible; we had self-selected ourselves into this group because of common traits. We shared a similar sense of purpose.

My purpose now, after a long career in daily journalism, writing for magazines, and founding an online magazine for parents of teens, is to continue researching, learning, and sharing what I know about living well. It is a more mature version of my former writing passion. And it does not require me to fight traffic and sit for 10 hours a day in a newsroom. It also fills my need to work. I can't imagine a world where I wouldn't want to research, interview others, and write.

TRANSCENDENCE

If you act on your authentic passions and take active steps toward finding them, you can find a feeling of transcendence and connection with the world. You might find a state of flow while hiking, painting, playing music, writing, skiing, surfing, or cooking. Many people find transcendence in nature, or in learning something startling and brilliant that lights up the mind. A transcendent experience reboots the mind, reduces stress, helps you lose track of yourself, and stops you from focusing on petty annoyances.

A POSITIVE PERSONAL NARRATIVE

As human beings, we create stories, or personal narratives, to make sense of our existence. Some empty nesters tell themselves negative stories, like that they were fulfilled when the kids were home and now feel disconnected. But others take a positive spin on the passage of time. They concede that the transition after the kids left was tricky, but they are grateful that they have more time for a spouse, a hobby, a new career, or for reaching out to help others in the community. Stack your thoughts with the brightest memories and weed out negative ones. If you have four great experiences and one bad one, the human brain fixates on the negative one, so you must override that mood-wrecking tendency. For every negative thought I have, I create several positive ones, which dilute darker thoughts until they disappear.

ALTRUISM

> Every man must decide whether he will walk in the light of creative altruism or in the darkness of destructive selfishness.
> Martin Luther King, Jr.

If you focus on positivity, it will sustain you as you pursue challenging activities that contribute to the greater good. Altruism, sharing your talents and energy for the benefit of others, is deeply ingrained in us as humans. But using your skills in service of something larger than yourself requires hard work and self-sacrifice in the short run. If you engage purely in hedonistic pursuits like seeking entertainment, relaxation, shopping for luxury goods, and vacationing, it's easier and more fun at first. But the sense of well-being you initially feel eventually evaporates. However, if you strive for eudaimonia, aiming to become your best self and work toward a noble goal, you will achieve a lasting sense of satisfaction.

The best antidote to the existential limbo that can envelop you in the empty nest is to stop focusing on yourself, which can lead to isolation, regret, and decline. The late Sen. John McCain, who I covered when I was a journalist on Capitol Hill, urged all of us to focus on the larger good. He told me that anyone who doesn't have a larger purpose in life is a "punk." Research shows that those who devote themselves to pursuits such as teaching, mentoring, volunteering, writing, engaging in creative pursuits, and philanthropy yield high levels of happiness and psychological well-being.

RE-FEATHERING THE NEST

The empty nest is a time to embrace your age and the wisdom that comes with it. It is a time to revel in your life experience and reassess your values and priorities. It's a time to tap passions and interests and turn them into your best life work. It's a time to avoid playing it safe and miring yourself in the status quo. It's a time to push aside uncertainty and cultivate your interests, skills, and hobbies to serve the larger good.

As we age and transition into the empty nest, we become more concerned with our inner lives, with insight, philosophy, and spirituality, and savor relationships in new ways. We begin to see our true selves in sharper focus and shake off our youthful concerns about how others view us. With the daily domestic scramble behind us, we can enjoy companionship with a mate that was rushed and hassled in the heat of child-rearing. If you are still married, you can recapture time together. If not, you may find that living alone is preferable, self-affirming, and rewarding. You may discover a new ability and enjoy going it solo. Or, once the nest is empty, you may have the energy to date again. And as our grown children face hurdles of adulthood, they can become wonderful companions.

Since my third and last child left home, I have strived to find the best life in the empty nest by researching, interviewing more than 300 people, and writing about this uncharted territory. I plan to continue posting on my website Judyhollandauthor.com the latest research and new insights about how to live well in the second half of life. You also can find me on Facebook and Instagram @Judyhollandauthor, on Twitter @JudyHAuthor, and on YouTube and LinkedIn as Judy Holland. I aim to spark new interest in empty nesting at a time when we are living longer and seeking more out of life. I hope you will share insights, tips, and ideas about this transition. You can reach out to me at judy@Judyhollandauthor.com.

We can help each other continue to grow, becoming bolder, wiser, and better able to wield our most positive influence on the world

As I climbed over this mountain to learn how to live well in the empty nest, I realized there are hills, valleys, thickets, briar patches, and ditches ahead, as well as waterfalls that resolve into pristine ponds. With mindfulness, hard work, and knowledge of the experiences, research, and wisdom of people who have gone before you, this can be the most golden phase of your life,—your spiritual prime. I hope my work as an advance scout will help you cope with the challenges on the path ahead and discover the hidden treasures along the way.

NOTES

INTRODUCTION

1. Robert W. Levenson, telephone interview by author, September 27, 2018.

2. Neil Howe, "The Silent Generation, 'The Lucky Few' (Part 3 of 7)," *Forbes*, August 13, 2014, https://www.forbes.com/sites/neilhowe/2014/08/13/the-silent-generation-the-lucky-few-part-3-of-7/#19914b4d2c63.

3. Neil Howe, "The Boom Generation, 'What a Long Strange Trip' (Part 4 of 7)," *Forbes*, August 20, 2014, https://www.forbes.com/sites/neilhowe/2014/08/20/the-boom-generation-what-a-long-strange-trip-part-4-of-7/#2d41e5c46197.

4. Neil Howe, "Generation X: Once Xtreme, Now Exhausted (Part 5 of 7)," Forbes, August 27, 2014, https://www.forbes.com/sites/neilhowe/2014/08/27/generation-x-once-xtreme-now-exhausted-part-5-of-7/#6c9e2dfa4843.

5. Neil Howe, telephone interview by author, October 8, 2018.

6. Lindsay M. Monte, "Counting the Chicks after They've Flown: Shared and Non-Shared Fertility among Empty Nesters" (paper, Annual Meeting of the Population Association of America, Chicago, IL, April 27–29, 2017), https://www.census.gov/content/dam/Census/library/working-papers/2017/demo/SEHSD-WP2017-27.pdf.

1. EMPTY NEST AWAKENING

1. Matteo Pistono, interview by author, Washington, DC, May 22, 2018.
2. David Almeida, telephone interview by author, September 28, 2018.
3. Martha Simkins Davis, telephone interview by author, May 22, 2018.
4. All quotes from Laurie Cameron refer to this interview.
5. Laurie Cameron, *The Mindful Day: Practical Ways to Find Focus, Calm, and Joy from Morning to Evening* (Washington, DC: National Geographic, 2018), 9.

2. REINVIGORATE YOUR MARRIAGE

1. Robert W. Levenson, telephone interview by author, September 27, 2018.
2. Elizabeth Rubin, telephone interview by author, February 23, 2018. All quotes from Elizabeth Rubin refer to this interview.
3. John Mordechai Gottman and Julie Schwartz Gottman, *The Science of Couples and Family Therapy: Behind the Scenes at the Love Lab* (New York: W. W. Norton, 2018), 235–36.
4. Donald Cole, telephone interview by author, February 8, 2018. All quotes from Donald Cole refer to this interview.
5. Gottman and Gottman, *The Science of Couples and Family Therapy,* 148–49.
6. Anne Morrow Lindbergh, *Gift from the Sea* (New York: Vintage Books, 1978), 75.
7. Arthur Aron, telephone interview by author, September 28, 2017.
8. Charlotte Reissman, Arthur Aron, and Merlynn R. Bergen, "Shared Activities and Marital Satisfaction: Causal Direction and Self-Expansion versus Boredom," *Journal of Social and Personal Relationships* 10, no. 2 (1993): 253.
9. Aron, et al., "Couples Shared Participation in Novel and Arousing Activities and Experienced Relationship Quality," *Journal of Personality and Social Psychology* 78, no. 2 (2000): 279.

10. Xiaomeng Xu, Gary W. Lewandowski Jr., and Arthur Aron, "The Self-Expansion Model and Optimal Relationship Development," in *Positive Approaches to Optimal Relationship Development*, ed. C. Raymond Knee and Harry T. Reis (Cambridge: Cambridge University Press, 2016), 91–93.

11. Xiaomeng Xu, telephone interview by author, October 26, 2017. All quotes from Xiaomeng Xu refer to this interview, unless otherwise noted.

12. Kathleen Deal, telephone interview by author, September 28, 2017. All quotes from Kathleen Deal refer to this interview.

13. Dave Deal, telephone interview by author, September 28, 2017.

14. Amy Muise, telephone interview by author, October 4, 2017. All quotes from Amy Muise refer to this interview.

15. Helen Fisher, telephone interview by author, October 23, 2017.

16. Richard Slatcher, telephone interview by author, September 25, 2015.

17. Richard B. Slatcher, "When Harry and Sally Met Dick and Jane: Creating Closeness between Couples," *Personal Relationships* 17, no. 2 (2010): 290–95.

18. Geoffrey L. Greif, interview with author, Baltimore, September 25, 2017.

3. THE DREADED D-WORD: DIVORCE

1. Susan Brown, telephone interview by author, February 26, 2018. All quotes from Susan Brown refer to this interview.

2. Marjorie Schulte, telephone interview by author, February 21, 2018. All quotes from Marjorie Schulte refer to this interview.

3. Donald Cole, telephone interview by author, February 8, 2018. All quotes from Donald Cole refer to this interview.

4. Michele Weiner-Davis, telephone interview by author, March 5, 2018. All quotes from Michele Weiner-Davis refer to this interview.

5. Jocelyn Crowley, telephone interview by author, March 1, 2018. All quotes from Jocelyn Crowley refer to this interview.

6. David Arp, telephone interview, March 19, 2018. All quotes from David Arp refer to this interview.

7. Eli Finkel, telephone interview, September 29, 2017.

8. David Sbarra, telephone interview by author, March 12, 2018. All quotes from David Sbarra refer to this interview.

9. Linda McGhee, interview with author, Bethesda, MD, March 9, 2018. All quotes from Linda McGhee refer to this interview.

10. Brown, telephone interview.

4. DON'T SUFFOCATE YOUR SPOUSE

1. Eli Finkel, telephone interview, September 29, 2017. All quotes from Eli Finkel refer to this interview.

2. Stephanie Coontz, telephone interview by author, July 28, 2018. All quotes from Stephanie Coontz refer to this interview, unless otherwise noted.

3. Liz Spencer, e-mail exchange with author, July 23, 2018.

4. Maxwell N. Burton-Chellew and Robin I. M. Dunbar, "Romance and Reproduction Are Socially Costly," *Evolutionary Behavioral Sciences* 9, no. 4 (2015): 235–38, https://doi.org/10.1037/ebs0000046.]

5. Natalia Sarkisian and Naomi Gerstel, "Does Singlehood Isolate or Integrate? Examining the Link between Marital Status and Ties to Kin, Friends, and Neighbors," *Journal of Social and Personal Relationships* 33, no. 3 (2015): 361–84.

6. Bella DePaulo, telephone interview by author, July 24, 2018. All quotes from Bella DePaulo refer to this interview.

7. Julianne Holt-Lunstad, Timothy B. Smith, and J. Bradley Layton, "Social Relationships and Mortality Risk: A Meta-Analytic Review," PLOS Medicine (Public Library of Science), July 27, 2010, accessed March 15, 2019, https://journals.plos.org/plosmedicine/article?id=10.1371/journal.pmed.1000316.

8. Timothy Smith, telephone interview by author, July 25, 2018.

9. Annette Lareau, telephone interview by author, July 30, 2018. All quotes from Annette Lareau refer to this interview, unless otherwise noted.

10. Stephanie Coontz, "For a Better Marriage, Act Like a Single Person," *New York Times*, February 10, 2018, https://www.nytimes.com/2018/02/10/opinion/sunday/for-a-better-marriage-act-like-a-single-person.html.

11. Sae Hwang Han, Kim Kyungmin, and Jeffrey A. Burr, "Friendship and Depression among Couples in Later Life: The Moderating Effects of Marital Quality," *Journals of Gerontology: Series B* 74, no. 2 (2017): 222–31.

12. William J. Chopik, "Associations among Relational Values, Support, Health, and Well-Being across the Adult Lifespan," *Personal Relationships* 24, no. 2 (2017): 418–20.

13. Elaine O. Cheung, Wendi L. Gardner, and Jason F. Anderson, "Emotionships: Examining People's Emotion-Regulation Relationships and Their Consequences for Well-Being," *Social Psychological and Personality Science* 6, no. 4 (2015): 412–13.

14. Elaine O. Cheung, telephone interview by author July 23, 2018. All quotes from Elaine Cheung refer to this interview, unless otherwise noted.

15. Margaret Clark, telephone interview by author, July 26, 2018. All quotes from Margaret Clark refer to this interview, unless otherwise noted.

16. Mario Small, telephone interview by author, July 27, 2018. All quotes from Mario Small refer to this interview, unless otherwise noted.

17. Marjorie Schulte, telephone interview by author, February 21, 2018. All quotes from Marjorie Schulte refer to this interview.

18. Elizabeth Lombardo, telephone interview with author, July 12, 2018.

19. Mitra Toossi and Elka Torpey, "Career Outlook: Older Workers: Labor Force Trends and Career Options," U.S. Bureau of Labor Statistics, May 2017, https://www.bls.gov/careeroutlook/2017/article/older-workers.htm.

20. Jon Nussbaum, telephone interview with author, August 1, 2018. All quotes from Jon Nussbaum refer to this interview, unless otherwise noted.

21. Richard Rubin, interview with author, New Haven, CT, February 23, 2018. All quotes from Richard Rubin refer to this interview, unless otherwise noted.

22. Elizabeth Rubin, telephone interview with author, February 23, 2018. All quotes from Elizabeth Rubin refer to this interview.

23. Richard Rubin, telephone interview with author, February 23, 2018.

5. EMPTY NEST BIRDS OF A FEATHER

1. Laura Carstensen, telephone interview by author, November 10, 2017. All quotes from Laura Carstensen refer to this interview.

2. William Chopik, telephone interview by author, February 12, 2018. All quotes from William Chopik refer to this interview, except where otherwise noted.

3. Rebecca G. Adams, telephone interview by author, February 1, 2018. All quotes from Rebecca Adams refer to this interview.

4. Deborah Tannen, interview by author, Washington, DC, February 6, 2018. All quotes from Deborah Tannen refer to this interview.

5. William J. Chopik, "Associations among Relational Values, Support, Health, and Well-Being across the Adult Lifespan," *Personal Relationships* 24, no. 2 (2017): 413, https://doi.org/10.1111/pere.12187.

6. Chopik, "Associations," 417–19.

6. NOW THAT YOUR KIDS HAVE MOVED OUT

1. Thomas D. Snyder, Cristobal de Brey, and Sally A. Dillow, *Digest of Education Statistics 2017* (NCES 2018-070) (Washington, DC: U.S. Department of Education National Center for Education Statistics, Institute of Education Sciences, 2019), nces.ed.gov/pubs2018/2018070.

2. U.S. Census Bureau, "The Changing Economics and Demographics of Young Adulthood from 1975 to 2016," United States Census Bureau, April 19, 2017, https://www.census.gov/newsroom/press-releases/2017/cb17-tps36-young-adulthood.html.

3. U.S. Census Bureau, "U.S. Census Bureau Releases 2018 Families and Living Arrangements Tables," United States Census Bureau, November 14, 2018, https://www.census.gov/newsroom/press-releases/2018/families.html.

4. Jeffrey Jensen Arnett, telephone interview by author, October 5, 2017. All quotes from Jeffrey Jensen Arnett refer to this interview.

5. Stoppard, T. (1997) Tom Stoppard Plays 2: The Dissolution of Dominc Boot; 'M' Is for Moon Among Other Things; If You're Glad I'll Be Frank; Albert's Bridge; Where Are They Now; Artist Descending a

Staircase; The Dog It Was That Died; In the Native State; On 'Dover Beach.' New York: Farrar, Strous and Girouz, p. 103.

6. Wendy Mogel, *The Blessing of a B Minus: Using Jewish Teachings to Raise Resilient Teenagers* (New York: Scribner, 2011), 189.

7. Monica McGoldrick, telephone interview by author, March 26, 2018. All quotes from Monica McGoldrick refer to this interview.

8. Susan Hammond, interview by author, Silver Spring, MD, April 27, 2016.

9. Linda McGhee, interview by author, Bethesda, MD, March 30, 2018.

10. Kate Levinson, telephone interview by author, February 8, 2018. All quotes from Kate Levinson refer to this interview.

11. Havelock Ellis, *Affirmations*, 2nd ed. (Boston: Houghton Mifflin, 1915), 220.

7. WHAT YOUNG ADULTS REALLY WANT AND NEED

1. Jeffrey Jensen Arnett, telephone interview by author, October 5, 2017. All quotes from Jeffrey Jensen Arnett refer to this interview, unless otherwise noted.

2. Jeffrey Jensen Arnett, *Emerging Adulthood: The Winding Road from the Late Teens through the Twenties*, 2nd ed. (New York: Oxford University Press, 2015).

3. Karen Fingerman, telephone interview by author, October 1, 2017.

4. Christopher Ingraham, "Divorce Is Actually on the Rise, and It's the Baby Boomers' Fault," *Washington Post*, March 27, 2014, https://www.washingtonpost.com/news/wonk/wp/2014/03/27/divorce-is-actually-on-the-rise-and-its-the-baby-boomers-fault/.

5. Jennifer Tanner, telephone interview by author, April 6, 2018. All quotes from Tanner refer to this interview, unless otherwise noted.

8. OBSTACLES IN THE WAY

1. Karen L. Fingerman et al., "Only as Happy as the Least Happy Child: Multiple Grown Children's Problems and Successes and Middle-

Aged Parents' Well-Being," *Journals of Gerontology: Series B* 67B, no. 2 (2011): 184–93, https://doi.org/10.1093/geronb/gbr086.

2. Karen Fingerman, telephone interview by author, October 2, 2017. All quotes from Karen Fingerman refer to this interview, unless otherwise noted.

3. Michael Kaplan, telephone interview by author, March 28, 2019. All quotes from Michael Kaplan refer to this interview.

4. Edward Spector, interview by author, Bethesda, MD, November 3, 2014. All quotes from Edward Spector refer to this interview, unless otherwise noted.

5. Steven Howard Zarit, telephone interview by author, April 24, 2018. The quotes in the next paragraph in the text are also from this interview.

6. Lasch, Christopher. "The Family as a Haven in a Heartless World." *Salmagundi*, no. 35 (1976): 42–55. http://www.jstor.org/stable/40546941.

9. THE NEST THAT NEVER EMPTIES

1. Richard Fry, "For First Time in Modern Era, Living with Parents Edges Out Other Living Arrangements for 18- to 34-Year-Olds," Pew Research Center's Social & Demographic Trends Project, May 24, 2016, https://www.pewsocialtrends.org/2016/05/24/for-first-time-in-modern-era-living-with-parents-edges-out-other-living-arrangements-for-18-to-34-year-olds

2. *Failure to Launch*, directed by Tom Dey (2006; Paramount Pictures, 2019 web). Starring Matthew McConaughey and Sarah Jessica Parker.

3. Jeffrey Jensen Arnett, telephone interview by author, October 5, 2017. All quotes from Jeffrey Jensen Arnett refer to this interview.

4. Andrew Cherlin, telephone interview by author, June 13, 2018. All quotes from Andrew Cherlin refer to this interview.

5. Laryssa Mykyta, telephone interview by author, June 7, 2018. All quotes from Laryssa Mykyta refer to this interview.

6. Karen Fingerman, telephone interview by author, October 2, 2017. All quotes from Karen Fingerman refer to this interview.

7. Frances Goldscheider, telephone interview by author, June 12, 2018.

8. "The Boomerang Generation," Pew Research Center's Social & Demographic Trends Project, March 15, 2015, https://www.pewsocialtrends.org/2012/03/15/the-boomerang-generation/.

9. "The Boomerang Generation."

10. Jonathan Vespa, telephone interview, June 8, 2018. All quotes from Jonathan Vespa refer to this interview.

11. Richard Fry, telephone interview, June 7, 2018.

12. "Health, United States 2017—Data Finder," Centers for Disease Control and Prevention, August 9, 2018, accessed March 27, 2019, https://www.cdc.gov/nchs/hus/contents2017.htm#014.

13. National Center for Education Statistics, "The Condition of Education: Annual Earnings of Young Adults," National Center for Education Statistics, February 2019, https://nces.ed.gov/programs/coe/indicator_cba.asp.

14. Richard Fry, "It's Becoming More Common for Young Adults to Live at Home—and for Longer Stretches," Pew Research Center, May 5, 2017, https://www.pewresearch.org/fact-tank/2017/05/05/its-becoming-more-common-for-young-adults-to-live-at-home-and-for-longer-stretches/.

15. "90 Percent of Young Adults Moved Away from Home by Age 27," U.S. Bureau of Labor Statistics: TED: The Economics Daily, January 8, 2015, https://www.bls.gov/opub/ted/2015/90-percent-of-young-adults-moved-away-from-home-by-age-27.htm.

16. Cameron Simons, "Boom-Mates: How Empty Nesters Could Help Ease a Housing Shortage," Trulia Research, July 19, 2017, https://www.trulia.com/research/boommates/.

17. Annamarie Pluhar, telephone interview by author, May 9, 2017. All quotes from Annamarie Pluhar refer to this interview.

18. Marketplace Staff, "Millennials with 'Boom-Mates' Could Ease the Housing Crunch," Marketplace, August 8, 2017, accessed March 26, 2019, https://www.marketplace.org/2017/08/08/economy/millennials-with-boom-mates-could-ease-housing-crunch.

19. Katherine Newman, "The Accordion Family: Boomerang Kids, Anxious Parents, and the Private Toll of Global Competition," *Contemporary Sociology: A Journal of Reviews* 43, no. 4 (2014): 262–65, ac-

cessed March 26, 2019, http://journals.sagepub.com/doi/full/10.1177/0094306114539455mm.

20. Drew DeSilver, "In the U.S. and Europe, More Young Adults Living with Parents," Pew Research Center, May 24, 2016, https://www.pewresearch.org/fact-tank/2016/05/24/in-the-u-s-and-abroad-more-young-adults-are-living-with-their-parents/.

21. Michael Day, "Minister Calls for Law to Force Italy's 'Big Babies' to Grow Up," *Independent, Independent Digital News and Media*, October 23, 2011, https://www.independent.co.uk/news/world/europe/minister-calls-for-law-to-force-italys-big-babies-to-grow-up-1871992.html.

22. Katherine Newman, telephone interview by author, June 8, 2018. Quotes in the last paragraph also refer to this interview.

10. WORDS FROM THE WISE

1. Martin E. P. Seligman, *Authentic Happiness: Using the New Positive Psychology to Realize Your Potential for Lasting Fulfillment* (London: Nicholas Brealey Publishing, 2017), 249.

2. Emily Esfahani Smith, telephone interview by author, September 10, 2018. All quotes from Emily Esfahani Smith refer to this interview.

3. G. Oscar Anderson, "Loneliness Among Older Adults: A National Survey of Adults 45+ ," AARP, September 1, 2010, https://www.aarp.org/research/topics/life/info2014/loneliness_2010.html.

4. Lisa Jaremka et al., "Loneliness and Immune Dysregulation: A Psychoneuroimmunological Approach" (paper presented at the Society for Personality and Social Psychology meeting, New Orleans, January 19, 2013).

5. Caroline Adams Miller, telephone interview by author, July 16, 2018. All quotes from Caroline Adams Miller refer to this interview.

6. Rebecca Schlegel, telephone interview by author, September 13, 2019. All quotes from Rebecca Schlegel refer to this interview.

7. Timothy Smith, telephone interview by author, July 25, 2018.

8. Richard M. Ryan and Veronika Huta, "Pursuing Pleasure or Virtue: The Differential and Overlapping Well-Being Benefits of Hedonic and Eudaimonic Motives," *Journal of Happiness Studies* 11, no. 6 (2009): 735–62 , accessed April 1, 2019, https://www.academia.edu/11912179/

Pursuing_pleasure_or_virtue_The_differential_and_overlapping_well-being_benefits_of_hedonic_and_eudaimonic_motives.

9. Ryan and Huta, "Pursuing Pleasure or Virtue," 756.

10. Elizabeth Lombardo, telephone interview by author, July 11, 2018. All quotes from Elizabeth Lombardo refer to this interview.

11. Margie Warrell, telephone interview by author, September 18, 2018. All quotes from Margie Warrell refer to this interview.

12. Daniel Kahneman, *Thinking, Fast and Slow* (New York: Farrar, Straus and Giroux, 2015), 301.

13. *Encyclopedia of Child Behavior and Development*, 2nd vol., s.v. "Erikson's Stages of the Life Cycle."

14. Dan P. McAdams, telephone interview by author, September 13, 2019.

15. Dan Yaden, telephone interview with author, September 14, 2018. All quotes from Dan Yaden refer to this interview.

16. Rosemary Sword, telephone interview with author, July 14, 2018. All quotes from Rosemary Sword refer to this interview.

17. Bronnie Ware, *Top Five Regrets of the Dying: A Life Transformed by the Dearly Departing* (London: Hay House, 2019), 37.

18. Dean Ahlberg, telephone interview by author, July 13, 2018.

BIBLIOGRAPHY

Anderson, G. Oscar. "Loneliness Among Older Adults: A National Survey of Adults 45+." AARP, September 1, 2010. https://www.aarp.org/research/topics/life/info-2014/loneliness_2010.html.

Arnett, Jeffrey Jensen. *Emerging Adulthood: The Winding Road from the Late Teens through the Twenties.* 2nd ed. New York: Oxford University Press, 2015.

Arnett, Jeffery Jensen, and Elizabeth Fishel. *Getting to 30: A Parent's Guide to the 20-Something Years.* New York: Workman. 2014.

Aron, Arthur, Christina C. Norman, Elaine N. Aron, Colin McKenna, and Richard E. Heyman. "Couples Shared Participation in Novel and Arousing Activities and Experienced Relationship Quality." *Journal of Personality and Social Psychology* 78, no. 2 (2000): 273–84. doi:10.1037//0022-3514.78.2.273.

Arp, David. *The Second Half of Marriage: Facing the Eight Challenges of the Empty-Nest Years.* Grand Rapids, MI: Zondervan, 2000.

"The Boomerang Generation." Pew Research Center: Social & Demographic Trends, March 15, 2012. https://www.pewsocialtrends.org/2012/03/15/the-boomerang-generation/.

Buettner, Dan. *The Blue Zones Solution: Eating and Living like the World's Healthiest People.* Washington, DC: National Geographic Partners, 2017.

Burton-Chellew, Maxwell N., and Robin I. M. Dunbar. "Romance and Reproduction Are Socially Costly." *Evolutionary Behavioral Sciences* 9, no. 4 (2015): 229–41. https://doi.org/10.1037/ebs0000046.

Cameron, Laurie. *The Mindful Day: Practical Ways to Find Focus, Calm, and Joy from Morning to Evening.* Washington, DC: National Geographic, 2018

Cherlin, Andrew J. *The Marriage-Go-Round: The State of Marriage and the Family in America Today.* New York: Vintage Books, 2010.

Cheung, Elaine O., Wendi L. Gardner, and Jason F. Anderson. "Emotionships: Examining People's Emotion-Regulation Relationships and Their Consequences for Well-Being." *Social Psychological and Personality Science* 6, no. 4 (2015): 407–14. doi:10.1177/1948550614564223.

Chopik, William J. "Associations among Relational Values, Support, Health, and Well-Being across the Adult Lifespan." *Personal Relationships* 24, no. 2 (2017): 408–22. https://doi.org/10.1111/pere.12187.

Christy, Andrew G., Elizabeth Seto, Rebecca J. Schlegel, Matthew Vess, and Joshua
   A. Hicks. "Straying from the Righteous Path and from Ourselves." *Personality and
   Social Psychology Bulletin* 42, no. 11 (2016): 1538–50. https://doi.org/10.1177/
   0146167216665095.
Coontz, Stephanie. *Marriage, a History: From Obedience to Intimacy or How Love
   Conquered Marriage*. New York: Viking Penguin, 2005.
Crowley, Jocelyn Elise. *Gray Divorce: What We Lose and Gain from Mid-life Splits*.
   Oakland: University of California Press, 2018.
Davis, Eden M., Kyungmin Kim, and Karen L. Fingerman. "Is an Empty Nest Best?:
   Coresidence with Adult Children and Parental Marital Quality Before and After
   the Great Recession." *Journals of Gerontology Series B: Psychological Sciences and
   Social Sciences*, 2016. https://doi.org/10.1093/geronb/gbw022.
DePaulo, Bella M. *Singled Out: How Singles Are Stereotyped, Stigmatized, and Ig-
   nored and Still Live Happily Ever After*. New York: St. Martin's Griffin, 2007.
DeSilver, Drew. "In U.S. and Europe, More Young Adults Living with Parents." Pew
   Research Center, May 24, 2016. https://www.pewresearch.org/fact-tank/2016/05/
   24/in-the-u-s-and-abroad-more-young-adults-are-living-with-their-parents/.
Dey, Tom, dir. *Failure to Launch*. 2006; Paramount Pictures, 2019 web.
"Erikson's Stages of Development." *Learning Theories*, September 30, 2016.
   www.learning-theories.com/eriksons-stages-of-development.html.
"Existential Psychology Collaboratory." Existential Psychology Collaboratory. Ac-
   cessed April 1, 2019. http://existentialpsych.tamu.edu/.
Fingerman, Karen L., Meng Huo, Kyungmin Kim, and Kira S. Birditt. "Coresident
   and Noncoresident Emerging Adults' Daily Experiences with Parents." *Emerging
   Adulthood* 5, no. 5 (2016): 337–50. https://doi.org/10.1177/2167696816676583.
Fingerman, Karen L., Yen-Pi Cheng, Kira Birditt, and Steven Zarit. "Only as Happy
   as the Least Happy Child: Multiple Grown Children's Problems and Successes and
   Middle-Aged Parents' Well-Being." *Journals of Gerontology: Series B* 67B, no. 2
   (2011): 184–93. https://doi.org/10.1093/geronb/gbr086.
Finkel, Eli J. *The All-or-Nothing Marriage: How the Best Marriages Work*. New York:
   Dutton, 2018.
Fisher, Helen E. *Anatomy of Love: The Mysteries of Mating, Marriage, and Why We
   Stray*. New York: Fawcett Columbine, 1994.
Fisher, Helen. *Why We Love: The Nature and Chemistry of Romantic Love*. New
   York: Henry Holt, 2005.
Fry, Richard. "For First Time in Modern Era, Living with Parents Edges Out Other
   Living Arrangements for 18- to 34-Year-Olds." Pew Research Center's Social &
   Demographic Trends Project, May 24, 2016. https://www.pewsocialtrends.org/
   2016/05/24/for-first-time-in-modern-era-living-with-parents-edges-out-other-liv-
   ing-arrangements-for-18-to-34-year-olds/.
Fry, Richard. "It's Becoming More Common for Young Adults to Live at Home—and
   for Longer Stretches." Pew Research Center, May 5, 2017. https://www.
   pewresearch.org/fact-tank/2017/05/05/its-becoming-more-common-for-young-
   adults-to-live-at-home-and-for-longer-stretches/.
Goldscheider, Frances, Eva Bernhardt, and Trude Lappegård. "The Gender Revolution: A Framework for Understanding Changing Family and Demographic Behavior." *Population and Development Review* 41, no. 2 (2015): 207–39. https://doi.org/
   10.1111/j.1728-4457.2015.00045.x.
Gottman, John Mordechai, and Julie Schwartz Gottman. *And Baby Makes Three: The
   Six-Step Plan for Preserving Marital Intimacy and Rekindling Romance after Baby
   Arrives*. New York: Three Rivers Press, 2007.

Gottman, John Mordechai, and Julie Schwartz Gottman. *The Science of Couples and Family Therapy: Behind the Scenes at the Love Lab*. New York: W. W. Norton, 2018.

Gottman, John Mordechai, and Nan Silver. *The Seven Principles for Making Marriage Work*. London: Orion Publishing Group, 2018.

Goudreau, Jenna. "Nearly 60% of Parents Provide Financial Support to Adult Children." *Forbes*, August 10, 2011. https://www.forbes.com/sites/jennagoudreau/2011/05/20/parents-provide-financial-support-money-adult-children/#5053ef5b1987.

Greif, Geoffrey L., and Kathleen Holtz Deal. *Two Plus Two: Couples and Their Couple Friendships*. New York: Routledge, 2017.

Hagerty, Barbara Bradley. *Life Reimagined: The Science, Art, and Opportunity of Midlife*. New York: Riverhead Books, 2017.

Han, Sae Hwang, Kyungmin Kim, and Jeffrey A. Burr. "Friendship and Depression among Couples in Later Life: The Moderating Effects of Marital Quality." *Journals of Gerontology: Series B* 74, no. 2 (2017): 222–31. https://doi.org/10.1093/geronb/gbx046.

Holt-Lunstad, Julianne, Timothy B. Smith, and J. Bradley Layton. "Social Relationships and Mortality Risk: A Meta-Analytic Review." PLOS Medicine (Public Library of Science), July 27, 2010. Accessed March 15, 2019. https://journals.plos.org/plosmedicine/article?id=10.1371%2Fjournal.pmed.1000316.

Jaremka, Lisa M., Rebecca R. Andridge, Christopher P. Fagundes, Catherine M. Alfano, Stephen P. Povoski, Adele M. Lipari, Doreen M. Agnese et al. "Pain, Depression, and Fatigue: Loneliness as a Longitudinal Risk Factor." *Health Psychology* 33, no. 9 (September 2014): 948–95. www.ncbi.nlm.nih.gov/pmc/articles/PMC3992976/.

Jaremka, L., C. Fagundes, J. Peng, J. Bennett, R. Glaser, W. Malarkey, and J. Kiecolt-Glaser. "Loneliness and Immune Dysregulation: A Psychoneuroimmunological Approach." Paper presented at the Society for Personality and Social Psychology meeting, New Orleans, January 19, 2013.

Jaremka, Lisa M., Christopher Fagundes, Juan Peng, Jeanette M. Bennett, Ronald Glaser, William B. Malarkey, and Janice K. Kiecolt-Glaser. "Loneliness Promotes Inflammation during Acute Stress." *Psychological Science* 24, no. 7 (2013): 1089–97.

Jaremka, Lisa M., Ronald Glaser, William B. Malarkey, and Janice K. Kiecolt-Glaser. "Marital Distress Prospectively Predicts Poorer Cellular Immune Function." *Psychoneuroendocrinology* 38, no. 11 (2013): 2713–19.

Jenkins, Jo Ann, and Randall H. Workman. *Disrupt Aging: A Bold New Path to Living Your Best Life at Every Age*. New York: Public Affairs, 2018.

Kahneman, Daniel. *Thinking, Fast and Slow*. New York: Farrar, Straus and Giroux, 2015.

Lareau, Annette. *Unequal Childhoods: Class, Race, and Family Life*. Berkeley: University of California Press, 2014.

Levinson, Kate. *Emotional Currency: A Woman's Guide to Building a Healthy Relationship with Money*. Berkeley, CA: Celestial Arts, 2011.

Lindbergh, Anne Morrow. *Gift from the Sea*. New York: Vintage Books, 1978.

Lombardo, Elizabeth. *Better than Perfect: 7 Strategies to Crush Your Inner Critic and Create a Life You Love*. Berkeley, CA: Seal Press, 2014.

Marketplace Staff. "Millennials with 'Boom-Mates' Could Ease the Housing Crunch." Marketplace, August 8, 2017. Accessed March 26, 2019. https://www.marketplace.org/2017/08/08/economy/millennials-with-boom-mates-could-ease-housing-crunch.

Miller, Caroline Adams, and Michael B. Frisch. *Creating Your Best Life: The Ultimate Life List Guide*. New York: Sterling, 2011.

Mogel, Wendy. *The Blessing of a B Minus: Using Jewish Teachings to Raise Resilient Teenagers*. New York: Scribner, 2011.

Muise, Amy, Cheryl Harasymchuk, Lisa C. Day, Chantal Bacev-Giles, Judith Gere, and Emily A. Impett. "Broadening Your Horizons: Self-Expanding Activities Promote Desire and Satisfaction in Established Romantic Relationships." *Journal of Personality and Social Psychology* 16, no. 2 (2019): 237–58. doi:10.1037/pspi0000148.supp.

National Center for Education Statistics. "The Condition of Education: Annual Earnings of Young Adults." National Center for Education Statistics, February 2019. https://nces.ed.gov/programs/coe/indicator_cba.asp.

Newman, Katherine S. *The Accordion Family: Boomerang Kids, Anxious Parents, and the Private Toll of Global Competition*. Boston: Beacon Press, 2012.

Pistono, Matteo. *Meditation—Coming to Know Your Mind*. London: Hay House UK, 2017.

Pluhar, Annamarie. *Sharing Housing: A Guidebook for Finding and Keeping Good Housemates*. E. Dummerston, VT: Homemate Publishing, 2013.

Reissman, Charlotte, Arthur Aron, and Merlynn R. Bergen. "Shared Activities and Marital Satisfaction: Causal Direction and Self-Expansion versus Boredom." *Journal of Social and Personal Relationships* 10, no. 2 (1993): 243–54. doi:10.1177/026540759301000205.

Ryan, Richard M, and Veronika Huta. "Pursuing Pleasure or Virtue: The Differential and Overlapping Well-Being Benefits of Hedonic and Eudaimonic Motives." *Journal of Happiness Studies* 11, no. 6 (2009): 735–62. Accessed April 1, 2019. https://www.academia.edu/11912179 /Pursuing_pleasure_or_virtue_The_differential_and_overlapping_well-being_benefits_of_hedonic_and_eudaimonic_motives.

Sarkisian, Natalia, and Naomi Gerstel. "Does Singlehood Isolate or Integrate? Examining the Link between Marital Status and Ties to Kin, Friends, and Neighbors." *Journal of Social and Personal Relationships* 33, no. 3 (2015): 361–84. https://doi.org/10.1177/0265407515597564.

Sbarra, D., R. Emery, C. Beam, and B. Ocker. "Marital Dissolution and Major Depression in Midlife." *Clinical Psychological Science* 2, no. 3 (2013): 249–57. doi:10.1177/2167702613498727.

Schlegel, Rebecca J., and Joshua A. Hicks. "The True Self and Psychological Health: Emerging Evidence and Future Directions." *Social and Personality Psychology Compass* 5, no. 12 (2011): 989–1003. doi:10.1111/j.1751-9004.2011.00401.x.

Schlegel, Rebecca J., Joshua A. Hicks, Jamie Arndt, and Laura A. King. "Thine Own Self: True Self-Concept Accessibility and Meaning in Life." *Journal of Personality and Social Psychology* 96, no. 2 (2009): 473–90. doi:10.1037/a0014060.

Schlegel, Rebecca J., Joshua A. Hicks, William E. Davis, Kelly A. Hirsch, and Christina M. Smith. "The Dynamic Interplay between Perceived True Self-Knowledge and Decision Satisfaction." *Journal of Personality and Social Psychology* 104, no. 3 (2013): 542–58. doi.org/10.1037/a0031183.

Schlegel, Rebecca J., Joshua A. Hicks, Laura A. King, and Jamie Arndt. "Feeling Like You Know Who You Are: Perceived True Self-Knowledge and Meaning in Life." *Personality and Social Psychology Bulletin* 37, no. 6 (2011): 745–56. doi:10.1177/0146167211400424.

Seligman, Martin E. P. *Authentic Happiness: Using the New Positive Psychology to Realize Your Potential for Lasting Fulfillment*. London: Nicholas Brealey Publishing, 2017.

Seligman, Martin E. P. *Flourish*. North Sydney, N.S.W.: William Heinemann Australia, 2012.

Slatcher, Richard B. "When Harry and Sally Met Dick and Jane: Creating Closeness between Couples." *Personal Relationships* 17, no. 2 (2010): 279–97. doi:10.1111/j.14756811.2010.01276.x.

Small, Mario Luis. *Someone to Talk To*. New York: Oxford University Press, 2017.

Smith, Emily Esfahani. *The Power of Meaning: Finding Fulfillment in a World Obsessed with Happiness*. New York: Broadway Books, 2017.

Snyder, Thomas D., Cristobal de Brey, and Sally A. Dillow. *Digest of Education Statistics 2017* (NCES 2018-070). Washington, DC: U.S. Department of Education National Center for Education Statistics, Institute of Education Sciences, 2019. nces.ed.gov/pubs2018/2018070.

Spencer, Liz, and Raymond Edward Pahl. *Rethinking Friendship: Hidden Solidarities Today*. Princeton, NJ: Princeton University Press, 2006.

Strauss, William, and Neil Howe. *Generations: The History of America's Future, 1584 to 2069*. New York: William Morrow, 1992.

Tannen, Deborah. *You're the Only One I Can Tell: Inside the Language of Women's Friendships*. New York: Ballantine Books, 2017.

Tannen, Deborah. *You Were Always Mom's Favorite! Sisters in Conversation throughout Their Lives*. New York: Ballantine Books, 2010.

Vespa, Jonathan. "The Changing Economics and Demographics of Young Adulthood: 1975–2016." United States Census Bureau, April 2017. https://www.census.gov/library/publications/2017/demo/p20-579.html.

Ware, Bronnie. *The Top Five Regrets of the Dying: A Life Transformed by the Dearly Departing*. London: Hay House, 2019.

Warrell, Margie. *Brave: 50 Everyday Acts of Courage to Thrive in Work, Love and Life*. Milton, Queensland: John Wiley Australia, 2015.

Weiner-Davis, Michele. *Divorce Busting: A Revolutionary and Rapid Program for Staying Together*. New York: Simon & Schuster, 1993.

Xu, Xiaomeng, Gary W. Lewandowski Jr., and Arthur Aron. "The Self-Expansion Model and Optimal Relationship Development." In *Positive Approaches to Optimal Relationship Development*, edited by C. Raymond Knee and Harry T. Reis, 79–100. Cambridge: Cambridge University Press, 2016. doi:10.1017/cbo9781316212653.005.

Yaden, David B., Scott Barry Kaufman, Elizabeth Hyde, Alice Chirico, Andrea Gaggioli, Jia Wei Zhang, and Dacher Keltner. "The Development of the Awe Experience Scale (AWE-S): A Multifactorial Measure for a Complex Emotion." *Journal of Positive Psychology* 14, no. 4 (2018): 474–88. https://doi.org/10.1080/17439760.2018.1484940.

Yaden, David Bryce, Jonathan Haidt, Ralph W. Hood, David R. Vago, and Andrew B. Newberg. "The Varieties of Self-Transcendent Experience." *Review of General Psychology* 21, no. 2 (2017): 143–60. https://doi.org/10.1037/gpr0000102.

Zimbardo, Philip G., and John Boyd. *The Time Paradox: The New Psychology of Time That Can Change Your Life*. New York: Free Press, 2009.

Zimbardo, Philip G., and Rosemary K. M. Sword. *Living & Loving Better with Time Perspective Therapy: Healing from the Past, Embracing the Present, Creating an Ideal Future*. Jefferson, NC: Exposit, 2017.

SUPPLEMENTAL SOURCES

Grown and Flown: Parenting Never Ends. https://grownandflown.com.
Next Avenue: Where Grown-Ups Keep Growing. https://www.nextavenue.org.

INDEX

abandonment, 142
academics, 98
acceptance, 144
access, 115; availability and, 151
accomplishment of natural growth, 64–65
accomplishments, 96
accountability, 104; goals and, 182
achondroplasia, 144
activities, 21, 78; concerted cultivation and, 64; connection and, 29; couples and, 33–34; passivity and, 186; side-by-side, 82
actors, 104
actual self, 67
Adams, Rebecca G., 81
adaptations, 107
Adderall, 130, 131; abuse of, 131; addiction, 19, 185; compassion and, 132; drugs and, 88–89; families and, 89; types of, 137–140; young adults and, 133–136
admiration, 118
adulthood, 108; acceleration to, 106–107; delay of, 117; moving out and, 156; paths to, 97; preparation for, 150; responsibility and, 142; transition to, 123–125, 125–126

advice, 84, 137, 187; complaints and, 200; for reentry, 158
age, 2; divorce and, 43; marriage and, 96; retirement and, 75; stereotypes and, 76; studies and, 3; 30 loom of, 126–127; well-being and, 92
age 30, loom of, 126–127
agitation, 137
Ahlberg, Dean, 190
airline flights, 13–14
Alcoholics Anonymous, 135
The All-or-Nothing Marriage: How the Best Marriages Work (Finkel), 59
Almeida, David, 10
altruism, 177, 208
Antioch University, 135
anxiety, 133, 136; deployment and, 143; expectations and, 132
appreciation, 36; listening and, 121; of mortality, 91; of nature, 41; respect and, 152; sacrifice and, 139
approach: differences in, 105; success and, 99
Aquinas, Thomas, 86
Arendt, Hannah, 10
Aristotle, 4; on friendship, 86
Arnett, Jeffrey Jensen, 96, 101; on independence, 112; research by,

123
Aron, Arthur, 32–33
Arp, Claudia, 48
Arp, David, 48
artists, 104; tattoo, 123–124
attachment, 37
attention, bids for, 29
authenticity, 176
authentic self, 67
authority, 65; rejection of, 135
autonomy, 48
autopilot mode, 68–69
avoidance, 50, 55; finances and, 122; of
    mistakes, 56–57; relationships and,
    72
awe state, 186

baby boomers, xiv; connection and, 27;
    divorce and, 53; finances and, 2;
    marriage and, 43; roommates and,
    163–164
baking, 157
balance, 132
Beecher, Henry Ward, 1
behaviors, 23; as corrective, 30;
    emotion and, 50; modification of,
    117
belonging, 171–172
benefits, 111, 163; arrangements and,
    156
biking, 71
birth control pill, 61, 95
blended families, 65
The Blessing of a B Minus, 97
bond, 39, 83; bolster of, 98–99; family
    and, 172–173; opportunity to, 141;
    priorities and, 62; strength of, 112
book club, 74
boomerang generation, 147–166
bravery, 142
Brothers, Joyce, 30
Brown, Susan, 43
Brunetta, Renato, 164–165
Bureau of Labor Statistics, 75, 161

Cameron, Laurie, 22; on routine, 22
Camino de Santiago, Spain, 11
cancer, 115; ovarian cancer, 140–141
career, 40, 183, 188; direction of, 127;
    dreams and, 104; options for, 148;
    second, 178–179; young adults and,
    152
cars, 154
Carstensen, Laura, 79; on limits of life,
    91
Carter, Hodding, 98
catastrophizing, 181
Census Bureau, U.S., 3, 159; data
    from, 159
certainty, 123
changes: frustration and, 32; as
    generational, xvi; in perspective, 21
Cherlin, Andrew J., 149
Cheung, Elaine, 68–69
children: departure of, xiv, 9; emotions
    and, 50; engagement with, xv, 113;
    priorities and, 117; of single
    mothers, 106–107; struggles for,
    130
Chopik, William, 67, 79, 91
Chopra, Deepak, 90
cigarette smoking, 53, 115; decline in,
    47
clarity, 20; vision and, 22
Clark, Margaret, 69, 75
clothing, 19
cocaine, 134
cognitive empathy, 72
Cole, Donald, 29; on couples, 45
college, 149, 160; degree and, 150;
    first to, 32, 118; men and, 161;
    scholarships to, 119
comfort, 78, 82; demeanor and, 85;
    risks and, 103
communication, 34, 98; contact and,
    99–100; nonverbal, 35; skills for, 90
community, 62, 80, 200
companionship, 60, 163
compassion, 90, 174; addiction and,
    132

concerted cultivation, 64
condescension, 45
confidant: encounters with, 71–73; as
    spouse, 83; women and, 82
conflict, xiii; business and, 83; finances
    and, 102; gray divorce and, 47;
    immaturity and, 155; space and,
    101
connection, 16, 58; activities and, 29;
    baby boomers and, 27; emotions
    and, 28; focus on, 98; loss of, 53;
    quality of, 27–28; ways to, 101;
    young adult and, 120
control, 12
conversation, 38
Coontz, Stephanie, 60, 77
coping, 145; divorce and, 57–58; tools
    for, 139
costs, 161; of education, 149, 160; of
    living, 156, 163
counseling, 20, 139; discussion and,
    139
couples, 45; activities and, 33–34;
    double-dating for, 38–39, 199–200;
    emotional networks and, 69–70;
    marriage and, 33; one-on-one time
    for, 61; questionnaires for, 36;
    success and, 29
Cox, Jennifer, 40
Cox, Nelson, 40
creativity, 74; uncertainty and, 127
credibility, 39
crisis, 88, 173; exhaustion and, 89;
    marriage and, 89, 135; young adult
    in, 136
Crohn's disease, 88, 90
cultivation, 68; concerted cultivation,
    64; of interests, 77; of self, 73–75
cultures, 148, 156; bias and, 102;
    culture shock and, 184; gender and,
    83
curiosity, 28

dance, 34–35, 150
data, 161; from census, 159

dating: date nights, 47; double-dating,
    38–39, 199–200
Davis, Martha Simkins, 16, 17, 21
Deal, Kathleen Holtz, 34
death, 81; cancer and, 115;
    prematurity of, 63
debt, 148
decisions, 97, 100; trust and, 124;
    young adults and, 112
demeanor, 85
demographics, 111; Goldscheider and,
    156; Vespa on, 159
Denmark, 165
Department of Education, U.S., 96
departure, xiv, 9
DePaulo, Bella, 63
dependence, 78, 144–145; support
    and, 97; values and, 102
deployment, 142–143; anxiety about,
    143
depression, 53, 67; manic depression,
    49; worry and, 133
despair, 171
devotion, 176
diet, 12
discord, 55; discussion and, 72;
    toleration of, 47
discussion, 89, 105; counseling and,
    139; finances and, 102; marital
    problems and, 72; relationships
    and, 103
disengagement, 120
disruption, 53
diversity, 69
division of labor, 60
divorce, 43–58
Divorce Busting (Weiner-Davis), 46
dopamine, 33, 34, 204; intimacy and,
    37
double-dating, 38–39, 199–200
doubt, 49; divorce and, 55
dreams: career and, 104; finances and,
    116–117; help with, 115–118
drugs, 131–132; addiction and, 88–89;
    descent into, 133–137. *See also*

specific types of drugs
Dunbar, Robin, 62
dwarfism, 143–144
dyslexia, 44

economy: home and, 153–155;
    knowledge-based, 149; shifts in,
    149
Ecstasy, 134
education, 61; accomplishments and,
    96; costs of, 149, 160; women and,
    96
Einstein, Albert, 153
embarrassment, 132, 171
emergencies, 14
emerging adults, 114; Arnett on, 149
emotional networks, 69–70
emotions, 9, 129; behaviors and, 50;
    children and, 50; connection and,
    28; evolution of, 124; finances and,
    102; sharing of, 38; support and,
    68–70, 77; vulnerabilities and, 70
emotionships, 68
emptiness, 171
empty nest, 147–166; adaptations to,
    107; doubt and, 49; enhancement
    of, 62; eudaimonia and, 10–11;
    freedom and, 169; friendships and,
    65, 79–92; opportunities and, 3;
    preparation for, 57; purpose and,
    175; reentry and, 165–166; siblings
    and, 90–91; spirituality and, 9–23;
    transition and, 1, 17; wisdom from,
    190–191; women and, 48; work
    and, 75
endorphins, 17
engagement, 120; with children, xv,
    113; flow state and, 186
equilibrium, 51, 136
Erikson, Erik, 52, 185
escapism, 138
eudaimonia, 4; empty nest and, 10–11;
    opportunities and, 23
exhaustion, 52; crisis and, 89

expectations, 45, 152; anxiety and, 132;
    marriage and, 43, 91; partnerships
    and, 59; service without, 183
experience, 32, 35, 112; disruption as,
    53; gift of, 108; gratitude for, 144;
    impermanence and, 22; knowledge
    and, 206; narrative of, 57–58; range
    of, 84; similarities in, 72; values
    and, 125
experimentation, 133
extramarital affairs, 51–52

face-to-face friendships, 82–84
failures, 139; fledglings and, 147
Failure to Launch movie, 148
faith, 11; fear and, 143
families, xiv, 201–203; addiction and,
    89; blended families, 65; bond and,
    172–173; clashes in, 119; crisis in,
    88; friends and, 90–91; gap year for,
    99; Lareau on social class and,
    64–66; nuclear family, 60;
    relationships outside of, 64, 65
fear, 28, 136, 181; of consequences,
    113; faith and, 143
fear of missing out (FOMO), 189
The Feminine Mystique (Friedan), 61
feminism, 48
finances, xvi, 44, 197; avoidance and,
    122; baby boomers and, 2; dreams
    and, 116–117; parenthood and,
    101–106; risk and, 103; women
    and, 55–56, 103; young adults and,
    103
Fingerman, Karen, 114; on kin
    support, 155; research by, 129–130
Finkel, Eli J., 49, 59
Fisher, Dorothy Canfield, 114
Fisher, Helen, 37
fitness, 83
fixators, 143
fledglings, xvi; failure and, 147;
    individualization for, 54–55; who
    thrive, 87

flow state, 176; engagement and, 186; interests and, 188–189

focus, 22, 173; crisis and, 89; on future, 126; McGoldrick on, 98; on moment, 187; after retirement, 183

FOMO. *See* fear of missing out

Fonda, Jane, 48

Foote, Shelby, 32

freedom, 118; empty nest and, 169; threat and, 175

Friedan, Betty, 61

friendships: cultivation of, 68; divorce and, 52; empty nest and, 65, 79–92; families and, 90–91; reconnection and, 66–67; singlehood and, 91; time and, 91–92; well-being and, 67

friendships, of the good, 86–87

Frisch, Michael B., 175

frugality, 138, 154

frustration, 32

Fry, Richard, 159

fulfillment, 43, 169; meaning and, 9–10

fun, 28

future, 185; focus on, 126

gap year, 108; families and, 99

gay men, 82

gender, 39; culture and, 83; division of labor and, 60; gender binary, 119; roles and, 43, 160; stereotypes and, 65

generation, 97; boomerang generation, 147–166; changes and, xvi; marriage and, 125; multigenerational home, 164; technology and, 111; of young adults, 95–96, 114. *See also specific generations*

generative adults, 185

Gen-Xers, 2–3

Gibran, Khalil, xiv, 9; on love, 59

Gift from the Sea (Lindbergh), 31

goals, 13, 32, 115, 176; accountability and, 182; commonality of, 80;

fitness and, 83; help as, 136; practices and, 21; service as, 171; support of, 115; values and, 84, 126

Goldscheider, Frances, 156; on marriage, 160

Gottman, John, 29

Gottman Institute, 29, 45

grandchildren, 172

gratitude, 136; for experience, 144; generosity and, 153; gift of, 15–16

gray divorce, 43, 46, 205; economic penalty for, 56; life expectancy and, 49; road to, 47

Great Recession, 3, 147

Greif, Geoffrey L., 39

growth, 64–65; growing pains and, 118–120; room for, 98–99; self-growth, 37–38

guilt, 100–101; disengagement, 120; struggles with, 135

gym, 83

habits, 152

Hammond, Susan W., 99

happiness, 22–23; eudaimonia and, 10; health and, 79; novelty and, 37; partnership and, 31; Schlegel on, 175; success and, 129

haven, 144–145

health, 53; access and, 115; divorced men and, 53; happiness and, 79; illness and, 85–86; mental illness and, 155; risk to, 58; social networks and, 63

hedonic happiness, 10

helicoptering, 113

help, 163; dreams and, 115–118; goals for, 136

Hepburn, Audrey, 158

heroin, 134

heteronormativity, 119

hiking, 21, 107

hobbies, 37, 80, 188

Holt-Lunstad, Julianne, 63

home, 153–155; multigenerational
   home, 164
homeschool, 135
honesty, 55
hostility, 113
Howe, Neil, 2
humanity, 14
Humphrey, Hubert H., 82
Huta, Veronika, 178
Huxley, Aldous, 73

ideas, xiii, 160; double-dating and, 39;
   exploration of, 121
identity, 52, 138, 175; authentic
   identity, 117; parenthood and, 48;
   priorities and, 177; reinvention and,
   58; self and, 175
illness, 66; health and, 85–86; young
   adults and, 140–141
immaturity, 155
immigration, 148
impermanence, 11, 22
improvisation, 15
inclusion, 74
independence, 16, 113, 118; Arnett on,
   112; guilt and, 100; millennials and,
   151; respect for, 99; self-reliance
   and, 126; want for, 142; for young
   adults, 151
individualization, 54–55
information, 119, 193; separation of,
   122–123
Instagram, 122
intelligence, 206
interactions, 104; with strangers, 73
interests, 73; cultivation of, 77; flow
   state and, 188–189; threats and, 74;
   values and, 71
intergenerational relationships, 76–77
the Internet, 135; therapy sessions
   over, 136; uncontrolled use of, 139
interviews, xiii
intimacy, 28; attachment and, 37;
   barriers to, 40; contact and, 69;
   relationships and, 45

intuition, 85; friendships on, 86
involvement, 113; parenthood and, 97
isolation, 135, 174
Italy, 164–165

Japan, 164
Jaremka, Lisa, 174
Jim Crow segregation, 115
journaling, 22
journalism, 4
judgment, 108, 125

Kahneman, Daniel, 181
Keller, Helen, 88
Kennedy, Patrick J., 137
kindness, 19
King, Martin Luther, Jr., 61, 208
kin support, 155
knowledge-based economy, 149

Lareau, Annette, 64–66
latchkey kids, 3; experience of, 121
laundry, xv
Layton, J. Bradley, 63
learning issues, 130–133
Leary, Timothy, 61
lessons, 193–210
letting go, 107–108
Levenson, Robert W., 2; research by,
   27
Levinson, Kate, 101
life, 145; Carstensen on, 91; chance at,
   13–15; details about, 101
life expectancy, 2; factor of, 159; gray
   divorce and, 49
Lindbergh, Anne Morrow, 31
listening, 121, 195
Lombardo, Elizabeth, 74
loneliness, 63, 139
longevity, 63, 79
love, 106; Gibran on, 59
Love Lab. See Gottman Institute
Luther, Martin, 27
Lyme disease, 52

mammone, 164
management, 156; as preemptive, 157
manic depression, 49
marijuana, 131
Marine Corps, U.S., 142
marriage, 60; age for, 96; as child-
    centric, 29, 46–47; couples and, 33;
    crisis and, 89, 135; dissolution of,
    43; expectations of, 43, 81;
    generation and, 125; Goldscheider
    on, 160; opt out of, 126;
    postponement of, 158–160;
    reinvigoration of, 27–41; as
    traditional, 44
maturation, 55
McAdams, Dan P., 185
McCain, John, 208
McGhee, Linda, 54, 55; on
    connection, 101
McGoldrick, Monica, 97; on focus, 98
Mead, Margaret, 163
meaning, xvi, 178; fulfillment and,
    9–10; search for, 170–171
meditation, 18; hiking as, 21
Meetup.com, 70
men, 82; college and, 161; divorce and
    health of, 53; patterns and, 102;
    vulnerability and, 70
mental illness, 120; health and, 155;
    manic depression and, 49
methamphetamine, 134
Michelangelo Effect, 38, 67–68
milk, 5
Mill, John Stuart, 169
millennials, 147; boomerang and, 155;
    independence and, 151
Miller, Caroline Adams, 175
mind, 67–68
ministry, 18–20
miscarriage, 15
mistakes, 105, 112, 176; avoidance of,
    56–57
Mogel, Wendy, 97
moods, 67–68
mortality, 91

motivation, 104, 106; desire and, 138;
    source of, 114
moving out, 95–108, 153; adulthood
    and, 156
Muise, Amy, 36
multigenerational home, 164
murder-suicide, 133
Mykyta, Laryssa, 149, 156

nagging, 4
narratives, 185, 207–208
Nash, Ogden, 28–29
National Basketball Association
    (NBA), 98
National Public Radio, xiii
National Science Foundation, 69
nature, 187; sanctuary of, 41;
    spirituality in, 20–22
NBA. *See* National Basketball
    Association
near-death experiences, 13–14
needs, 99, 163; of spouse, 68; of young
    adults, 111–127
negativity, 16–17, 184; success and, 87
neighbors, xiii
Nesterly app, 163
Newman, Katherine, 164
Nixon, Richard, 75
nonverbal communication, 35
novelty, 32–34, 204; happiness and, 37
nuclear family, 60
nurturing, 41; relationships and, 52;
    shift in, 11; spouse and, 27
Nussbaum, Jon, 76

obstacles, 129–145
opioids, 133
opportunities, 31, 182; to bond, 141;
    empty nest and, 3; eudaimonia and,
    23; service as, 184
Ornish, Dean, 171
ovarian cancer, 140–141
ownership, 1
oxytocin, 17

Pahl, Ray, 62
pain, 85, 129; drug addiction and, 88;
    endurance of, 143–144; growing
    pains, 118–120
paradox, 71
parenthood, xiv, 131; finances and,
    101–106; identity and, 48;
    involvement and, 97; parenting
    style and, 64–65; relationships and,
    1, 46; success and, 158; support
    and, 112; worry and, 13, 51, 133
parent network, 80
parents: of single mothers, 155;
    struggle internalization by, 133
Parry, Joseph, 81
partnership, 37, 56; awareness in, 39;
    completion and, 73; expectations
    and, 59; happiness and, 31;
    improvement of, 37; wait for, 126
passion, 76, 124, 188; illness and, 141;
    performance as, 12; purpose and,
    179–182, 205–206; service and, 175
paths, 122–123; to adulthood, 97;
    sharing and, 87–88; vocations as,
    160–161
patience, 137
patterns, 57, 164; men and, 102
pay gap, 161
Pearls for Girls group, 184–185
Pearson, Lester Bowles, 59
Percocet, 133
personalities, 87
perspective, 66; changes in, 21;
    differences in, 67
Pew Research Center, 147, 159, 161
phenomenon, xv; Michelangelo, 38
philanthropy, 84
photography, 199
pleasure, 87
Pluhar, Annamarie, 163–164
Polner, Fred, 75
positivity, 16
practices, 35; goals and, 21
pregnancy, 12

preparation: for adulthood, 150; for
    empty nest, 57
pride, 153
priorities, 55, 159; bond and, 62;
    children and, 117; identity and,
    177; relationships as, 173
prison, 19–20
problem solving, 84; skills and, 100
purpose, 18, 174–176; empty nest and,
    175; passion and, 179–182,
    205–206

rape, 134
reconnection, 58, 80; friendships and,
    66–67
reentry, xv; advice for, 158; empty nest
    and, 165–166; stigma of, 155–156
re-envision, 23
regrets, 189–190
reinvention, 1; autonomy and, 48;
    identity and, 58; twists on, 5
relationships, 27, 57, 79, 162;
    avoidance and, 72; creation of, 70;
    discussion and, 103; exclusion of,
    61; families and outside, 64, 65; to
    find, 70; as intergenerational,
    76–77; intimacy and, 45; as
    intrapersonal, 10; nurturing and,
    52; parenthood and, 1, 46; as
    priorities, 173; as professional, 70;
    repertoire of, 62; resentment and,
    106; revel in, 173–174; romance
    and, 203–204; separateness and, 78;
    Smith on, 63; stress and, 85; toxicity
    in, 201; transformation of, 155;
    view of, 63; as voluntary, 81
research, 33; by Arnett, 123; by
    Fingerman, 129–130; by Levenson,
    27
resentment, 106, 114, 121
resilience, 70; sensitivity and, 144
respect, 67; appreciation and, 152; for
    independence, 99
responsibility, xvi; acceptance of, 108;
    adulthood and, 142; young adults

and, 100
Rethinking Friendship: Hidden Solidarities Today (Pahl and Spencer), 62
retirement, 75, 154, 176; focus after, 183
Revolutionary War, 172
risks, 113, 181; finances and, 103; to health, 58
rituals, 30
role models, 144, 182; unhappiness and, 49–50
roles, 90; gender, 43, 160; vacation of, 11
roommates, 163–164
routine, 22
Rowland, Helen, 54
Rubin, Elizabeth, 28, 77–78
Rubin, Richard, 77, 78

sacrifice, 115; appreciation and, 139
Sbarra, David A., 53
scars, 141
Schlegel, Rebecca, 175
scholarships, 32, 106; college and, 119
Schulte, Marjorie, 44, 46, 73
self: cultivation of, 73–75; identity and, 175; investment in, 151; transcendence of, 186–188; work and, 75
self-care, 50
self-compassion, 58
self-definition, 175
self-disclosure, 76
self-doubt, 181
self-growth, 37–38
self-improvement, 206–207
self-reliance, 97; independence and, 126
sensibilities, 4; sense and, 152
sensitivity, 144, 174
separateness, 77–78
separation, 20, 53; of information, 122–123; summer and, 108

service, 13, 18; goal of, 171; legacy of, 177, 183–185; opportunities for, 184; passion and, 175; purpose and, 174; skills and, 208
sex, 28; sexual desire and, 36; sexuality and, 119; sexual liberation and, 61, 95–96
Sheehy, Gail, 17
siblings, 120; empty nest and, 90–91
side-by-side friendships, 82–84
signals, 28–30
Silent Generation, 2, 3
singlehood, 62, 159, 205; friendships and, 91; social networks and, 62–63
single mothers, 12; children of, 106–107; parents of, 155
skiing, 80
skills, 4, 104, 150; communication as, 90; problem solving and, 100; proficiency and, 34; service and, 208
Slatcher, Richard B., 38
sleep, 58
Small, Mario Luis, 71
Smith, Timothy, 63; on relationships, 63
social class: Lareau on families and, 64–66; marriage and, 60
social networks: singlehood and, 62–63; well being and, 63–64
Social Security, 56
Someone to Talk To (Small), 71
space, 100, 108; conflict and, 101; spouse and, 35
Spain, 164
Spector, Edward, 138
Spencer, Liz, 62
spiritual gifts, 16–17
spirituality, xiv; empty nest and, 9–23; nature and, 20–22; time and, 17–18; tools and, 11–13
spouse, xv; confidant as, 83; needs of, 68; nurturing and, 27; space and, 35; suffocation of, 59–78; team with, 31

stability, 116
Stanford University, 79
Starr, John, xiii, 2
step-family, 57
stereotypes: age discrimination and, 76; gender and, 65
stigma, 155–156
strangers, 72; interactions with, 73
stress, 10; finances and, 102; relationships and, 85
struggles, 150; for children, 130; with guilt, 135; parents internalization of, 133
student loans, 121; debt and, 148
studies, 69, 156; aging and, 3; participation in, 178
success, 87, 124; approaches and, 99; happiness and, 129; parenthood and, 158
suffocation, 203; of spouse, 59–78
suicide, 11
summer camps, 107–108
support, 61, 121; behavior modification and, 117; dependence and, 97; emotion and, 68–70, 77; of goals, 115; gratitude for, 136; kin support, 155; as mutual, 145; parenthood and, 112; weaponization of, 118; women and, 88
surveys, 174
Sweden, 165
Sword, Rosemary, 187; on transcendence, 188

taboo, 102
Tannen, Deborah, 82
Tanner, Jennifer L., 126
tardiness, 100
tattoo artist, 123–124
technology, 61; advances in, 96; generation and, 111; unhealthy use of, 138; witness through, 130
tennis, 66
therapy, 90; over the Internet, 136

Thinking Fast and Slow (Kahneman), 181
Thoreau, Henry David, 20
threat, 149; freedom and, 175; interests and, 74
time, 74, 152, 198; couples and one-on-one, 61; for divorce, 54–55; friendship and, 91–92; to savor, 172; spirituality and, 17–18; tension about, 65–66; time-out, 156–157
togetherness, 59
tools, 69; to cope, 139; spirituality and, 11–13
The Top Five Regrets of the Dying (Ware), 189
transcendence, xvi, 207; of self, 186–188
transition, 97, 153; to adulthood, 123–125, 125–126; divorce as, 55; empty nest and, 1, 17; mindfulness and, 3
trauma, 11, 133
travel, 108; road trips and, 204
trends, 95; boomerang as, 147
Trulia, 163
trust, 1, 199; decisions and, 124
Twain, Mark, 111
Two Plus Two: Couples and Their Couple Friendships (Greif), 39

uncertainty, 127
unconscious bias, 181
uncoupling, 44
Unequal Childhoods: Class, Race, and Family Life (Lareau), 64–66
unhappiness, 129; modeling, 49–50

values: dependence and, 102; experience and, 125; goals and, 84, 126; interests and, 71; personalities and, 87
Vespa, Jonathan, 159
video games, 137–140
vision, 23; clarity and, 22
vocational paths, 160–161

The Voice (TV show), 116
volunteering, 19
vulnerability, 62; emotions and, 70;
    fragility and, 97; men and, 70

wages, 149; minimum-wage, 150; pay
    gap and, 161
walk-away-wife syndrome, 48–49
walking, 40
wants: for independence, 142; of
    young adults, 111–127
Ware, Bonnie, 189
Weidner, David, 163
Weiner-Davis, Michele, 46–47
well-being, 68; age and, 92; friendships
    and, 67; social networks and, 63–64
widows, 81
Williams, Robin, 55–56
wisdom, 151; words of, 169–191
women, 39; confidants and, 82;
    education and, 96; emotional
    networks and, 69; empty nest and,
    48; finances and, 55–56, 103; gray
    divorce and, 47; intuition and, 85;
    in prison, 19–20; support and, 88

women's movement, 95–96
Woodward, Bob, 75
work, 75; marriages as, 60; self and, 75
World War II, 60
worry, 136; deployment and, 142;
    depression and, 133; parenthood
    and, 13, 51, 133
writing, 22

Xu, Xiaomeng, 33–34; on hobbies, 37

Yaden, David, 186
yoga, 21
young adults, 2; addiction and,
    133–136; career and, 152;
    connection and, 120; dalliance and,
    151; decisions and, 112; finances
    and, 103; generation of, 95–96, 114;
    illness and, 140–141; independence
    for, 151; responsibility and, 100;
    wants and needs of, 111–127

Zarit, Steven, 144–145
Zimbardo, Philip G., 187
Zogby, John J., 125

ABOUT THE AUTHOR

Judy Holland has been a journalist for more than 30 years, having spent 13 years in the Washington Bureau of Hearst Newspapers, where she was national editor, preparing stories for 600 newspapers over *The New York Times* wire. She also served as Capitol Hill Correspondent and was elected president of the Washington Press Club Foundation, a nonprofit celebrating female pioneers in journalism and providing scholarships for women and minorities. She has been a Capitol Hill commentator for C-Span and CNN and won the Hearst Eagle Award for excellence in journalism. Judy's stories have appeared in dozens of publications, including the *Washington Post, Boston Globe, Houston Chronicle, San Francisco Examiner, Tampa Tribune,* and *Washingtonian* magazine. Her work includes hundreds of stories about teens, including a piece for the *Washingtonian* about the pressures that teenagers face. She also was founder and editor-in-chief of Parentinsider.com, an online magazine for parents of teens, for which she wrote stories, edited columns, and co-produced videos. She lives in Washington, D.C., with her husband John Starr, and their Great Dane, whom her three children, Lindsay, Maddie, and Jack, left home to fill the empty nest.

Author photo by Lizzy Oakley Photography
  @Lizzyoakleyphotography